Co-Existence or Co-Extinction Between Races, Religions and Ideologies

Co-Existence or Co-Extinction Between Races, Religions and Ideologies

Joseph Molitorisz

iUniverse, Inc.
New York Lincoln Shanghai

Co-Existence or Co-Extinction Between Races, Religions and Ideologies

iUniverse books may be ordered through booksellers or by contacting:

iUniverse
2021 Pine Lake Road, Suite 100
Lincoln, NE 68512
www.iuniverse.com
1-800-Authors (1-800-288-4677)

ISBN-13: 978-0-595-41154-2 (pbk)
ISBN-13: 978-0-595-85513-1 (ebk)
ISBN-10: 0-595-41154-1 (pbk)
ISBN-10: 0-595-85513-X (ebk)

Printed in the United States of America

I DEDICATE MY BOOK
TO THE VICTIMS
OF MINDLESS LOYALTY AND
PROUD OBEDIENCE.

Contents

PROLOGUE.

We are in a critical period of history. Religious-political self-consciousness, ideological self-consciousness and racial-political self-consciousness are on a dangerous collision course. We are in—or are entering—history's biggest religious war, the Crusade of the 21st Century, which according to the political pundits might last for decades. The American neo-conservatives' interventionist foreign policy being pursued under the aegis of "modernizing" or "democratizing" the Muslim societies has prompted a global conflict with the Islamic World, and resulted in alienation from friends and allies. The Muslims are in a Jihad, or Holy War against the Infidels, especially against America and Israel, not just on dogmatic matters, but also on strategic politics.

We have more foes than friends. The Europeans are skeptical about America's strategic intentions, and distance themselves from America's world leadership. Russia, because of America's humiliating policies toward it following the collapse of the Soviet Union is striving to regain its super-power status. China, the evolving Asiatic super-power pursues clearly pro-China policies, rejecting any American attempt for intervention in its internal affairs. The devastation of Hiroshima and Nagasaki by the American nuclear bombs is still deeply imbedded in the minds of the Japanese. The Canadians and the British as traditional allies watch with bewilderment America's reckless foreign policies. Israel, as America's chief ally is in open and widening conflict with its Arab neighbors. The Jews are drawing world-wide criticism over their harsh actions against their Arab neighbors, over their often provocative racial attitude in their hosting countries, and over the role of their radicals in the Bolshevik terror in the Soviet Union and in Eastern Europe. Peace-serving institutions, like the United Nations, are under siege from America and Israel, and are treated as irrelevant. Tension and war-mindedness are increasing. A small, arrogant clique claiming to be the advocates of the democratic principles is attempting to control the world. America as a nation is being pushed

1

into deeper and deeper violent confrontations, not realizing that the days of its military-monopoly are over. We are vulnerable. Politically and strategically we are isolated from the world-community. These are the realities.

At home, under the "PATRIOT ACT", a fight is waged against freedom of the mind. In it *"...an attempt to intimidate or coerce the civilian population or change the policy of the government by intimidation or coercion"* is domestic terrorism. Thinking critically on vital national and international issues, sharing critical thoughts became a crime. Bookstores and libraries are under order to provide information to government authorities about their customers and visitors, as to what books they buy or borrow. Telephone lines are tapped and e-mails are read by government agents, with presidential approval. Intellectual liberty, the much-cherished treasure of civilized, democratic societies, is in today's America in jeopardy.

For me, who personally experienced the pain of intellectual deprivation, such laws are reminiscent of the worst years of Bolshevism, against which I stood up in joining the 1956 Hungarian Revolution. Our President and government officials argue that the PATRIOT ACT is necessary because America is at war. But, whose war is it? Some of our senators and congressmen who dutifully—but irresponsibly—voted for the Afghan and Iraq wars, years and tens of thousands of victims later awakening to the horrors and futility of wars are washing their hands, admitting that it was a mistake. But, can a premeditated mass-murder with tens of thousands of victims be called a "mistake"? No, it cannot. They claim that they were misled by the President on the reasons for the war. Aren't most of them well-educated, sharp-minded lawyers? Hadn't they heard the warnings from all over the world against the wars? Haven't they seen how unsustainable the claims for going to war were? Didn't they understand that wars are government conducted pre-meditated mass-murders? Would they, the experts of legal-justice, accept in a court argument that a mass-murder on a huge scale was just a mistake? Anyone who plans and conducts wars is a war criminal. Anyone who instigates, or with a vote authorizes wars, is an accomplice. Their voting for the wars was a clear case of moral-intellectual corruption.

I believe it is not an exaggeration when I raise the two alternatives we are facing; co-existence or co-extinction. The confrontational issues of our times, ideology, economics and race are joined by an ancient cause of deep animosities; religious-politics, not on doctrinal grounds only, but as the tool of the most immoral power politics. The ideal of international co-existence is swept aside by fanaticism, megalomania, greed and immorality. The hoped-for victory blindfolds those who are to be sacrificed; the faulty pride in defeating the foe is elevated to the act of noble patriotism. But wars are acts of pre-meditated mass-murder, of co-extinction. The huge military cemeteries all over the world are the condemning evidence to that.

Co-existence or co-extinction as national and international issues were the dominant political elements in the past seventy-eight years—that is throughout my lifetime. I was born at the time, when in Europe the devastation of the First World War, and the horror of the Bolshevik terror were very much on the minds of the surviving victims. From my early teenage years to the autumn days of my life I had to live in unending crises, had to face the threat of extinction. Co-existence or co-extinction became personal matters for me, and that is the reason why I want to share my experience with the reader. I do it with the intention to warn: The danger of co-extinction is real. It is not only threatening from the outside, but also from within. I survived the Second World War, endured the terror of Bolshevism, in my struggle for personal freedom marched with the revolutionary crowd, and shared the agonies of the fleeing refugees.

I am a member of a generation in an era, which was full of controversies. Ideologies evolved, collided and disappeared. Old beliefs were shaken, and new discoveries broadened the horizon of the human mind, bringing new questions to the ultimate puzzle of my existence. I grew up in that world under the old teachings, and exposed to the new realities. In my writings I am seeking answers to the social, political, intellectual and spiritual matters, which dramatically affected—or determined—the course of my life.

I do not live by convictions, be those religious, political or racial. The one deeply rooted moral principle, which might be viewed as conviction, which I wish to share with my readers, is my stand against violence, and especially against wars. I saw the tragic consequences in individual cases, in the horrible massacres of civilians in air raids, in the horrors of the concentration camps, in the destruction and killing in senseless battles. Presenting a summary of my early age, of my experience in the Second World War and in American prison, of my struggle under the Bolshevik terror, of my fleeing to the West, of my attempt as an immigrant to melt into a new society, is to help the reader to understand why my conclusions are what they are. I am doing it not in an academic study, my world was too narrow for that, but as I lived through those times.

My writings might be—and most likely will be—subjected to vehement criticism, especially by those who in their biased views see my interpretation of the past as attacking the integrity of their own accounts, by those who relying on the "official account" may see in my views the distortion of "historical facts." Publishing my writings, opening my thoughts to others was the fulfillment of an obligation, which I feel I have to the new generations. I want to present another point of view, that of an eyewitness to some of the monumental world events. More than sixty years later, while my memories are still rather fresh and my personal records are in my hands, I want to give another perspective on a colossal tragedy of mankind. I am not questioning or discrediting the accounts of others.

Revealing my thoughts, exposing my intellectual concepts on controversial and politically explosive issues in a book is like exposing myself. It is risky, especially when the smell of gunpowder is in the air, when wars are being fought on issues which are inherently related to the subject of my writings, when the powerful ideologues of the opposing views are in a fierce battle, when in an anachronistic nonsense reminiscent of the blind nationalism of the much deplored past nationalistic pride is demonstrated by wearing badges with the image of the flag, when opposing wars is treated as unpatriotic, when under THE PATRIOT ACT any criticism of the government policies could be treated as domestic terrorism.

Please, read my lines with an open mind, just as I wrote them with an open mind. Do not prejudge my accounts and my thoughts, but view them as what they are; the reflections of a human being, who is in search of an understanding of tumultuous times.

Seattle, 2006

A FEW THOUGHTS TO THE
DEDICATION OF THIS BOOK.

I dedicate my book to the victims of "Mindless Loyalty and Proud Obedience. This dedication was inspired by one of the tragic episodes of my wartime memories. In late April of 1945, only a few days before the end of the Second World War a young German soldier breaking his loyalty to his by then dead Führer fled to Switzerland. The Swiss border guards in their mindless loyalty and blindly proud obedience to their authorities, knowing well what the consequences for the young man could be, returned him to the German military authorities, who in their mindless loyalty and blindly proud obedience to an already defeated cause, only days before their surrendering to the enemy, sentenced the young man as a traitor and shot him. This is a tragic war episode, and a frightening reflection on our society in the Twentieth Century.

I view mindless loyalty and proud obedience as the most dangerous ills of the human society. Those are the fundamental elements of chauvinistic nationalism and of arrogant militarism, without which governments could not generate hatred between peoples and nations, and without which decent human beings could not be sent to wars to kill. Loyalty, if granted on moral principles, is a noble human characteristic. It is an essential structural fiber holding families and societies together. It is an expression of devotion. Obedience in its noble form is an essential element in raising the young, both in the family and in the educational environment. In its broad application it means total submission to higher authorities. Proud obedience is the fundamental element of the militaristic or totalitarian societies. The young men—and also women—in uniform are brainwashed to the degree where they proudly and unquestionably submit to the orders of someone one rank higher, even if that order puts them in jeopardy. Proud obedience excludes reasoning, demands absolute submission, and in extreme cases self-sacrificing. The reality is that in most societies the noble aspects of loyalty and obedience are wrapped in an "Oath", which is construed by the authorities as a means of gaining absolute control over their subjects. The governments, whether dictatorial or democratic, together with the military, applying the moral and legal power of an oath compel their subject to absolute loyalty and blind obedience. They also grant for themselves the right for harsh—in wartime capital punishment—on anyone who is disloyal or disobedient to them. The consequences have been—and still are—that in my lifetime, without exception, all wars in which millions have been killed, maimed and driven from their homes, have been instigated by governments through lies, deception and distortion, and have been fought by misled, mindlessly loyal, and blindly, proudly obedient subordinates.

Killing anyone other than in justifiable self-defense, hiring someone to kill, or ordering someone to kill under command, are totally immoral criminal acts. What are the young men and women in uniform trained to do? To kill under orders. Kill, or be killed is what they face. What do they know about the enemy whom they have to kill? Nothing! Having been myself in a war, I view wars not as conflicts between the peoples of nations, but as bloody rivalry between immoral, megalomaniac government officials, in which the misled, mindlessly loyal and the proudly and blindly obedient masses are the sacrificial pawns. I view wars as personal matters, and do so with good justification. As a soldier I was trained to shoot to kill, had to endure the horrors of a war, was buried under the rubble in bombed cities, suffered the agonizing pain of the wounded, had to endure the humiliation of captivity. Somehow I survived, but had to bear the consequences of the war for the rest of my life. Can anything be more personal?

What did the American soldiers who were sent in the Second World War to fight against us in Europe know about me? Nothing. They knew only what the propaganda told them; that we on the other side were Nazis, Fascists who had to be destroyed. What did I know about the American soldiers and airmen who were sent to our world to fight? Only what the government's propaganda told me, that they were my enemies, and I had to defend the nation and myself. We young men on both sides preparing for joyful and peaceful life were cheated into mutual hatred and killing, without knowing each other. That is the reality! Facing the young American airman, who in 1944 after the bomber on which he served crashed, landed with his parachute on Hungarian soil and I captured him, was for me at that time a clear recognition of the absurdity of wars. He was on his way back from a deadly "mission" dropping bombs on civilians in German cities. At the same time I was on my way to the river to lunch my newly built kayak. We met at the crash site, where he was the only survivor of the crew. His comrades were dead in the burning wreckage. Had we met in civilian life, without military indoctrination, together we could have enjoyed kayaking. Those are the absurdities of wars, which I had seen and experienced throughout my life from my childhood to this day, from Hitlerism to Stalinism, from dictatorship to Democracy, from Europe to America.

Loyalty and obedience—the noble human social elements—grotesquely distorted by the ruling political powers, imposed on the societies and individuals as fundamental patriotic obligations, turned into mindless loyalty and proud obedience, and became the ultimate threats to humanity.

THE CHRONICLE OF CO-EXISTENCE.

1843

First international peace congress in London, promoting international arbitration, denouncing military education, urging anti-war propaganda and control of the manufacture and sale of weapons.

1848

Universal Peace Congress in Brussels.

1849

Peace Congress in Paris.

1850

Peace Congress in Frankfurt.

1851

Peace Congress in London.

1867

International League of Peace and Liberty, Geneva.

1873

International League of Peace and Liberty, Brussels.

1889

Universal Peace Congress. Chicago.

1899

Hague Conference. International Court of Arbitration established.

1907

Second Hague Conference.

1921
Nov.12.
Washington Disarmament Conference.(USA, Britain, Japan, France and Italy).

June 28.
Versailles Peace Conference.

1922
April 17.
German-Soviet "Rapallo Agreement".

1924
October 2.
Geneva Protocol:
"Aggressive war an international crime".

1925
October 16.
Lucarno-Agreement on the invulnerability of the western boarders between Germany, Belgium, France, Britain, Italy, Czechoslovakia and Poland.

1928
Aug. 27.
"Kellogg-Briand Pact",
renouncing war as instrument of national policy.

1933
February 2.
Second International Disarmament Conference in Geneva.

1934
January 26.
German-Polish Friendship and Non-aggression Agreement.

1937
May 28.
Neville Chamberlain British Prime Minister.
("Appeasement Policy")

1938
April 16.
British-Italian agreement on easing tension in the Mediterranean.

Sept. 15.	Hitler-Chamberlain meeting in Berchtesgarten.
Sept 22.	Hitler-Chamberlain meeting in Bad Godesberg.
October 21.	Chamberlain's "Peace for our time" proclamation.
Dec 6.	French-German Non-aggression Treaty signed.
1939 March 21.	Germany's offer to Poland for settling the boarder disputes.
August 23.	German-Soviet Pact.
August 28.	Germany guarantied Belgium, Holland, Luxembourg, Denmark and Swiss neutrality.
1943 Nov. 9.	44 nations signed the United Nations Relief and Rehabilitation Association.
1945 June 26.	United Nations established.
Oct. 24.	United Nations Charter signed.
1964	International Confederation for Disarmament and Peace.
1950	World Council of Peace.

THE CHRONICLE OF CO-EXTINCTION.

1914–18

        First World War.
        7,000,000 perished.

1916
April 6.   USA entered World War I.

1917.
Nov 6.   Bolshevik Revolution in Russia.
        During Bolshevik rule 20,000,000 killed.

1919
March   Communist International (COMINTERN) established in Moscow. ("…by all available means, including armed forces…. the creation of an International Soviet Republic…)

March 21.   Hungary under communist rule declared a Soviet Republic.

April 6.   Bavaria under communist rule declared a Soviet Republic.

1922

        October 28 Mussolini took power in Italy.
        Hitler's "Mein Kampf" first edition published.

1929

        Wall Street Crash.

1930 September	Hitler's National Socialist Workers Party (NSDAP) won election in Germany.
1933. March 24.	"Judea declares war on Germany". (Daily Express).
October 19.	Germany left the League of Nations.
1934. August 2.	Hitler appointed as Chancellor of Germany.
1935. January 27.	Negotiation on a German-Polish coalition on military matters against the Soviet Union.
March 7.	Germany peacefully regained the Saarland territory.
March 16.	Conscription reintroduced in Germany.
May 2.	French-Soviet mutual assistance pact.
June 18.	British-German naval agreement. (Tonnage ratio (100:35)
July 25.	Failed National Socialist Coup in Austria. Chancellor Dolfuss assassinated.
October 3.	Italy attacked Abyssinia (Ethiopia).
October 11.	League of Nations sanctioned Italy.
1936. March 7.	Germany denounced the Locarno Agreement.
July 24.	Spanish Civil War.
October 25.	Berlin-Rome Axis established.
Nov 25.	"Antikominter Pact" between Germany and Japan.
1937. October 10.	Roosevelt's "Quarantine" speech in Chicago.
1938. March 12.	"Anschluss". Austria became part of the German Reich.

April 22.	Hitler's military plans against Czechoslovakia prepared.
April 26.	In Germany all Jewish owned properties over 5000 RM (Reichsmark) value had to be declared.
May 20.	Military mobilization in Czechoslovakia.
Sept 26.	Hitler declared the returning of the Sudetenland as Germany's final demand for revision.
Sept 29.	Munich Agreement. Sudetenland returned to Germany. Hitler ordered the war against Czechoslovakia.
Nov 7.	Assassination of the German diplomat Rath in Paris by a Jewish man.
Nov 9.	"Reichskristalnacht" Retaliatory attacks on Jewish businesses and synagogues in Germany. 26,000 Jewish men arrested.
Nov. 2.	First Vienna Conference on the Hungarian-Czechoslovakian border dispute following the 1920 Trianon Peace Treaty.
Nov 28.	For Jews in Germany visiting theaters, movies and concerts became prohibited.
Dec 3.	In Germany Jews had to surrender their driver licenses.
1939. March 14.	Slovakia declared independence.
March 16.	German occupation of Czech territories.
March 26.	Poland declined the German offer for settling the boarder issues.
March 27.	Britain reintroduced conscription.
March 28.	Spanish Civil War ended with Nationalists' victory.
March 31.	British-French guaranty for Poland granted.

March–June	Negotiation between USA, Britain, France and Soviet Union.
April 1.	Franco took power in Spain.
April 7.	Italy occupied Albania.
April 13.	British-French guaranty declaration to Greece and Rumania.
April 14.	Roosevelt's proposal to Hitler and Mussolini for a peace conference.
April 17.	German-Soviet Pact.
April 28.	Hitler canceled the 1935 German-British Naval Agreement and the German-Polish Non-aggression Agreement.
May 22.	German-Italian Military Pact.
August 23.	German-Soviet Non-aggression Agreement.
August 25.	British-Polish Mutual Assistance Agreement.
August 26.	German-British negotiations on the Polish issue.
Sept 1.	German-Polish War.
Sept 3.	France and England declared war on Germany.
Sept 5.	USA declared neutrality.
Sept 7.	French patrols crossed the German boarder.
Sept 11.	British Navy mined the Dover-Calais Narrows.
Sept 11.	British troops landed in France by Nantes and St. Nazaire.
Sept 17.	Soviet troops occupied Eastern-Poland. German U-boat sunk the British carrier "Courageous".
Sept 19.	British military plan initiated to halt German shipping of iron ore from Norway.
Sept 24.	German Luftwaffe bombed Warsaw.

Sept 26.	German air attack on the British Home Fleet in the North Sea.
Sept 28.	German-Soviet Boarder and Friendship Agreements. German-Polish War ended.
October 3.	The Pan-American Safety Zone announced.
October 6.	Hitler's "Peace-offer" speech.
October 12.	Britain declined the German peace offer.
October 14.	The Germans sunk the British battle ship "Royal Oak".
Nov 3.	US Congress approved the "Cash and carry" deal for Britain, and with that altered the neutrality of the USA.
Nov. 8.	Assassination attempt on Hitler.
Nov 15.	Allied military plan "Dyle" prepared for the occupation of Belgium in case of an imminent German attack.
Nov 30.	Soviet-Finnish war.
Dec 15.	Hitler was warned by Quisling the ex-Minister of War of Norway on the planned British military occupation of Norway.
Dec. 20.	British and French military aid sent to Finland.
1940. January 15.	The Belgian government rejected the allies' request for free passage of their military units.
March 1.	Summner Welles US representative visited Berlin, Rome, Paris and London.
March 12.	The Soviet-Finnish War ended.
March 18.	Hitler-Mussolini meeting at the Brenner Pass.
April 9.	Germany occupied Denmark and Norway.
April 30.	The first fenced Jewish Ghetto in Lodz Poland.

May 9.	French-German war.
May 10.	Churchill became Prime Minister of Britain. Germany occupied Holland, Belgium and Luxembourg.
May 11.	The British cabinet authorized the British Air Force to attack German cities.
May 13.	Churchill's speech: "I can offer nothing but blood, toil tears and sweat."
May 14.	The German Luftwaffe attacked Rotterdam.
May 15.	Holland surrendered.
May 24.	British troops landed at Dunkirk. The Germans sealed the area and allowed the evacuation of the British troops.
May 28.	Belgium surrendered.
June 10.	Italy declared war on France and Britain. First German air attacks against British convoys.
June 13.	Roosevelt offered USA help to France, but declined entering the war.
June 14.	728 Polish political prisoners brought to Auschwitz camp. German occupation of Paris.
June 16.	Churchill's offer for a British-French Union rejected by France.
July 19.	Hitler's speech, an "Appeal for rationality".
June 22.	German-French armistice. Lord Halifax rejected Hitler's "Appeal for rationality".
June 24.	Italian-French armistice.
June 25.	German-French war ended.
July 3.	British naval attack on the French naval base in Oran.

August 13.	First German air raids on Britain.
August 25.	First British bombing raid on Berlin.
Sept 27.	Three-Power Pact between Germany, Italy and Japan.
October 28.	Italy attacked Greece.
October 29.	British troops landed on Crete Island.
Nov 12.	Molotov visited Berlin for negotiating the USSR's joining the Three Power Pact.
Nov 15.	The Warsaw Ghetto established.
Nov 16.	British bombers attacked Hamburg.
Nov 20.	Hungary joined the Three Power Pact.
Nov 23.	Rumania joined the Three Power Pact.
Nov 24.	Slovakia joined the Three Power Pact.
Dec 7.	Spain declined the German request for entering the war.
Dec 8.	Churchill in a letter informed Roosevelt that Britain was no longer able to pay for the supplied goods.
Dec 12.	Hungary and Yugoslavia signed a Friendship Agreement.
Dec 18.	Hitler's "Weisung Nr. 21" for the war against the Soviet Union.
1941. January 10.	German air attacks on British convoys at Malta.
January 13.	Greece declined British offer for troops.
January 22.	Jewish massacre in Rumania. Soviet-Japanese Friendship and Non-aggression Pact.
February 10.	British Air Force bombed Hannover and Rotterdam.

February 17.	Bulgaria and Turkey signed Friendship and Non-aggression Pact.
February 24.	The British cabinet approved the "Greece-Expedition".
March 1.	Bulgaria joined the Three Power Pact.
March 2.	German troops entered Bulgaria.
March 7.	British troops landed in Greece.
March 11.	Roosevelt signed the "Loan and Rental Law" as military aid to the Soviet Union.
March 19.	Heavy German air attack on London.
March 27.	The Japanese foreign minister visited Berlin. Hitler ordered the attack on Yugoslavia.
March 29.	Heavy British air attack on Lübeck in Germany.
March 30.	The German, Italian and Danish vessels in American ports confiscated.
March 31.	German-Italian attack against the British in North Africa.
March	Patent filed in Germany for the Plutonium bomb: "Process for producing explosion from energy and neutrons through splitting the elements 94."
April 4.	The Hungarian Prime minister committed suicide in protest against the German troops marching through Hungary against Yugoslavia. Anti-British government took power in Iraq.
April 5.	Yugoslav-Soviet Non-aggression Pact.
April 6.	German attack against Yugoslavia and Greece.
April 11.	Hungary entered the war against Yugoslavia. Italy attacked Yugoslavia.
April 16.	German air attack on London.
April 19.	Heavy bombing of London by German planes.

April 17.	Yugoslavia surrendered.
April 19.	Bulgarian army entered Macedonia.
April 23.	Greece surrendered to the Germans.
April 24.	Evacuation of the British troops from Greece.
May 2.	British-Iraq war.
May 8.	Heavy British air attacks in Germany on Hannover and Bremen.
May 10.	Partisan war in Yugoslavia began. Rudolf Hess, Hitler's deputy flew to England, to meet Lord Hamilton with a peace offer.
May 20.	German paratroopers landed on Crete. The spy "Sorge" warned the Soviets on the imminent German attack, presumably on June 22.
May 23.	Hitler: "Freedom movement in the Middle-Eastern Arab countries is our natural ally against England…I am determined to support the development of Iraq."
May 24.	The British battle ship "Hood" sunk by the Germans.
May 27.	The German battle ship "Bismark" sunk by the British.
May 28.	A protocol between the France and Germany signed for German supply routes through Tunisia, and for French naval support from Dakar.
May 28.	British troops evacuated Crete.
June 7.	British and French troops occupied Syria.
June 14.	Hitler set the date for the attack on the Soviet Union at June 22. Roosevelt ordered the freezing of all German assets.
June 15.	Croatia joined the Three Power Pact.
June 18.	German-Turkish Friendship Pact.

June 22.	German attack ("Barbarossa") on the Soviet Union. Italy and Rumania declared war on the Soviet Union.
June 23.	Hungary broke the diplomatic contact with the Soviet Union. Slovakia declared war on the Soviet Union.
June 26.	Finland declared war on the Soviet Union.
June 27.	Hungary declared war on the Soviet Union after an air attack on two Hungarian cities. Denmark broke the diplomatic contact with Russia.
July 18.	Stalin requested the opening of a second front in Western Europe.
July 21.	British-Soviet agreement for joint action against Germany.
July 31.	Removal of all Jews from Europe ordered by Hitler.
August 2.	The first shipment of American war material to Russia delivered.
August 8–12.	Roosevelt and Churchill meeting in Newfoundland. "Atlantic-Charter".
August 14.	Heavy air attacks by the British on German cities.
August 25.	British and Soviet troops occupied Iran.
Sept. 1.	Order issued in Germany for Jews to wear the yellow star.
Sept 8.	Leningrad's siege by the Germans.
Sept. 29.	Large scale Jewish massacre in Kiev in the Ukraine.
October 14.	Order issued on forced labor for all Jews in Germany.
October 16.	Systematic deportation of German Jews began.
Nov. 14.	The British battle ship "Ark Royal" sunk by German U-boat.
Dec. 6.	Britain declared war on Hungary, Finland and Rumania.

Dec. 7.	Japan attack on Pearl Harbor.

1942
January 10.	German air attack on Liverpool.
January 15.	British air attack on Hamburg.
January 18.	Military pact between Germany, Italy and Japan.
January 20.	Wannsee Conference on the "Final Solution" of the Jewish question.
January 21.	British air attack on Bremen in Germany.
February	Secret meeting in Germany on the A-bomb program. (Target date 1945?)
March 28.	British commando attacked St. Nazaire.
April 2–8.	Heavy German bombing of Malta.
April 24.	British air attack on the city of Rostock in Germany.
May 12.	1500 Jews killed in Auschwitz.
May 26.	Alliance agreement between Britain and the Soviet Union.
May 30.	British bombers dropped 1455 tons of bombs on Cologne, killing 460, making 45,000 homeless.
June 10.	The Czech village Lidice destroyed and all men executed by the German SS in retaliation for the killing of the German official Heydrick.
June 18–25.	Conference between Roosevelt and Churchill on the second front and on the atomic bomb research.
June 25.	British bombers attacked the city of Bremen in Germany.
June 30.	Closing of all Jewish schools in Germany.
July 24.	Agreement between USA and British high commands on a troop landing in French-Northwest Africa.
July 26.	Heavy British air attack on the city of Hamburg.

August 12.	Meeting between Churchill, Stalin and Harriman in Moscow.
August 19.	Unsuccessful British landing at Dieppe. German siege of Stalingrad.
August 21.	German troops took the Elbrus peak in Caucasian mountains.
Sept. 29.	Hitler's speech at the German High Command on building the "Atlantic Wall".
Nov. 11.	German and Italian troops occupied South France and Corsica.
December 2.	The first nuclear reactor started in Chicago.
1943. January 14.	Casablanca conference between Roosevelt, Churchill and deGaulle.
January 31.	German troops in Stalingrad capitulated.
February 18.	Germany declared "Total War".
April 13.	Discovery of the mass graves in Katyn, Poland, of over 10,000 Polish military officers executed by the Soviets in 1941. Another 10,000, Polish intellectuals killed.
May 13.	German troops in North Africa capitulated.
May	COMINTERN dissolved.
July 10.	Allied landing on Sicily.
July 15.	The Soviet counter offensive began.
July 16.	Roosevelt and Churchill appealed to Italy to stop the war.
July 24.	Mussolini as "Duce" removed and arrested.
Aug 25.	The first German guided bomb in action. Allied air raid on Hamburg, 40,000 dead.
Sept. 8.	Italy capitulated.

Sept 10.	German troops occupied Rome.
Sept 12.	Mussolini liberated from Gran Gasso by German troops.
Sept 28.	600 Jewish prisoners moved from Auschwitz to Mauthausen.
October 13.	Italy under Badoglio declared war on Germany.
Dec. 1.	Teheran Conference (Roosevelt, Churchill and Stalin).
Dec. 12.	Soviet-Czech agreement for post-war mutual assistance.
1944.	
January 1.	Heavy British bombing of Berlin.
January 15.	British plan for Germany's division into occupation zones.
January 22.	US troops landed at Anzio in Italy.
February 8.	The military plans for Europe's invasion prepared.
February 12.	General Eisenhower commander of the invasion forces.
February 15.	Destruction of the Monastery on Monte Casino by US bombing.
March 15.	Heavy bombing of Stuttgart.
March 18.	Hungarian Governor Admiral Horthy in dispute with Hitler.
March 19.	German military occupation of Hungary.
March 22.	Night bombing (3000 tons) of Frankfurt.
March 23.	Rumanian leader Antonescu visited Hitler.
April 5.	US bombing of the Rumanian oil fields at Ploesty.
April 13.	New Italian pro-allies government under General Badoglio.

April/June	Mass deportation of Jews from Greece and Hungary.
May 8.	Eisenhower set the date of invasion on June 5.
May 15.	The German Generals Rommel and Stülpnagel conspired to arrest Hitler.
June 4.	The date of invasion of Europe changed to June 6. German military withdrawal from Rome.
June 6.	Invasion of Europe by the Western Allies.
June 10.	German SS in retaliation destroyed the French village Oradour.
June 12.	First German V-1 flying bomb hit London.
June 16.	619,000 allied soldiers, 95,000 vehicles and 218,000 tons material landed on the French coast.
July 20.	Failed attempt on Hitler's life by count Staufenberg.
June 21.	US bombers attacked Berlin.
July 11.	USA recognized the French Liberation Committee.
Aug 1.	Warsaw uprising.
Aug 12.	Churchill-Tito meeting in Caserta.
Aug 23.	Rumanian coup. Antonescu arrested.
Aug 25.	Paris surrendered by the German commander to the Allies. Rumania declared war on Germany.
Aug. 26.	German military withdrawal from Greece.
Aug. 31.	Soviet Army occupied Bucarest.
Sept. 3.	Brussels in allied hands.
Sept 4.	Antwerp in allied hands.
Sept. 5.	Soviet Union declared war on Bulgaria.
Sept. 6.	First German V-2 rocket launched against London.
Sept. 8.	Bulgaria declared war on Germany.

Sept. 12.	Soviet-Rumanian armistice.
Sept. 11.	US forces arrived to the Germany's border.
Sept. 19.	Finnish-Soviet armistice.
October 9.	Stalin-Churchill Moscow conference.
October 12.	Roosevelt-Churchill conference in Quebec. Soviet-Rumanian armistice.
October 14.	German General Rommel committed suicide.
October 15.	Hungary declared cease-fire with Soviet Union. Hungarian National Socialist (Arrowists) coup for continuation of the war.
October 19.	USA bombers attacked Cologne.
Nov. 3.	The siege of Budapest began.
Dec. 6.	The author survived an air attack by American fighter planes on a civilian passenger train.
Dec. 9.	The author joins the Hungarian Army.
Dec. 16.	Last German counter offensive (Battle of the Bulge).
Dec. 24.	Soviet troops encircled and sealed Budapest.
1945. January 26.	Auschwitz liberated by the Soviets.
January 30.	"Gustloff" was sunk with 9000 German refugees on board.
February 3.	US bomber attacked Berlin.
February 4.	Yalta Conference.
February 9.	"Steuben" was sunk with 5000 German refugees on board.
February 13.	Heavy US and British air attack on Dresden. Nearly 200,000 died. 102 days siege of Budapest ended., 160,000 died.

February 20.	Hungary signs the armistice with the Allies. Author in an American air attack on Nürnberg buried under rubble.
March 4.	The first German A-Weapon test in Jonastal.(?)
March 9.	Air raid on Tokyo 80,000 dead.
March 19.	Hitler's order for the destruction of all important installations in Germany.
April 12.	Death of Roosevelt.
April 13.	Soviet troops occupied Vienna.
April 14.	Author wounded.
April 16.	"Goya" was sunk with 4000 German refugees on board.
April 15.	Bergen-Belsen concentration camp was liberated by the Allies.
April 25.	German cease-fire offer by Himmler. United Nations Conference in San Francisco. US and Soviet troops met at the river Elbe.
April 28.	Mussolini executed by Italian partisans.
April 30.	Hitler committed suicide.
May 1.	The author was captured by US troops. For eight months prisoner of war.
May 2.	Berlin capitulated. New German government under Admiral Dönitz.
May 9.	Germany surrendered. The European war ended.
Aug. 6.	USA dropped the A-bomb on Hiroshima (Nearly 200,000 killed.)
Aug. 9.	USA dropped the A-bomb on Nagasaki.(Nearly 60,000 killed)
Sept. 2.	Japan surrendered.

Nov. 20.	Nürnberg Trial began.
1946	
Jan. 12.	The author released from American prisoner of war camp.
1956	
Oct. 23.	The Hungarian Revolution.
Nov. 21.	The author fled to the West with his family.

CASUALTIES OF WORLD WAR II.

Country	Military	Civilian
Belgium	10,000	90,000
Bulgaria	10,000	7,000
Canada	40,000	
China	3,500,000	10,000,000
Denmark	4,000	3,000
Finland	80,000	10,000
France	250,000	170,000
Germany	3,250,000	2,000,000
Great Britain	240,000	65,000
Greece	17,000	400,000
Hungary	140,000	610,000
Italy	380,000	180,000
Japan	1,700,000	950,000
Netherlands	10,000	240,000
Norway	5,000	8,000
Poland	600,000	6,000,000
Rumania	200,000	460,000
Soviet Union	8,700,000	16,900,000
Spain	12,000	1,000
Czechoslovakia	7,000	310,000
United States	292,000	

Civilians: 38,404,000 dead
Military: 19,447,000 dead
Total: 57,845,000

Material losses: immeasurable

The carnage of World War II barely ended, when the victorious powers who promised peace were preparing for more wars.

1946–60	USA-Soviet Union "Cold War".
1946–54	French-Vietnam war.
1950–53,	USA-Korea War: 540,000 killed.
1954–62	French-Algerian war.
1954–73,	USA-Vietnam War: 1,350,000 killed.
1956	Hungarian Revolution, 30,000 killed.
1979–89	Soviet-Afghan War, over 1,000,000 killed.
1990–	Israel-Palestine war.
1994	USA-Somalia conflict.
1998	USA-Iraq war.
1999	USA-Yugoslavia (Kosovo) conflict.
2002–	USA-Afghan war.
2003–	USA-Iraq war.
2004–	USA-Moslem war.

WARNING!

Tens of thousands of nuclear warheads are in the arsenals of several nations ready to be used.

THE GREAT CONSPIRACIES.

Close to the small Hungarian village, where I grew up, is a large military cemetery with thousands of graves of foreign prisoners of war from the First World War. There are Italian, Rumanian, Russian and Serb names, crosses, half-moons and Jewish stars carved into the gravestones. Each year it was—and still is—the scene of memorial day events with flags waving in the wind, flowers laid on the graves, and loud speeches given by politicians, encouraging the young to be ready to sacrifice themselves for the nation, like those thousands in the graves did. Remarkably, the honored dead were not our own, but were the soldiers of the enemy. The remembrance was a noble gesture by a defeated nation. The Hungarian veterans of the war stood along the walkways between the graves, proudly wearing their medals. They were the fortunate ones; they survived it. Shots were fired in honoring the dead, who while on the battlefield were frightened by the noise of the guns. They chose to surrender. What an absurd remnant of the militaristic anachronism it was honoring the dead with rifle shots! The military band played the national anthems of the dead prisoners, the same anthems, which at one time raised their patriotic pride to go to war, and brought them to their graves on a foreign land. They were prisoners for whom the horror of the battle was over, who waited for a return to their families. Then came a disease or an accident, sending them not home, but to the graves. The ritual was held each year with the same message. In the early 1930s as a young child with a keen mind I watched the ceremonies with sadness and curiosity.

In the center of the village stands a memorial tower for the fallen soldiers of our own, on its marble slab are engraved the names of dozens of local men. Yearly rituals have been also held at the tower with fiery speeches given by politicians on true patriotism, on the glory of heroism and self-sacrifice. In reality—which at that time as a young boy I did not understand—both at the

31

prisoner cemetery and at our heroes' memorial tower we the participants were
wrapped in ritualistic nonsense, bombarded with patriotic bluffs, not knowing
that we were remembering the victims of a senseless, immoral war.

On early Sunday mornings I watched in the street leading by the memorial
tower as the not quite military age young men were drilled in the handling of
rifles. It was in the 1930s, barely fifteen years after the First World War, and
nearly ten years before the outbreak of the Second World War. That was a
short pause between two immense human tragedies. The rifles were wooden
replicas, because under the terms of the Trianon Peace Treaty the number of
real weapons was restricted in Hungary. The wooden rifles were used in preparation for another war, with the aim to rectify a perceived injustice committed against the Hungarian nation in the Peace Treaty after the First World
War. The shortsightedness and bigotry of the politicians of the victorious
Western Powers drew new boarders on the map, taking away two-thirds of
Hungary's territory, disrupting a relatively peaceful co-existence between the
neighboring countries, depriving my homeland of the natural and economic
resources necessary for normal existence. They punished the common people
who were the real victims of the war. They injected in the minds the powerful
venom of hatred, destroying the essentials for peaceful co-existence. The seeds
of another war were planted. The young men with the wooden rifles were
trained to become the victims of another senseless war.

Migration viewed from historical perspectives is a key element in the development of the human societies. Breaking out of isolation in search of a better
life, or driven by the lack of the essentials for survival, masses of people moved
from country to country, bringing with them their traditions, language, culture and skills. Co-existence between nationalities, races and religions became
a fundamental survival matter. During the past centuries there was a constant
influx of immigrants to Hungary, some coming on the invitation of the country's rulers to re-populate the land after devastating wars or deadly epidemics,
some arriving by using the liberal immigration policies. At the time of the
First World War Slovaks, Rumanians, Germans, Jews and other ethnic
groups lived together, in some places as majority in others as minority, mostly
in peaceful co-existence. If measured with today's political and social standards it may not have been an ideal integration, but it provided peaceful living-together on an ethnically divided land. After a bloody world war and a
harsh peace treaty, when the emotions still ran deep on all sides, millions of
my countrymen—including my mother—became the targets of ethnic-nation-
alistic hatred, and had to flee, arriving to a land that was deprived of the essen-

tials for existence. The foundation for peaceful co-existence between the neighboring nations was destroyed. I grew up in those years, when under the economic hardships, unemployment and hopelessness, the outcry against the injustices of the Peace Treaty dominated the minds not only of the politically active, but also of the common folks. The seeds were planted for antagonism. The wooden rifle replicas were the ominous warning signs of what was to come.

Politics—other than the protestation against the Trianon Peace Treaty—was not a common subject among the villagers, although there were plenty of stories about the alleged brutalities committed under the short lived communist terror in 1919. The valley at the edge of the village was called the "Hanging valley" where gangs, called "Lenin Boys" coming from cities, tortured and murdered the village elders who opposed them. Their goal was the extinction of their ideological opponents. The records speak clearly of the horror. After the defeat of Communism there was tolerance for those who played some minor role in the communist era. The chief notary was a member of the Red Army, not by choice but by necessity. The carpenter was some sort of party activist, by his own words "in the hope of a better life". People knew and talked about their past, but nobody bothered them. Party-politics was considered the game of the gentlemen rascals in the big cities. Village life was close to nature, and interdependence was an essential element of existence. There were no political organizations, and if occasionally—usually at election time—the politicians showed up giving short speeches, only a few people listened, mostly children, waiting for free candy. The mood in the isolated village was calm. For the people whose daily life was centered around caring for the animals and cultivating the fields, life was simple. For them there were no imminent threats of another war.

My father's radio received the Austrian station from Vienna, the German station from Berlin and the British news from London. We were informed about the world events, about the civil war in Spain, about Hitler's and Mussolini's rise to power, about the political tensions in some of the countries, and on Italy's war in Abessinia. The newspapers arrived a day late and only a few people read them. My father received a paper that was somewhere in the political center. When the sales agent signed him up as a subscriber, he gave us an enlarged picture of Mussolini, the Italian "Duce," who at that time was considered a good friend of Hungary, better than Hitler was. Italy supported our complaint against the Trianon Peace Treaty, which was viewed by the Hungarians as a severe and unjustified punishment for the country's involvement in the First World War. That Treaty nearly 80 years later is still an almost daily subject not only among the politicians, but also in the media and among the common folks. Some view it as the direct cause of World War II, by not only not solving the historic ethnic tension in Eastern Europe, but also adding to it. It did not further the peaceful co-existence between the neighboring countries, but injected an animosity that reached the level of violent hatred, even co-extinction.

The Northern Light in our part of the world was an unusual spectacle of nature, but in 1935 on one night it was spectacular. The shimmering colors floated in the sky for hours. The villagers rushed to my Lutheran Minister father for a blessing, as they saw in the mysterious light the signs of the coming of the end of the world. An old peasant saw in it the sign of the coming of a big war. He was right!

In the late 1930s as a peaceful gesture between Hungary and the Soviet Union an exchange of the jailed Bolshevik leaders of the 1919 era in return for the historic Hungarian flags of the 1848 Fight for Freedom, was played out with fanfare. It gave hope for peace. After the 1939 war between Germany and Poland many Polish soldiers escaped to Hungary. A young officer became a butler in the home of a noble landlord in a village nearby to our town. He talked about the horrors of modern warfare with tanks and airplanes, about the invincibility of the German army. The pictures of the 1940 bombing of the Dutch city Rotterdam with the corpses of women and children lined up in the streets were frightening signs of what was to come, but somehow for me it was unimaginable that anything like that could happen to us. The war of Germany against France, where the Peace Treaty of Trianon after the First World War was signed, was followed by us with satisfaction. The word Trianon was deeply engraved in the minds of the people, including mine. The propaganda painted France as the most responsible for the injustice, so the newsreels showing the German troops marching through Paris gave us a malicious joy. The onward march of the German troops through Hungary in 1941 to Yugoslavia gave me the impression of their military might. The war against Russia in 1941—which came as a surprise—was justified by the propaganda as *"Europe's holy war against the hoards of the Jewish-Bolsheviks."* I watched the newsreels and read the magazines with the pictures of the captured Russian soldiers as the *"Asiatic barbarians,"* against whom Europe had to be defended. The alleged killing of 20 million Russians by the Bolsheviks after the 1917 Revolution was presented as proof of the brutality against which Europe had to fight. The short-lived communist terror in Hungary in 1919, which directly touched my family, left deep resentment and fear in me. I also heard strong opposition to the war. In 1941 came the news that a Soviet airplane bombed the Hungarian city of Kassa. When visiting my uncle in 1942, he showed me the post office building that had been damaged by the bomb. The memorial plaque at the site stated that it was a Russian attack. Rumors on the other hand claimed that it was a German plane with Russian insignia. The attack was to induce the Hungarian government to join in the war. The propaganda prevailed, and the country entered the war. Hungarian soldiers were sent to the Russian fronts. The propaganda included the pictures of the Russian peasants welcoming the Hungarian "Liberators" with the traditional salt and bread. All that was made quite believable, especially for those who themselves lived through the 1919 communist terror. For me who knew about the past only what I heard or read, the images of the war were confusing but interesting. Maps were included in the propaganda articles showing the looming shadow of the Soviet giant over the tiny Central Europe. The special reports on the radio and on the newsreels gave accounts on the surrendering of the hundreds of thousands of enemy soldiers, the Germans taking one big city after the other, the German tanks rolling on Russian soil passing the wreckage of the Soviet armor. Maps in store windows with small flags, needles and strings showed the rapid advances of the German troops. The daily news gave hope that the war could soon be over. I followed the events with excitement.

My first taste of the tense ethnic-national co-existence came in the late 1930s in the city of Sopron, where I attended the Lutheran Lyceum, or high school. The city lies in an enclave on Hungary's border with Austria. The politicians of the victorious powers of the First World War assigned the city to Austria. The strong protestation of the Hungarians resulted in a referendum that kept the city Hungarian. About half of the population was German nationals and half Hungarian. There was rivalry, occasionally exploding into street violence, mainly between youngsters. Those were the times when Austria in the Anschluss joined the German Reich. Some of the German nationals felt great pride of belonging to the powerful Germany. The Hungarian residents fearing for the future of the city resented that. The "Magyar Társaság," or Hungarian Society, which was a literary group of the pupils in our school for nurturing the Hungarian literature in its monthly publication the "Nyugati Örszem," The Western Sentry, had anti-German overtones. I read it with curiosity. In 1938 a census was taken in Hungary that also was to determine the future of the city of Sopron. If half of the residents were to state their nationality as German, the city was to have two administrations, one German and one Hungarian, some of the schools and public facilities were to be turned over to the German residents. Tactically, co-existence was to be turned into a defined ethnic-national division. In reality the battle was for total domination. The rush for listing names on the census charts began. To have as many Hungarian names as possible on the census lists, on the day of the census the Hungarian schools, clubs and churches held national meetings and events. The city was like a beehive with flags and bands drumming up patriotism. The confidence of the Hungarians was high until trainloads of German nationals arrived from other parts of the country in support of their cause, marching in the streets under their "Volksbund" flag with a symbol similar to the swastika. Tension arose when their columns marched by the monument with the Hungarian flag, without saluting it. Nationalistic pride and arrogance were on a collision course. The residents of the city, both the Hungarians and the Germans had been gripped in feverish, blind nationalism. The atmosphere was foreboding. The result of the census was that the Germans remained in the minority, and the city remained Hungarian. The tension-filled co-existence continued. Another upheaval came in April 1941 when the German army marched through the city for the war against Yugoslavia. I watched as the columns of trucks and tanks, and airplanes in the sky, were rumbling day and night. Having seen the parading Hungarian army with horse-drawn artillery and outmoded rifles, the modern motorized army of the Germans was impressive. In the presence of the mighty army some of the German national residents of the city were elated. The sidewalks were filled with people watching the flowing parade, I among them. In the noon hours came the news that the Hungarian Prime Minister count Pál Teleki, in protestation against the Germans' entering the country committed suicide. (Recent reports suggest that he was murdered.) The tension grew. Black flags appeared on the buildings, black armbands were distributed and worn. Rumors spread about the fight between the German troops and the Hungarian patriots at the border. Strong resentment arose in the city against the intruding foreigners. My history teacher who was a British-oriented anti-German gave the order to puncture the tires of the German military vehicles and of the bicycle of the local Germans who were watching the march. I became injected with the spirited feeling of nationalism and patriotic duty and with deep antagonism against the intruders and their local allies. For me the tranquility of the small village life was replaced by the tension of an ethnically and politically divided city. At the age of 14 I was made aware of my loyalty and obedience obligation to a national cause, which I did not understand. At the same time my German national classmates who were born and raised in the city, were made aware of their alien identity. The spiraling of the events from calm to calamity began. Peaceful co-existence was losing ground.

In the fall of 1941 I was enrolled in the Calvinist Collegium, or High School, in the city of Pápa that had a large Jewish community. Most of the Jewish residents were Orthodox, wore the traditional attire, had their small businesses in the city, or traveled as traders. Although there was a simmering mistrust, there was no open hostility between the races. I heard about atrocities committed by the paratroopers whose headquarters were near the Jewish sector. Occasionally, after getting drunk they went on rampaging, breaking the windows of the synagogue. Those were isolated incidents rather than organized harassment, but still caused much resentment in the Jewish community. The Jews lived in their sector. I avoided it, because in the narrow streets young Jewish men standing in groups did not welcome us "Goys". (Goy or Goyem were derogatory words used by some of the Jews for us Gentiles.) Social contact between the middle-class, educated, professional, non-Orthodox (Neologue) Jews and Gentiles did exist. A few Jewish girls and boys attended the Calvinist high schools. Their religious identity in the school-register was given as "Izraelita". In the schools there was no racial discrimination. As the war progressed and the mobilization of the country began, the healthy, young Jewish men—who by law were not allowed to serve in the armed forces—were called in for compulsory labor service. That caused deep resentment in the Jewish community. The drastic events came in the summer of 1944, when the order came for the Jews to wear the yellow star. Later in the summer all the remaining Jews were deported. The sight of their long columns leading to the railroad station by the gendarmes was depressing. One day I stood on the sidewalk watching the exodus. The column moved silently and slowly, the grownups carrying small suitcases and holding the hands of their children, the gendarmes with the bayonet attached to the rifle leading them. I felt saddened, fearing for my sweetheart whose father was Jewish. The people watched them from the sidewalk in silence. There were only a few who shouted the usual nasty anti-Jewish slogans. In those days I experienced another ethnic and also racial hatred, in which the Jews were portrayed as the deplorable internal enemy, the agents and sympathizers of Bolshevism, who were to be blamed for the bombing of our cities by the Americans and the British, and for all the horrors of the war. The elements of peaceful co-existence between the natives and the Jews ceased to exist.

In the late 1930s and early 40s there were many who feared the German control just as much as the threat of Soviet Bolshevism. "Pan-Germanism" and "Pan-Slavism," as the ambitions of the big powers, the real threats to our national identity and integrity were exploited by the politicians on both sides. In Hungary both the National Socialist and the Communist Parties were small and powerless. Under the internal and external political pressure changes in the government came, from conservative to nationalist, from nationalist to neutral, and then to the National Socialist. The fear of Bolshevism, together with the German support in the return of some of the territories which were taken away from Hungary in the Trianon Peace Treaty, were used as inducement for participating in the war on Germany's side. The political "Left" came with the propaganda against Germany, claiming that for the Germans "The Hungarian Question" was only a matter of enough railroad cars to replace the Hungarian population with German nationals. The political "Right" painted a picture of the West as an impotent, outdated world that was going to change, or disappear altogether. It also refreshed the memories of the short-lived Bolshevik terror of 1919 in Hungary. There was a period when the government danced a duet both with the Left and the Right, trying to please the Germans, but also maintaining contact with the West. However, the fear of Bolshevism did not fade. Just looking at the map I could see what the realities were. Germany with its military and industrial might was on the west and north, the Soviet Union on the east, south of us were the Balkans which in 1941 became occupied by the Germans. Adding to that the mistrust and resentment against the French and British because of the Trianon Treaty, the Hungarians seemed to have few choices. In short, this is how I as a teenager on the basis of the official propaganda and of the floating rumors perceived the events.

In 1942 large posters with big letters appeared on the walls and fences, warning the population of the danger of imminent air attacks. I read the news with excitement and fear, not knowing what an air war could be. Although, the pictures of the victims of the German bombing raid on Rotterdam were frightening, I did not want to believe that any country other than Germany could have the airplanes to attack us. That danger just was not taken as real. The bombs falling on Kassa brought new realities, but that city was far away from my hometown. In 1943 the war propaganda included horrifying pictures and reports on the mass graves in Katyn, Poland, discovered by the Germans, in which the remains of thousands of Polish military officers were found, executed during the occupation of the eastern part of Poland by the Soviets. The exhumation was conducted by an international committee, including a Hungarian professor, lending special interest to the matter in Hungary. I read the report and viewed the pictures with fear and sadness. A Hungarian soldier who came back from the Russian front talked about the brutality with which the war was fought, especially against the partisans, among whom were also women. With some pride he told me how they executed the captured women by pushing dynamite sticks into their genitals, blowing them up. He said it was in revenge for the alluring and killing of Hungarian soldiers by those women. I listened in disbelief. Could it be really true? Or, was it just a wild story of a bragging soldier? Good Christians could not do such horrible things! So I believed. I had to live through the war to learn what human brutality can be.

As the mobilization of Germany intensified, the German nationals living in Hungary were called in for service in the SS. Not having been German citizens, they could not serve in the regular army of the Wehrmacht. Trainloads of them were taken to Germany. One day a train with older Germans on it rolled in. I saw the inscription on the wall of one of the freight cars: *"Wir alte Affen sind Hitlers neue Waffen,"* We old monkeys are Hitler's new weapons. The realities of the war came closer to me when my sister's fiancé, who was an officer in a Hungarian tank unit was sent to the Russian front. In the first year of the war I heard about victories. He received high decorations for bravery. I was proud of him. But, then the forward march stopped. He came home on a stretcher. Visiting him in the hospital and seeing the many wounded soldiers without arms and legs, with deformed, burned faces, hearing their moaning and wailing, the image of the war changed for me. I no longer saw the heroes, but the victims. When the direction of the advances on the fronts changed, as the German and Hungarian troops had to retreat, the maps with the needles, flags and strings showing the front line disappeared from the shop windows. Rumor had it that the entire 2nd Army of Hungary had been wiped out. The reports with the new phrase "flexible tactical disengagement" became more and more frequent. We lived under the spell of the confident daily military reports, which sounded like telling the truth, although following on the maps the names of the cited places the front came closer and closer to us. But still, only a few people wanted to believe that the war was lost. Those who may have believed otherwise were afraid to say so.

My active service began in the summer of 1943, when I joined the compulsory paramilitary youth organization called "Levente", and was assigned to a training school for instructors. It existed for years, preparing the young men for military service. Under the terms of the Peace Treaty following the First

World War Hungary was allowed to maintain only a small army, but there were several paramilitary training programs. This was my first exposure to the strict military discipline, to mindless loyalty and blindly proud obedience. Wearing the uniform, learning the basic military skills, I served with great devotion, believing that it was for my country and in the defense of my nation. The brutal realities of wars lingered in my teenage mind, but still I was too young to understand the futility.

On March 19, 1944 Hungary became occupied by the German military. It came fully unexpected, as we were Germany's ally in fighting against Bolshevism, and it happened in spite of our Governor's strong objection. The reason for the strategic move was argued on the one side to reinforce Hungary's defenses, while on the other side it was viewed as a military step to prevent the possibility of Hungary's declaration of a cease-fire with the Soviets. It was a sunny Sunday morning when the loud noise of heavy tanks and trucks driving by the church overwhelmed my father's church service, after which I went to downtown to see what was happening. Long motorized columns were moving, German military police stood in the streets. Some of the public buildings became military command posts, and the schools became quarters for the soldiers.

In the days before the arrival of the Germans the residents of the town were preparing for a big cultural event. The country's leading writer and a favored actress, both known for their strong nationalistic attitudes came for an evening program. With the surprising arrival of the Germans the holding of the event was in doubt. In the early afternoon a German military vehicle stopped at our house, a German and a Hungarian officer came to see my parents. They requested a room for a German officer. It was done in a polite manner, and my parents consented. I felt safe by having had a German guard at our gate. The guest-officer was the deputy commander of the town. My father asked him about the evening program. He replied that they did not want to interfere with our daily lives. The program was held with a much larger attendance than had been expected. It was a quiet demonstration against the occupation.

The German military vehicles covered with camouflage nets were parked along the streets. Going by those monstrous machines, and seeing the enthusiastic young German soldiers my confidence grew. With all the seemingly devoted young men, and with those powerful war-machines the war couldn't be lost. So I thought.

While attending school I signed up at the civilian air guard, spending a few nights each week in the church tower. Patriotic loyalty and duty became part of my young life. In the summer of 1944 I joined the youth labor service, building new runways at the airfield near the city of Pápa. We were several hundred high school age youngsters in that service. Work started early in the morning, scraping the ground and shoveling the dirt into wheel barrels. It was hard work under the hot summer sun. But I did it with pride, believing that it was in serving my country. Not ideological convictions, but pure patriotism was what drove me.

At that time the bombing raids by the Americans became daily events. The frightening sound of sirens started in the morning hours with the long continuous tone giving the warning for the coming of the enemy planes. The radio programs were interrupted and the coded messages began: *"Achtung! Achtung! Lichtspiele! Krokodil gross kommen Spinat."* I did not know what such messages meant. Those were for the German military. Soon after that the screaming of the sirens signaled the arrival of the planes. A deep continuous rumbling was heard as hundreds and thousands of big bombers appeared in the sky in exact formation drawing the contrails. On clear sunny days it was an amazing show as the glittering machines reflected the sunshine and the white contrails broke the monotony of the blue sky. The airfield became a frequent target for the low-flying American fighter planes. During the raids I was ducking in small foxholes. I watched it from my foxhole with amazement, but also with a determination to do whatever I could to defend my country. The show lasted for hours as the planes came from the South and split into two streams, one heading West, the other North, all flying to Germany. By noon the passing of the air-armada ended, the alarm was cleared. We went back to work, until another air alarm came in the afternoon when the return flight of the bombers began. The afternoon show was different. The planes came in disorganized groups, some separated from the others. While in the morning I seldom saw German or Hungarian fighter planes, in the afternoon they were there hunting for the separated planes, chasing and firing at them until they burst into flames, or broke up. The night raids, which I often watched from the church tower, were different. No lights other than the moon and the stars, I could only hear the rumbling noise of the planes. Once in a while by the light of a full moon I could see some of the airplanes reflecting the moonlight. Telling from the length of the time it took to fly over those must have been smaller units. When a nearby airfield was attacked the flashing of the exploding bombs created a mysterious and frightening glow in the sky. On a Sunday afternoon, ignoring the air alarm, which for the people of my town became a harmless routine, the boys were playing soccer on the sports field. A single bomber flew over the town—not an unusual event—so nobody paid much attention. But, then an explosion shook the ground. A bomb hit the field. Torn bodies of the boys were scattered. I saw body parts hanging from the trees. That was the first taste for me of the real bloody war.

In August 1944 on a Sunday as I was on my way with my friends to the Rába river, taking our newly-built kayak for its maiden voyage, a big American bomber flew at low altitude, chased and shot at by a German fighter plane. The fate of the bomber was obvious. The German plane came back repeatedly opening up machine gun fire. For a while the bomber fired back, but to no avail. A parachute opened just before the bomber made a nosedive and hit the ground, bursting into flames. It happened a few hundred yards from us, shaking the ground. The parachutist landed nearby. He was the first enemy whom I saw face to face, a frightened young American with dark, curly hair shining from hair tonic. He did not appear injured. The angry peasants rushed to the site, gathered around him, talked about beating him or killing him, some wanted to see whether he was circumcised as proof that he was a Jew. The villagers hated the airmen because in the nightly raids they dropped small cellophane sheets coated with phosphorus that ignited when the sun dried them, setting the barns and the crops on fire. The gendarme arrived in time to save him. The wreckage burned for hours igniting the stubble, increasing the anger of the peasants. On that day 18 bombers crashed in our area. I wished that every single one of them had the same fate. The captured "Air bandits," as they were called, stood with raised hands, fearfully looking around, while over their heads hundreds of planes carrying their comrades were flying home.

In 1944 a new, illustrated newspaper the "Magyar Futár," the Hungarian Courier, was published by the Ultra Right. It was printed on cheap paper with ink that left its mark on my fingers. It carried photos from the Russian front, and included hate-filled anti-Jewish stories. On the last page were caricatures of the Jew with a big nose and devilish eyes. Most of the newspapers remained moderate even in the difficult years. Not that there was no war propaganda, but the issues were treated with caution. It was obvious that nobody could write about losing the war.

In the spring of 1944 I heard rumors that the Jews were to be deported to labor camps. The order came that they had to wear the yellow star. Everybody had to prove Gentile ancestry, or faced persecution. The feverish search for birth certificates began. Some of the non-Orthodox Jews sought sources for forged documents. Up to the early years of the century such records were kept by the churches. Although, it was most dangerous, a few forged birth certificates were issued. In our town in search of escape a few Jews joined the Lutheran Church, and could be saved from deportation. The Jews had to go to the market square with whatever they could carry. It was a depressing sight. The few Arrow-Cross Party bigots of the town, who were the imitators of the German Nazis, joyfully watched the exodus. There were only a few of them, and nobody took them seriously. Nobody thought that they could ever come to power. Their small party office was in the outer corner of the market square, the window was decorated with their Arrow-Cross flag and with propaganda leaflets. The local leaders were a law student the son of a prominent attorney, a medical student and a tailor. After the party was legalized in late 1944, they proudly walked in the main street with the Arrow-Cross armband. The people laughed at them.

With the turn of events it was becoming obvious that the war was lost. In the autumn of 1944 the Russian troops were already on Hungarian soil, the daily bombing raids paralyzed the country. But life still continued. The arrival of trains loaded with wounded soldiers was depressing. Trains going to the fronts carrying soldiers mobilized the town people. Soup kitchens were set up at the railroad station with volunteer women staffing them, including my mother. The hospital was full of wounded Hungarian and German soldiers and of captured American airmen. On Sundays people visited them bringing some cheer. In one of the hospital rooms I saw the absurdity of wars; a German SS and an American airman peacefully rested next to each other in their beds. In September the school year began, but as the frequency of the bombing raids increased, and bombs fell on the city, it ended a few weeks later. After school closing I went home to my parents. There was not much to do. The daily news reported great successes on the fronts, but the Russian troops came closer with each passing day. At noon after broadcasting the chiming of the church bells and playing the National Anthem, morale-boosting slogans became part of the radio program: "The Hungarians stand in a struggle. Fate put the weapons in their hands and they courageously accepted it."

What did I—the young teenager—know about the world in which I lived, and about the storms, which were brewing around me, disrupting my youth? As a young child I lived in a small village where some of my playmates lived in poverty. I also saw the wealth of the nobles who lived in their mansions. I felt that something was not right. I read the slogan on my pencil and on my school notebooks: "No, No Never," protesting against the Trianon Peace Treaty. The protest was even personal to me, because my dear mother had to flee from her home in Transylvania, which became part of Rumania. I was taught to be a good Hungarian, but had to resent the Czechs, the Rumanians, the Serbs and even the Austrians as neighbors for occupying parts of my country. At the same time I was taught to be a good Christian and love my neighbors. I was taught to be afraid of Bolshevism, and was warned about the threat of Hitlerism. In the tension-filled days living under German military occupation and fearing the arrival of the Soviet Army, I watched the events with the curiosity of the young. Although I knew from the news that the Russians were only one hundred kilometers away from my hometown, somehow I still could not accept the possibility that someday Russian soldiers were going to patrol our streets. Having seen the modern German tanks in our streets, the airplanes landing and starting from the airfields, watching the enthusiastic young German soldiers, I could not imagine that they could be defeated. I could not quite understand why the fronts were collapsing, when a well-equipped, modern army was around me. Those were the questions in my young mind for which I could not find the answers. What did remain for me as the guiding rule was; to be loyal and obedient, and trust in our leaders!

October 15, 1944 was a gray, cloudy Sunday. Early morning I went to the sport airfield near my hometown. Normally we had two glider-planes, both for early flight training. But at that time we had the best planes in the hangar. Those had been brought from the eastern part of the country before the Russian troops arrived there. There was also a very small motorized planes in the hangar, which I admired. I wished to be up in the air, but in those late days of the war flying for civilians was no longer permitted. After touching the wings with deep sadness, closed the doors of the hangar and began my bicycle journey home. My youthful passion for flying came to the end. The brutal realities of the war changed my life's course from passion to survival.

On the way home I met a Hungarian soldier hurriedly going along the road. With great enthusiasm he said that the war was over, the Governor of the country ordered the Hungarian army to stop fighting against the Russians. With excitement he said that he was on the way to his family. His words were unbelievable to me. But could it be true? I was wondering. He warned me of the armed and arm-banded gangs of the "Hungarists" or "Arrowists" who patrolled the streets checking the identification papers of every men, arresting those without proper documents. Bypassing the main streets I arrived home. The radio was turned on; my parents were sitting around it, listening to the announcements on the cease-fire. So, it was indeed true! The war was over, we believed. Then came a long silence with interruptions by military marches. In response to the Governor's call for cease-fire the Hungarists, or National

Socialists, in a coup overthrew the government, and their calls for the continuation of the war were broadcast. Replacing Miklos Horthy the Governor, the party leader Ferenc Szálasi was declared the new "Nemzetvezetö" or National Leader. The official greeting became: "Kitartás!", Persistence! For the first time the red-white-green Hungarian flag with the national coat-of-arms was joined on the public buildings by the Arrow-Cross flag. All those events were played out at the time when the fronts were crumbling, the Soviet troops were only 100 kilometers from our town and Budapest the capitol city was threatened by the rapidly advancing enemy.

Who in his right mind could assume that the events of the war could be reversed? There were such people, and there were also reasons for those who still wanted to believe in miracles. The presence of the well-armed German troops in the town, the talk about the "New weapons" which were soon to be launched to destroy the enemy, gave hope. The sensational news printed in big letters on the newspapers was: "Hundreds of unmanned German airplanes attack London. London burns" Those were the V-1 missiles. For me at that time the most immediate effect of the war were the American and British bombing raids. The reported destruction of hundreds of American bombers by a new German airplane, called the "Turbo," the new jet—although I had not seen one—was exciting. The latest giant German tank the "König-Tiger," that was described as indestructible was glorified. The "Hitler-Organ," a multiple rocket-launching weapon that was to wipe out the enemy added to the convincing evidence of changes to come. But, there was also a numbing uncertainty. In the streets I saw young men carrying submachine guns, wearing armbands with the Arrow-Cross symbol of the party. There was fear of the armed rulers, of the bombing raids and of the hated Soviets enemy.

Who was right, the Governor who called for the cease-fire, or those who wanted to continue fighting? Logic and morality dictated that the war was lost, and all further sacrifice was in vain. But there was also the fear of what was to come if the Soviet troops were to arrive. Could surrendering prevent bloodshed, looting and rape, or could it provide free reign for those horrors? Were those who wanted a cease-fire the cowards, and those who wanted to continue fighting the heroes? Fear and fanaticism were on a collision course. If only the enemy had not been feared as much for its brutality! Posters appeared on the walls giving orders for all military aged men to report for service, and death sentence warnings for all soldiers who were away from their units without a permit. The mindless loyalty and blind obedience of a small and fanatical

minority to a cause that was being lost, ruled the frightened people. Those
were the realities in Hungary in the late days of 1944.

In early December the Hungarian military commander of our town—who
was not a friend of the "Arrowists"—came to my father and told him that soon
all the young people, including my age-group, were to be called in for quick
training, and were to be taken to the front. He told me to leave the town as
quickly as possible. Not wanting to be in the hands of the Arrowist fanatics, I
stayed off the streets. Columns of young people marched on the roads from
villages and towns that were taken by the Russians to the still unoccupied
western part of Hungary. They were tired, hungry from the long march.

The fear of Bolshevism was deep in the minds of the people. The propaganda speeches by Dr. Goebbels, the German propaganda minister were powerful, telling the people that the propaganda coming from the Russian and
British radios were "Pure Jewish lies." The horror stories of the soldiers and of
the news about killing, destruction, raping of women by the Russians in the
towns and villages which temporarily had been retaken by our troops, added to
the panic. People fleeing on horse-drawn coaches, in automobiles, or on foot,
carrying what little they could, were on their way to the hoped-for safety of
the still unoccupied western part of Hungary and to Germany. It was a sad
exodus under the constant threat of air attacks. Although the local population
offered shelter for many, most of the refugees were exposed to the harshness
of the cold and wet autumn weather, spending the nights out of doors. The
frightened faces of the children and women were tragic images of the times.
Exhaustion from the constant moving and fear drained their strength, adding
to their desperation. That was another "Holocaust," a human tragedy of
immense proportion, about which not much has been written.

As the front came close to our town, and as it was only a matter of time
before the fighting reached it, my mother who lived through the communist
terror in 1919 said something that must have been very painful to her; *"I would
rather poison my family than to see you go through what I had to endure under the
Bolsheviks"*. She never told us what it was, but knowing her deep love, it
indeed must have been a terrible tragedy of her life. The time had arrived for
me to plan an escape. My father's decision was to stay with his congregation,
my mother wanted to stay with him. They both wanted me to leave. With two
of my friends we decided to join the regular Hungarian army at the tank battalion where my brother-in-law was an officer. His unit was to be transferred
to Germany for re-equipping and training. At least we could be with a regular
unit and not with the hastily slapped together bands of the Arrowists. For my

parents it was somewhat comforting that my sister and I were going to be together in a Hungarian group. In recognition of the inevitability of the outcome of the war it was somewhat comforting to know that we were going to be away from the much-feared Bolshevik terror. Without knowing what was in the future for me, I began my long journey. On a cold, foggy December day with the official papers in hand, as a volunteer of the army, I went to the railroad station. It was full of soldiers going to their units, and with civilians fleeing from the front.

The diary which I wrote in the tension-filled days, when I was 17–18 years old, is a remarkable collection of my thoughts at that young age under difficult circumstances. That was the only period of my life when I wrote down the events of my days, as if I had felt that someday those events could become the focal points of my old age tribulations. The times covered in my diary were the turning points of my life, when I was ripped from a boyhood and was tossed into the brutalities of a war, when the implanted respectful and mindful loyalty and obedience to my parents became distorted by the events and by the higher authorities into mindless loyalty and blind obedience. It is also quite remarkable that my diary survived the war and the prison. Reading it sixty years later gave me the impetus to write my memoirs and subsequently this book. On the following pages is the translation of a few excerpts.

"Celldömölk (My home town), December 6, 1944.

With my two friends, Sándor and Loránt, we spent the night in the office of the military command post at the railroad station. All night long talked about the coming journey. The train that was scheduled to depart at midnight arrived at 8 o'clock in the morning. The delay was caused by an American air attack on it on the previous day. We rushed to find place in the cars, but could find room only on the open platform to put down our luggage and sit on it. I thought of everybody at home, then looked at the buildings and the people, wondering whether I would see them again. The train started to move. The three of us with tearful eyes searched for the fading-away faces of those left behind. After arranging my luggage I crouched down shivering and covered myself with a blanket, smoking one cigarette after the other. A depression set in upon me. We looked at each other without a word. Our thoughts were probably the same; we broke away from the home, from the parents, and from those who loved us and whom we loved. Where are we going, what will happen to us? Will we ever come back? I was wondering. The cold wind cutting into my face sobered me up. It was a sad fate, but I didn't want to see it like that. I was heated by the thought of becoming a soldier, maybe decorated for bravery, my name as a hero someday in the news. What a spirited feeling, and what an illusion it was that started me on this big journey!

Railroad stations one after the other were left behind. Dense fog blanketed the ground, giving a sense of protection against air attacks. As the train left the station of the city of Pápa the sun broke through the wall of fog. It took a few minutes and a beautiful, but also danger concealing clear sky unfolded. We squeezed ourselves inside the car. Tired faces, fearful eyes surrounded me. Across from me sat a policeman with his wife, next to me a soldier. With bowed head I was trying to sleep. Did not want to see the desperate faces, did not want to know what was happening. The train passed a station where the buildings laid in ruins. The speeding rumble and the clicking noise of the wheels made me drowse. The train's whistle blew; we were arriving at the next station. The clicking noise began to slow down. Then came a nerve breaking, cracking and snapping noise together with loud engine roar. It was an air attack. Women were crying, men were screaming. Everybody was on the floor. The door slammed open, people ran out trampling on each other. A soldier shouted; "Nobody move or I shoot!". Loránt pulled down the window and jumped from the moving train. After Loránt I jumped. My pants got caught on the window frame. Behind me was the pressing crowd. I ripped my pants, and fell on the high embankment. I did not feel any blow. After me jumped Sándor. Nine low-flying "Lightnings" (The type of the American fighter-bombers) one after the other turned upon us strafing the fleeing. Machine gun thunder shook the air. Bullets were exploding. Bleeding and wailing people, dead on the ground were around me. I ran behind the guardhouse at the railroad crossing. The people tearing at each other were running around the building. Sharp screaming, steam clouds in the air. This was the end of the locomotive. More and more calls came for help. The airplanes came again. With my friends we rushed to help the wounded when there was loud engine roar again. This time was no gunfire. The victors came to see their victims. A few minutes passed when I heard gunfire again. The planes were attacking another train at the railroad station. The steam was pouring from the locomotive. The terrible sound of rattling throats, and wailing came from around me. Ambulances were coming, picked up the wounded and rushed back. Doctors bandaged the wounded, the dead were pulled from the shot-out cars. The locomotive engineer and coal handler lay dead next to each other. They became victims of their duty. At the door of our car was a pool of blood. A Rumanian work-service man was hit by an exploding bullet. His life ended there. In the car the luggage was on the floor, on the benches was blood. I went to a small wooded area, and watched the faces. Exhaustion and the lived-through horror muted everybody. Slowly I began to realize what I lived through, and what I did survive. We talked, while hundreds of murderous bombers were flying over our heads. Deep rumble signaled that somewhere they were delivering death.

My journey continued on a military convoy-train from Hungary to Germany, passing though the deep valleys of Slovakia, where the train-wrecks were evidence of the partisans' activities. The first signs of heavy bombing were in the city of Magdeburg in Germany. The next big city was Braunschweig, where in place of the buildings of the railroad station was only rubble, the rail tracks were ripped up, the railroad cars were thrown on top of each other. Behind the station were the ruins of the burned out city. Those were the signs of the devastation of a war. The train passed by Hannover. Smoke clouds floated over the city, spewed from the factory chimneys. Celle, a beautiful city with many modern houses followed. There were no signs of the war. Standing at the door of the freight car I looked out. The rain was sprinkling as the train moved through forests and valleys. We stopped for a short time at a big airfield. Airplanes were parked in lines, covered with camouflage nets. Hundreds of people were working erecting the walls of huge buildings. This was a remarkable contrast to the destruction that was in Braunschweig. It was almost dark when we arrived at our destination. The railroad station of Bergen-bei-Celle was small, more like a loading dock, carts and milk cans stacked along the walls. Gathering my belongings I stepped off the train. We marched through a dense forest to the military compound. The streets were divided; multi-story buildings were on both sides. It was a modern city, not like the old military barracks in Hungary. Here I was to be trained to become a loyal and obedient soldier, to fight for my country.

We were assigned to a group of buildings, and were told that if an air alarm was to come we must stay there. Soon after arrival the sirens screamed and the rumbling noise of the airplanes could be heard. As the bombs fell the ground was shaking. Through the windows I saw as the city of Hannover was bombed. It was a frightening sight. Giant flashes of the exploding bombs and the rays of the searchlights lit the sky. The monotonous muffled thunderclaps of the explosions vibrated in the air. The horizon was in a reddish glow from the flames of the burning city. After about a half-hour the sirens signaled the end of the raid. I went to bed and fell asleep. In the morning looking out the window saw how big this compound was. As far as I could see was a modern city.

Next day we marched to the Bergen-Belsen concentration camp, which was only a short distance from the compound, to take a hot shower and to be disinfected. The Germans were afraid of the outbreak of an epidemic. All units arriving from the Eastern front zones had to undergo the treatment. The camp was surrounded with tall barbed-wire fence and guard towers. The uniformed KAPO, the internal police of the camp made up of the Jewish inmates led us to the barracks where the showers were. I saw people in striped prisoner outfits walking by piles of potatoes and cabbages. It was depressing to see human beings locked behind barbed-wire fences guarded by soldiers in the towers with machine guns. How could anybody survive there, I was wondering. The shower barracks had narrow doors; on the ceiling were vent chimneys, but no windows. After we disrobed all our belongings were loaded on carts and were taken away by the Jewish inmates who worked there. Finishing the hot shower the carts were back with our clothing on them, releasing a bad odor. It was the gas—I was told—with which the disinfecting was done. While going by the medic barrack I had a few words with a Hungarian medical doctor, he was Jewish and was an inmate. He talked about the fear of the outbreak of a typhoid epidemic, and wished me well. In another nearby camp were Russian prisoners of war. They were free to leave the camp, visited us at our compound, entertained us with traditional Russian dances in return for cigarettes. We had a friendly camaraderie with them.

The saddest Christmas of my life arrived. We brought a small fir tree from the surrounding woods, decorated it with cigarettes, with tin foil shaped into balls and with garlands made of the foil strips dropped by the American and British to jam the German radar. We received gift packages from the German army with a few pieces of the traditional German Christmas cookies, candies and cigarettes. On Christmas Eve after singing the traditional Christmas songs everybody was quiet. The temperature outside was 22 below zero Celsius. Sharp, cutting cold wind blew across the Lüneburger Heide, which is a large flat area in the northern part of Germany. There was no radio and there were no newspapers to read. I had no idea what the status of the war was, didn't know how close or how far the fronts were.

After Christmas trainloads of Hungarian Jews were led on the road across from the building where I stayed. Women, children and men stumbled on the slippery road, carrying their few belongings. They looked tired and filthy. One of them seeing our Hungarian uniform asked where they were being taken. I did not know, and so I could not say.

MEDITATION AT THE GRAVES OF THE VICTIMS OF BIGOTRY.

In memory of the dead of the Bergen-Belsen concentration camp.

On the walls along the grassy earth fillings,
numbers in hundreds and thousands are carved in the stones,
telling the visitor how many are buried in the graves.
There are no names, no dates of birth or death.
Nobody knows who they were, were they young or were they old.
It is a quiet, solemn place.
It is the place to contemplate.

In December of 1944, I was in the military camp
not far from where the mass-graves are,
watched the deportees as they arrived.
That was at Christmas time, in the season of peace and love,
but all around me the horror of the war prevailed.

It was a heartbreaking sight,
mothers holding their children's hands,

filthy and exhausted, dragging themselves in the fog.
I heard them speaking my native tongue.

A few weeks earlier as a soldier
I marched along the same snowy road.
My destination was a military camp,
I came to be trained to fight.
They were women, children and the old.
I heard one desperate call:
"Where are they taking us?"
I could not answer.
I didn't know.

Those were my last images of them until years after the war,
when I saw the pictures of the human wrecks,
just skin and bones, the victims of a horrible disease,
the mass-graves as open pits,
the corpses thrown in like worthless waste.

To stop the spreading of the deadly disease
they had to be quickly buried,
the barracks had to be burned to ash.
They became nameless,
they were erased from the human race.

What was their guilt?
It was their race.
They had to wear the yellow star,
the symbol of their fate.

Walking between the mass-graves
reading the numbers of the dead,
recalling the images of the past,
I became deeply depressed.

The brutalities of the concentration camps,
the horror of slaughtering the fleeing refugees
the immoral bombing raids,
the turning of homes into rubble
burying their inhabitants beneath,
the evaporating of hundreds of thousands
in the nuclear attacks,
the killing of the millions on the battlefields,
the persecution under faulty ideologies,
all those crimes are my lifetime's tragic legacies.

How could all that happen in a world in which I was raised,
was taught to respect and to love?
How could all the cultured minds tolerate such inhumanity?
What happened to the high moral principles?

What did happen cannot be undone.
The mass-graves all over the world will keep their dead.
It is us the living who have to reflect,
It is us who have to learn.

Not far from the compound I saw heavy contrails drawn by a small air-plane-like flying thing, starting from the forests, flying at high speed. The Germans told me that those were the "Pilotless airplanes" attacking London. They were enthusiastic about the "V-1 Neue Waffen," one of the new weapons.

In early 1945 I was transferred to Erlangen, which is a city in the central part of Germany, for training on the "Panther" tank. The frequent air raids by the American planes against the railroads made the journey dangerous. On the way we passed through the city of Dresden, a treasure house of art and culture. The streets were full of refugees fleeing from the advancing Russian troops. They were without any protection against the cold winter, but felt safe in what they believed was an "Open City." But on February 13 and 14, 1945 the entire city was turned into an inferno, the refugees were blown by the firestorm into piles of burning human flesh. They were caught in the rain of firebombs. Bodies of dead and dying, women, men and children covered the ground. It was death and destruction of unimaginable horror. According to the German official report more than 200,000 human lives were extinguished in one of the major crimes of the war.

Erlangen is a university city not far from Nürnberg. The military compound was almost vacant, the troops left to the Western Front. Only a few German instructors remained behind to train us in operating the 43-ton war machine. What monstrous power it had when it moved across the field. It appeared as if nothing could stop it, but thousands were destroyed in battles. Inside it was a cramped, dark place with unbearable noise and choking smoke. When the long-barreled 88 millimeter gun was fired the whole machine shook as if it would fall apart. Out on the cold fields in 20 degree below zero temperature we had to change the tracks, and had to clean the gun. The huge 750 horsepower engine was the source of heat. In one of the big garages were mock-ups of battlefields with miniature tanks, which were moved with long wooden sticks. We were taught to plan and carry out defensive moves. With the depletion of the fuel supply the field training was reduced to on-foot type exercises. That is, five of us as crew of a tank moved on the field on foot learning how to give and receive commands. While on the training field I often saw strange-looking airplanes in the sky. They flew extremely fast, leaving behind two smoky trails, climbing almost vertically at high speed. Those were also new weapons, the "Turbos." An airfield for the new jets was nearby. On the grounds of the compound stood a huge steel frame, the German instructor told me that it was the "Locator-antenna," a new secret thing. It was the early version of radar.

On the night of February 20, 1945 while on a military exercise on a hill about twenty miles from Nürnberg I watched the air raid as the bombs exploded, heard the deep thunder and saw the red glow over the burning city. Early in the morning our unit was brought by train to the city to help the rescue troops. The train stopped at the city of Fürth, which is a few kilometers from Nürnberg. From there we marched to the burning city. In the outer districts I saw people clearing the streets from the debris and putting out small fires. In the city center it was total devastation, fires raging, buildings collapsing, the streets covered with debris. We joined the German rescuers and civilians who desperately fought the flames. They had been doing it all night and were exhausted and needed help. At the noon hours we heard the sirens signaling another air raid. Soon the deep rumbling sound of the hundreds of airplanes could be heard. I went in the nearest bomb-shelter, called the "Luftschutzkeller" under a building that was damaged but still standing. The shelter had an L shape. The civilians sat quietly on benches under the flickering light of candles and of hand-operated flashlights. I was among the last to enter and crouched at the door. What more could the bombs destroy in an already burned down city, I was wondering. The deep rumbling noise and the ground shaking grew as the carpet-bombing approached the area. It was frightening. For me this was the first time in a heavy terror bombing. The shaking of the ground was violent. Then everything quieted down as the bombs fell further and further away from us. It was a relief, and I thought it was over. In the dark shelter there was an eerie quiet. When we began to open the door the rumbling noise and the ground shaking started again, becoming stronger and stronger. It was another wave of terror. Then came a big shock. A deep almost continuous rumbling noise grew as if the building was collapsing on top of us. In my first reaction I grabbed my steel helmet and banged it on the floor. In the darkness and choking dust we opened the door. Outside was raging fire. The asphalt, the trees and the buildings were burning with intense heat. It was an inferno with total devastation. In the first wave explosive bombs were dropped on the already burning city, then came the rain of the magnesium bars, which burned with the inextinguishable bright white flame igniting everything. In a third wave came another carpet of explosive bombs, spreading the fire. Such was the strategy in a war against the civilians, against women, the elderly. Leaving the shelter I crawled through the stairway, dazed from the sight. The heat was intense, the smoke was dense. The flames were jumping, flying across the street. Walls were breaking and crashing down. The building under which the shelter was housed, was severely damaged and burned out. There was nothing left to save. I was sent to help in one of the nearby apartment buildings where the upper floors were on fire. The people fleeing from the burning building gathered in the yard. In the middle of the square across from the building stood a church in flames. In that frightful inferno the question arose in my fearful, young mind; what should I do; save God's church or the peoples' homes? Should I help The Almighty or the desperate people? Why couldn't God save his own house? Why did He allow such horror to happen? This experience was a major break in my faith. I lost it forever. With my friends we ran up the stairs of the burning apartment buildings, avoiding the flames, carrying down whatever we could salvage.

On another occasion while in a bomb-shelter I sat next to an old, frail lady. She sat quietly, holding two photos in her hands. When the explosions shook the walls I reached for her hand, and in my broken German tried to comfort her. She looked at me with some indignation, saying that she was not afraid, she was only deeply sorrowed because two of her soldier sons had died in the war. What was she—I was wondering—a desperate mother who no longer viewed life as worth living? A courageous human being, or a fanatic? I began to feel the true evil of wars, and the bestiality of the human minds which brought such horror upon mothers, children and upon all our fellow human beings. Air-war against civilians is the most horrible war crime. In my view those who commit it are the most despicable criminals.

THE AIR RAID.

In memory of the victims of the February 20, and March 16, 1945 air raids on Nürnberg.

The night was dark, only a few stars could be seen.
The sirens screamed, searchlights scanned the sky.
The deep rumbling of the airplane engines could be heard.
And then, the rain of thousands of bombs began.
The ground shook, there was vibration in the air.
The flaming city turned the horizon into reddish flair.
When the raid was over, silence set in.
The city was in a glow of flames.

I watched the horror in anger and rushed to help.
What I saw was frightening.
It was hell on earth.
The flames jumped from house to house,
the carnage was total, the heat was immense,
burning debris covered the streets.
The people screaming and bleeding,
their faces blackened by the soot,
desperately fought the raging flames,
frantically searched under the rubbles
hoping to find someone alive.

While the survivors and the rescuers battled the flames
new waves of the bombers arrived.
There were no sirens to warn.
The splashed flesh and blood was pure horror.
Killing the survivors and the rescuers was the raiders' aim.

Who were the raiders; the barbarians of the rogue?
Or were they the outlaws of the wild?
No, they were not such breed, they were Americans.
Who sent them to commit the crime?
The generals and the strategists,
the government, the peoples' representatives.

Americans, shed the fake innocence
and accept the burden of the guilt.
The fate of the raided cities,
the suffering of the millions in Europe and in Asia,
from Dresden to Nürnberg, from Tokyo to Hiroshima,
the killing of women, children, the sick and the old,
the slaughtering of the fleeing refugees
the turning of the homes into rubble,
were crimes of immense magnitude
committed not by your enemies.

Don't soothe your souls with the thought
that what you did was right,
that you had to stop the evil Hitlerites.
Don't ask for, and don't expect forgiveness for what you did.
The suffering of your victims was much too deep.
Victory cannot erase a crime,
it cannot wash you clean.
Humbly admit the guilt and learn from it
never again the same to commit.

When the Americans came close to Erlangen our instructors went to the front. The commander of the school asked us if we were willing to join them. Our Hungarian officer told us, that according to the agreement with the German military, the Hungarian troops could be sent to the eastern front only, to fight against the Russians. Most remarkably even in those highly critical days the Germans honored that agreement. We did not have to join them, but instead were to return to the Hungarian Battalion in Northern Germany. But that was no longer possible. On April 3, 1945 we began the northward journey by train, but could go up to the city of Saalfeld only, and no further. The Americans broke through the German lines and sliced Germany in two halves. A torturous southward journey along the ever-changing eastern front began. Low-flying American fighter-bombers were over our heads all day long, destroying everything that moved on the roads and on the rails. It was a chaotic retreat. We ate what food we could find in the wrecks along the roads, rested at daytime wherever we could find a relatively safe roof, and moved at night. Nobody knew where the enemy was. On one occasion when in the dark we entered a small village the residents hearing foreign talk thought we were Americans. Small white flags appeared in the windows. There were places where the villagers set up road barricades, made of tree trunks and bricks. Not really effective obstacles for tanks. The long nightly marches were exhausting. Not knowing where we were, and not knowing where the Americans were, made the retreat even more tense. Excitement came, when from time to time we came under American fire. There was no resistance. We had neither ammunition, nor the desire to get entangled in battles.

Going through the city of Hof I saw a beautiful car in the store window of a dealership. Well, it would have been nice to drive it. On the railroad station we found a freight car full of marmalade. I was hungry, ate it without bread, giving me a bad stomachache. In Augsburg for the first time I saw a German jet in action against American bombers. Ducking behind the tombstones in the cemetery, watched as one single German jet shot down three of them. It was too little and too late. After the air raid an eerie quiet set in with the deep humming noise of the falling shrapnel of the anti-aircraft guns, vibrating the air. It was a beautiful sound, like that of an organ. I can still hear it in my ears. In Kempten next to the railroad station was a big cheese factory that was damaged by a bomb. There was plenty of cheese to eat. From there we rode on a narrow-gauge mountain train not far from the snow-covered peak of the Zugspitze, the well-known marvel of nature. It was a beautiful ride between gigantic, snow-covered peaks, helping me to forget that there was a devastating war all around me. The train stopped at the station of the cable car, which went up to a building high on the mountainside. The German soldiers at the station told me that the building was a prison for captured American fliers and for foreign political prisoners. I envied them. For them the war was over, they survived it, and they lived in a winter wonderland. For me the uncertainty about the immediate and the distant future was the occupying thought. On April 20 we arrived in Mittenwald, the famous violin-making town. Comforting was that there was no longer gunfire around me. The protection by the majestic mountains of the Alps was a welcome relief.

Sensing the imminent defeat, waiting for the enemy and surrender was on my mind throughout the journey. The fear of the "Neue Waffen" the new weapons of which I had seen the jet airplanes and the V-1 missiles, together with the rumors that Hitler sent an apology to the German prisoners of war for the harm they could suffer in the destruction of the enemy with the new secret weapons, kept me going. For me the young seventeen-year-old Hitler's rumored message was a hopeful and also frightful thought. Hopeful that the war could come to a sudden end, frightful that I could be one of its victims.[1]

I have spent he last days of the war in Mittenwald, a city in a beautiful valley in the Alps, not far from the Swiss border. The military compound that was mostly vacant was at the edge of the city at the foot of the snowy mountains. A small German SS unit also was there. On the afternoon of April 30th we were ordered to the drill yard. A young German SS soldier was led by two SS guards to the walls, his hands tied behind, his uniform stripped of all insignia. He fled to Switzerland, was captured by the Swiss boarder guards, and was handed over to the German side. For the event the Commander of the Southern Front came with a helicopter-like "autogyro", an unusual mode of travel in those days, flying low in the winding valleys. He acted as if he were still a powerful man commanding victorious armies, when in reality the fronts had already collapsed. There was no army to fight; only exhausted and

---

1.   There is an array of reports and articles available on the "New Weapons", including the first "A-Bombe" test by the Germans on March 4, 1945 at the secret research facilities near the town of Ohrdruf in the Province of Thüringia. Although, it was a very small yield bomb, the explosion killed several hundred prisoner workers. Reports also speak of a second, a much larger A-Bomb that has not been exploded. Uncorroborated reports speak of large amount of nuclear material captured and transported by the American troops from those facilities in 1945.

wounded soldiers who tried to survive. The eyes of the young soldier were covered with a handkerchief, a shot rang out and he died without a word. The commander who fired the shot showed satisfaction from punishing a deserter. That event was a sobering reminder for me.

In the evening of the last day of April the SS Commander of compound gave the order for the evacuation and demolition of the buildings. I could see the flashes of artillery and could hear the thunder, so it was obvious that the front was close, and the Americans could arrive at any hour. The buildings have not been demolished. A white flag was raised at the gate. We spent the night in the basement that was furnished as sleeping quarters. A movie projector with stacks of spools of films for ski instruction served as entertainment. We had plenty of cigarettes recovered from an overturned truck, and good French wine collected from a wreck. While wondering what was coming on the next days, we watched the films, ate cheese and drank wine."

These are a few translated excerpts from the surviving pages of my diary. The story was not a fiction, was not something that I heard, but was my own experience written down in the scribbled words of a 17 year old.

For me it was an anticlimactic end of a world war. I survived it without returning to my homeland to fight with the new "Miracle Weapons", without receiving medals for bravery, without my name ever printed in the news as a hero. I remained a surviving young corporal. Still a teen-ager, but through the hardships and dangers much matured young man, I was the witness to historic events of the collapsing of a once mighty empire, and to the defeat of a once invincible army. I have lived through a struggle for survival, experienced the indescribable barbarism and brutality with which seemingly civilized nations fought a war, burning cities to the ground, mercilessly slaughtering the fleeing refugees, herding people in concentration camps. Much disillusioned with the human society, and demoralized, I was at the closing of a chapter of my young life, and began to understand the evilness of blind patriotism, of mindless loyalty and proud obedience. Was Switzerland's neutrality so important to them to return a fleeing man at the time when the war was almost over, just days before Germany's final capitulation? Was the SS officer pulling the trigger totally blind to the fact that the war was already lost? I assume he did know well that it was only hours or days away when he himself had to surrender to the enemy. Witnessing the tragic event of the execution of the young German, and recalling it many years later led me to the recognition of the futility and of the danger of the fundamental elements of militarism; mindless loyalty and blindly proud obedience. Another young human being, together with many millions, fell victim to the senseless submission to higher authorities.

Not quite at 18 years of age another dramatic phase of my young life began. I became a prisoner of war. Although I knew well that it was only a matter of time when I had to face that humiliation, but did not know how to prepare for it. I had seen in the newspapers and on the movie screens the images of prisoner of war camps, the tired, frightened faces of the prisoners, heard stories from the prisoners of the First World War, but still could not see what was coming for me. The thought of becoming a prisoner meant the end of fighting, and that was a long sought-after relief. The question was; what was it going to be like? On May 1st 1945, at about 8 o'clock in the morning, I saw the first American tanks at the edge of the city of Mittenwald, on the opposite side of the valley from the military compound. There was no fighting. White flags were raised on the buildings. Around 10 o'clock a jeep with two American soldiers stopped at the gate of the military compound. The English-speaking guard greeted them. The American officer gave the order to line up in the drill yard for a formal surrender, and to gather all the weapons. He was a tall man wearing a steel helmet. For the first time I faced an American soldier who was not my captive, but was my captor. He was not the trembling young airman looking at me with fear in his eyes, whom I had captured a few months earlier, but was a man with self-confidence, looking at me with stern eyes. I felt what my prisoner must have felt; fear, helplessness. After a short inspection for which we had to remove from our uniform all insignia, the officer through an interpreter assured us that we were to be well treated. He then gave the order to march. I gathered my few belongings. One American soldier was at the front, and one at the end of the column. There were no threats, no harsh words. It was almost unreal. As we were led through the city I saw the residents looking from behind the window curtains. After exiting the city the road turned to the right, on both sides with columns of American tanks and trucks. The soldiers looked down at us, quite likely not knowing what nationality we were. I looked at them with a smile. For me the war was over. Or, so I thought. Later on the way a few soldiers jumped from the tanks, hit us with bars, cut off our wristwatch. They were all white Americans. In the ditch I saw young German soldiers, beaten, bleeding and dying. Peace had not arrived. Brutality still flourished.

We passed small groups of Hungarian Jews who were coming from a concentration camp. They were happy. One of them said: "Boys, be careful and see you at home." They were the ones who should have hated us the most.

It was a long march to Garmisch-Partenkirchen the well-known Winter Olympics city in the snowy, beautiful Alps. White flags were on the houses; the civilians watched the events from the windows. Our first stop was on a square where we were searched. After that in a cold rain we were loaded on open trucks. A machine gun mounted on the top of the cab was aimed at us. The drivers and the guards were changed on the way. The white drivers ran through the towns not letting the citizens give us food or water. When a black crew came, the guard tossed cigarettes to us. In the towns they slowed down, letting the people pass food and water to us. Those were the Negroes whom before I was captured I had feared the most.

The first overnight stop was at the air base in Göppingen. Trucks with mounted searchlights and machine guns surrounded the hangars full of prisoners. I was cold, wet and hungry, but there was no food, had to sit on the cold concrete floor, searchlights scanning over my head. Next morning as the guards herded us to the trucks I saw a wrecked automobile, the same make, the same model and the same color that my father once had. That sight detached me from the sad presence and brought back pleasant memories. Why did those happy, worry-free days had to come to this deplorable end? In heavy rain we were driven through war-torn cities, over makeshift bridges, on roads littered with the burned-out wrecks of tanks and trucks. The 43-ton steel monsters which appeared indestructible when I was trained to operate them lay in the ditches wrecked, burned out. I was wondering what did happen to their crew. I could very well have been in one of them. The trucks carrying us tightly packed rolled by these remnants of the war. The cold rain penetrated my uniform. I could not feel like a human being anymore.

It was late afternoon when we arrived in the city of Heilbronn. The convoy stopped at a soccer field just outside the city. There were already many trucks unloading German prisoners. The loud shouting of the guards could be heard. As I jumped off the truck became separated from my friends. The American guard with a rifle in his hands pushed me away into a line of German soldiers. When tried to run back he pointed the rifle at me. We were herded to the field, where along the fence at the gate I saw bloody corpses of German soldiers. The field was full of prisoners, surrounded by tanks and trucks with mounted machine guns. I was told that those at the gate were shot when a water truck arrived, and they rushed to it. Thirst was more unbearable than hunger. An older German soldier sat next to me, gave me encouragement that everything was going to be just fine, we were going soon released. During the day more and more German prisoners arrived. The whole soccer field was full of people. It was frightening to see the guards around us standing behind the machine guns aimed at us. Late afternoon we were divided into smaller groups and began the slow march to the permanent camp. Every few yards there was a guard. It was a slow march in heavy rain and in deep mud. I kept licking the sleeves of my coat to reduce the pain of thirst. We were herded like cattle, the guards screaming at us: "Let's go! Let's go! Move!" Those were the first English words I learned.

When we arrived to the campsite it was already dark. Trucks and tanks formed square blocks; bright searchlights scanned the barren, wet clay field. That was our camp. I stood there all night long in pouring rain, shivering in my water soaked uniform, hungry and thirsty, heard gun fire, but was too numbed by exhaustion to be afraid. Next morning black soldiers came on trucks to erect barbed-wire fences dividing the plateau into blocks. The big plateau was like an ocean of human beings. Later I heard that one million prisoners were in that camp. One million men behind fences like cattle, wet, shivering in the cold, whose names nobody registered, who had not even a number anymore. I did not belong to anybody or anything, ceased to be what I was only a short time earlier, member of an army, belonging to something that provided a feeling of identity. Now, the only thing that identified me was the "Carrion-tag" that I still had hanging around my neck, engraved on it my name and my military numbers that meant nothing anymore. I had nobody to look up to, nobody to respect. We were just look-alike, dirty, wet, tired. The mud was deep to move around, so just stayed where I was. Most of the men around me were older, hardened in the battles of the war. A very young German soldier, most likely younger than I sat in the mud, and was crying. He was left alone. Nobody reached for him. Those were the feelings of total abandonment, of helplessness. Just stared without seeing anybody or anything, wondered what was happening to me. I was in the middle of a human sea, but felt totally alone. I despised the military, but at least in it I was a member of a unit, had a commander who was responsible for me—at least in peacetime—knew that I was to be fed each day, no matter how meager. Now, I had nothing of that, only strange people around me just as desperate as I was, no shelter, no food, no water, and only mud to sit on. The feeling of having been caged-in, surrounded by barbed-wire fences, guard towers and machine guns, knowing that I could not go anywhere for help was a heavy burden on my mind at the age of 18. But I had to be strong, had to do what the others were doing around me, if wanted to survive.

Two rows of barbed-wire fences surrounded each block, with the "no man's land" between them. On the corners stood guard towers with machine gun, searchlight and two soldiers. Inside the camp was bare mud of sticky clay, no shelter of any kind. Having been exhausted we sat down, back-to-back, forming circles to keep each other warm, covering ourselves with our coats to stay dry in the pouring rain. Days went by without food or water. For protection we made dugouts in the muddy clay. Shivering in my water-soaked uniform, my boots filled with muddy water, I crouched there. At least I felt safer. In one of the dugouts were five young Germans. At night the water-soaked dirt moved and buried them. The order came to fill the dugouts. We had to stay on the surface. I remembered the shock that I had when entering the concentration camp in Bergen-Belsen and seeing inmates walking between piles of cabbage and potato, living in simple wooden barracks surrounded by barbed-wire fence and guard towers. I was wondering how anybody could survive under such conditions. Now, I was surrounded by barbed-wire fences and faced machine guns in the guard towers. There were no piles of cabbage and potato, no shelter of any kind, only deep sticky mud.

After several days without shelter, without food or water, trucks arrived with large rolls of fabrics, empty cardboard boxes and wooden bars. We were allowed to build makeshift tents, the cardboard served as flooring. Scraping away the wet clay small tents for eight to ten men were set up, barely high enough in the middle to sit under, tapering on both sides, leaving little room for the heads and feet. The fabric was not water-resistant, if touched from inside it leaked through. On the outside, we attempted to seal the edges with wet clay. We laid close to each other to keep warm. If somebody had to step out there was the danger of touching the fabric or breaking the seals. When the wind blew we grabbed the sticks that held up the tent. The daily food supply for the next few weeks was one loaf of bread and one cup of sugar for five of us. Rainwater collected in small puddles was the only means to wash myself. Constantly I felt itchy from the bites of the lice, which multiplied rapidly. It was not only unpleasant, but also shameful to have those bugs. But there was nothing I could do. When the sun came out I sat outside the tent hunting for them under the armpits and in the groin. It was a sad picture of a civilized society doing what was the sign of the lowest imaginable standing. The great fear was the outbreak of a typhoid epidemic that could be devastating for us who were badly undernourished. I remembered how fearful the Jewish doctor in the Bergen-Belsen concentration camp was of the outbreak of epidemics. I lost weight; my hair grew into a big stack. I felt and looked miserable.

The distribution of the loaf of bread and the cup of sugar was a closely watched procedure. Every morsel counted. Scales were made of the tin cans in which the sugar came; making sure that everybody received the same amount of the meager daily ration. To my great fortune I followed the tip of one of our guys. Before capture I had filled my backpack with cigarettes which I found in an overturned truck. Most of my cigarettes fell victim to the rain, but some survived. In the camps cigarettes were the only valuable commodity. I could buy half a slice of bread for one cigarette. Wedding rings and watches were traded for a couple of cigarettes. To keep dry, I bought a military raincoat from a German prisoner for two cigarettes.

Some of the white guards were quite brutal. They tossed slices of bread on the "no man's land" waiting for someone to take. Those who tried risked their lives. I often stood at the inner fence looking at the bread, fighting the temptation to crawl for it. The black guards made sure to toss the bread far enough to land on the safe zone. The worst atrocity was when the wife of one of the German prisoners came to the fence with her baby in her arms. Somehow, she knew that her husband was there. She came close to the fence, raised the baby up in the air to show it to her husband, when the white guard fired a shot and hit the baby. The war was over, but brutality did not cease. The guard was a white man, he could have been raised in a good family attending church, and he wore the uniform of the army of a civilized nation. At the moment when he fired his rifle he might have worn a necklace with a cross. How could he do such an evil thing? What turned him into a beast? He was the victim of propaganda, of lies, of false indoctrination, of mindless loyalty and blindly proud obedience, just as his enemies were.

Lack of personal hygiene, meager food, absence of protection against the elements, together with the infestation with lice brought the fear of some disease. Slowly, my body functions began to deteriorate. My digestive system failed, my kidneys did not work. My teeth became loose, flipping out when I bit in bread. On my neck big painful boils grew keeping me from the much-needed sleep. Life was most miserable. I could not go anywhere for help. The handkerchief that my mother gave me and the photo of my sweetheart were the only ties to something that gave me the purpose to survive.

When I had left home, my father gave me his small pocket Bible. On the inner side of the cover page I wrote the quotation that my father read to me from Joshua 1:5-6: *"I shall never desert you, nor leave you entirely. Be courageous and strong."* I carried that Bible with me throughout the war, although seldom opened it. Having kept it in the pocket of my water soaked uniform it was wet, washing away the stains of my blood that glued together some of the pages. While in prison camp, in preparation for the presumed inevitability, I read it four times, hoping to find some relief from my miseries. Life, as I had seen it was so cruel, the suffering that I had seen and had to endure was so terrible that I could not find any signs of a loving God.

As months later the conditions improved, I regained my physical strength, and rebuilt my hope for a better life. There was a tent over my head, had better and more food to eat, but still I was living between barbed-wire fences, deprived of the essentials of a meaningful life. I looked around the huge field where one million of us were. A few months earlier we were the feared armies with powerful weapons in our hands. What did happen to us? I was wondering. We became like sheep, arguing and fighting over the size of a slice of bread and over a spoonful of sugar. Actually, that was the daily ration on which we had to survive. The starvation of the first months was a very difficult period. As I lost strength, lethargy came upon me with hallucination. Dreamed about eating, and when I woke up I was too weak from hunger to move. Thirst was even more unbearable. I drank the dirty rainwater that I collected in small puddles. In the mornings we woke each other, but some could not bear the starvation, and died in their sleep. The corpses were gathered in the mornings and loaded onto a jeep and were carried away. For a few days the deceased men's rations meant extra nourishment for us survivors. A few Germans attempted to escape. Those who were caught ended up in the cages set up in the middle of the camp. For me, whose homeland was far away, who had no place to go, escape was not an option. I just hoped for survival and eventual release.

To prevent the outbreak of an epidemic in the summer months we were regularly sprayed with DDT, not knowing how dangerous that chemical was. We had to stand in a single row, bare-naked, a jeep came with a pump towed behind it, and we were covered from head to toe with the dust. My eyes, nostrils and mouth were full of the dust. It kept me free of lice, which was a great relief. We were frequently moved from one fenced block to another. I assume it was to prevent any possible organized activities for breakouts or revolts. In the eight months that I spent in the camp my group was moved seven times. The guards with rifles on their shoulders, screaming, herded us. Eventually, we were sorted by nationalities, Germans, Hungarians and others, including Russians who were members of the "Wlassov-Army" named after a Russian general who was its commander, and fought on the German side.

As the conditions improved water was brought in for showering. Tents with washbasins were set up where we could wash our clothing. Having seen the American guards in their sharply pressed clean shirts and pants I felt like a poor beggar wearing old rags. Still, the toilet facilities were most primitive, rows of open latrines along the inner row of the fence. No privacy at all. When summer arrived life became more bearable. Not having been in the deep mud the weekly line-ups for counting were not so bad either. Once a week we had to stand in five-man columns along the inner fence to be counted. During line-ups we had to raise our arms to check whether anybody had the tattooed number like the SS men had. An American sergeant with rapid steps walked along loudly counting. If the end-count did not match the previous week's count he did it again. To fill the missing numbers German civilians were brought in. We had very old and very young civilians among us.

On Christmas day of 1945, at the age of 18, I wrote a letter to my parents. They received it after my return. It is with me now.

"My dearest Parents.

With deep thanks to God for allowing me to reach this day, I begin my lines. Maybe you cannot believe that this letter comes from me your lost son. Maybe you are doubtful, maybe you can believe, maybe you are sobbing or smiling. Yes, that is our fate. In one minute we are hoping and are joyful, then we cry and despair. I don't believe in the heavens, and can't trust mankind. In a moment when I have old mementos in my hands, I call everybody, and I shout in their ears: Friends, this is from home, I received it from my mother. And then comes the breakdown. I cannot look at them, I can't see anything else in them than living memories, and that hurts, that cuts into my soul. I want to be freed from them, want to throw them away. But something holds me back, maybe these are the last mementos from your mother who brought you up, who embraced you, who kissed you and taught you to pray. Think about it. Would you throw away what your parents with so much love provided for you? You can't do that. Those few mementos are now squeezed in my bag. It is not much, only a few handkerchiefs and photos, but they worth for me more than anything else in the world.

My dear father, I never felt remembering so burdensome. It never was so painful to think of the home, and to see in my eyes the parents, the brother and the sister, the house in which I spent my happy days, where I could be a child, because I had no worries. There was my dear mother who could read from my face what I wanted. And now fate is so cruel, it beats and beats, torments, but teaches! I walk the school of life. When a difficult day came that tried my manly strength, I broke down, I wanted to cry, wanted to sob. I wanted to run to my mother; don't leave me mother, it is enough, I can't bear any more. But my call was in vain. She was not here. Did she abandon me? No, I abandoned her. Yes, I am the cause of everything, and still I am calling for her, I am asking for protection from her whom I left behind. I want to be her child again. When she embraces me I have no more worries, have no more fear. But now, my wishes are fulfilled and I am my own man. Is this what I was yearning for? Fate gave it to me, and I have to endure the blows without the motherly protection. Up to now I could stand it, although it was hard, but whether I can endure it in the future, that I don't know.

I wish to greet my dear parents with this letter. I wish to send the words of my gratitude. I write this letter before my expected release from prison. The weight of eight months burdens my shoulders. I am tormented by the suffering, the humiliations. And now, maybe it is only a few days and it will come to an end, I shall be free again, I can be a human being again. The thoughts that lived in me in the days of my capture were very painful. I felt that everybody abandoned me. I had nobody. I was afraid of diseases, of starvation, but thanks to God, today I await the release in good health. My first trip will be to Kati (my sister) in Bergen. Will I find her? I don't know, but I will try. If we can meet I will return home with them, if not I will leave with the first available train. I don't know what is with Miklos (my brother). I was looking for him, but up to now could not find. I hope we will meet at home. And now I say goodbye, wishing for you my dearest parents a happy New Year. God grant us that the whole family be together in joy."

The aimlessly spent long days and the sleepless nights in the prison camp, the disillusionment with what I thought was holy and noble, the still vivid memories of the horror of killing and destruction, together with the hopelessness of captivity matured my young teen-age mind into utter rejection of all the ideals with which I grew up. My letter, which I wrote at night at candlelight, was an emotional outcry. I longed for the warmth of the family and of the holidays, but could not escape from the realities. In respect to my father's faith I could not leave God out of my thoughts.

The eight months spent in the prisoner-of-war camp with the humiliation, starvation and hopelessness was the time for reflection on what the war was about, not in a deep philosophical sense, I was too young for that, not in a historical sense, the immediacy of the events was still too close, not from a political perspective, my views were too narrow for that.

As a young teenager in school in Sopron a few times I went across the border to Austria, which was at that time part of the German Reich, to see what was it like there. The happy youngsters, the evidence of purpose, of unity and of progress were everywhere. Comparing the conditions in my home village, the contrast was striking. The question loomed in my young mind; why couldn't we have the same? On the rivers I saw the German boys rowing in boats, saw them flying model airplanes, hiking in the mountains. Back at home in my village for some of the youngsters poverty was the way of life. Some of my playmates had no shoes; in the cold winter days their feet were wrapped in burlap. Their families were thrown out of their homes because they could not pay the taxes. Why all that injustice? Those thoughts bothered me very much while I was still young. Ideology was far from my thoughts; I lived in the world of simple, poor people. In one summer we made a journey in my father's automobile visiting a famous abbey, a holy institution with its richly decorated church, housing those who dedicated their lives to God and to piety. But the local people whom those holy and dedicated clergy was supposed to serve lived in caves carved into the hillside. They lived in utmost poverty. Their children begged along the road leading to the hilltop, from where the echo of the cathedral walls could be heard. They had to live in the caves—I was told—because they could not pay the taxes, and their homes and fishing rights were taken away. They had to struggle for survival in the shadow of the glittering church tower. Was it not only reasonable that those people wanted a change? Was it not only understandable that they listened to those who promised a better life? Was for them the issue an ideology? No, it was not. Survival, not politics was on their minds.

My disillusionment with the human social and spiritual institutions was deep. The deprivation of the poor in a god-fearing Christian world, where love toward our fellow men was preached from the pulpits, struck me in early childhood. The Bible's teaching on the love and mercy of God, which I heard on every Sunday—and also believed—became empty words when I saw and also lived through the utmost human suffering. When I saw the burning churches, the almighty, loving and merciful God became for me a spiritual illusion, which the believers warship in blind faith. Where was the loving God when my soldier friends were blown to pieces, when the collapsing air raid shelter crushed those with me? Should I praise Him for granting me survival, while abandoning millions of others? Is it sensible to pray to Him, when it was He who did not listen to the prayers of the orphaned, of the maimed and of the killed millions? I also lost my trust in the human institutions. Ideologies, and social ideals became repulsive; when under their banners they tolerated human brutality. What do the Christian world and the western Democracy mean to those who had to face their merciless terror? I am in search of meaningful spiritual and social principles.

After eight months in prison, on January 14, 1946, I began my homeward bound journey to my country and into another uncertainty. Still not quite free, I left the prison camp. The long train of freight cars loaded with prisoners, guarded by American soldiers, rolled away. During the journey I was wondering what was going to happen to me. I was on my way to a country that was occupied by the Russians, whom I feared so much during the war. Were they going to let me go home, or were they going to put me in another prison camp? Was I going to find my parents? Were they alive? I wondered. When the train stopped at the first station in Hungary, Russian and Hungarian soldiers came to check the passengers. I was taken to an old fortress that was for clearing the "Nyugatosok," the returnees who went to Germany in the final months of the war. It was full of people waiting for processing. The interrogation was done by civilian and by uniformed people. They wanted to know whether I was in the voluntary units of the Arrowists, or was in the German SS. After several days of interrogation one night a man in Hungarian military officer uniform questioned me. He wanted me to identify my unit, and name the officers under whom I served. When I mentioned my brother-in-law's name he smiled and asked where he was. He told me that they were together in the Military Academy. Convincing him that I was in the regular army and not in the SS, he left the room. When he returned he told me that I was free to go. In the cold and snowy winter I began my journey as a free man back to my parents. Passing by a small house with light inside I stopped and knocked on the door. An old woman peeked through the window, and let me in. She gave me a bowl of soup, and allowed me to spend the night in her kitchen. Next morning I continued my journey.

It was late evening when the train arrived in my hometown. As I stepped off the train, fear, anxiety and joy occupied my mind. The buildings stood as before the war, but now Russian soldiers patrolled the walkways, where on December 6, 1944 with my friends as army volunteers, heated by patriotic pride to fight that enemy I began my long journey. There I was again, but now as the defeated, among the victorious enemy. A Hungarian railroad service-man whom I recognized warned me to be careful, because things were not quite settled, and drunken Russians were robbing people in the streets. Con-cerned, but driven by the urge to see my parents I exited the building. On the square in front of the station, where before the war the taxis used to park, were Russian military trucks, behind them the ruins of the Red Cross kitchen, where my mother did her volunteer work. In November of 1944, while I was still at home, it was hit by an American bomb. That attack almost killing my mother, infuriated me, and reinforced my patriotic feelings. I was there again, defeated and disillusioned.

Our home was about one mile from the station. The streets were dark. On the lampposts were the sockets but no light bulbs. There was no light any-where. It was like a ghost town. Where were the people, I was wondering. I was eager to arrive home. Not to make much noise on the paved sidewalk, I carefully took my steps. The windows of the houses were dark, no light could be seen anywhere, not like as it was before the war. Near to our home I passed by the house of an elderly lady. In the past it was a charming place with beau-tiful raw-iron and carved stone fences, with well-groomed flowerbeds, the windows covered with beautiful lace curtains, the rooms lit by decorative chandeliers. That was how I remembered it. Now Russian military vehicles parked in front of it. The inside was brightly lit; no curtains were on the win-dows. In place of the chandeliers bare light bulbs were hanging from the ceil-ing. The iron gate was twisted out. The flowerbeds were trampled. The loud voice of the Russian soldiers broke the silence of the night. They were the vic-torious occupiers of the home of an old lady. This was for me another new and hideous reality.

In the dark night I stood in front of my home. It was just as when I have left it. That was the first relief. The windows were dark; no light anywhere. Was anybody there? I was wondering. The iron fence was there, and the gate was locked. Hurriedly I pushed the button of the doorbell. Nobody responded. I shook the gate to make noise. No response. After waiting for a while, I climbed over the fence. The trees, the flower beds, the shrubs were in the garden. There was no sign of war damage. Going around the building to the entrance I tried to ring the doorbell. It did not work. After knocking on the heavy oak door I heard motion from inside and a fearful voice asking who was there. The voice was not familiar. Where were my parents? I wondered. Then heard my mother's voice. What a relief it was! She was alive. For a moment I hesitated, but then could not hold back my joy, and cried out that it was me. Then came the loud cry of my mother: *"This is my dear little son, he is alive. Father hurry, Jozsi is here, he is alive. Come, Jozsi is here."* Her words are still vividly in my memory. This was a second relief. My father was also alive.

It took a while to open the door, because it was reinforced with steel bars and chains against the Russian intruders. I stepped in and there were my mother and my father looking well, and I was in their arms, tired, hungry and filthy. I was at home again! Mother held me in her arms, and her tears were flowing. She looked at me: *"I prayed so much for you my dear little son. I knew you were alive. God heard my prayers."* Those were her words, which are deeply carved in my memory. I was the first of the three children to return, and the one whom my parents thought was dead. A man from the town who was also in Germany during the last months of the war, and who had returned a few months earlier, told them that he had seen me fallen in Berlin. I was mourned by my beloved mother who at my birth was ready to sacrifice her life to save mine.

It was 14 months earlier when I said farewell to my parents, and began my long and treacherous journey. In that 14 months my parents had to endure the intrusion of the feared enemy, had to bear the agonies over the fear for their children, and had to live with the sorrow of losing their "little son". But, those first hours were not for reflection, only for the joy of being together again.

According to my father there was no fighting in and around our town. The Germans withdrew to the Rába River ten miles to the west. The Russians arrived in small groups going from street to street in an unexpectedly orderly takeover. Before their arrival the women of the neighborhood were gathered in the Lutheran church, my father and his chaplain clad in the Luther robe stood guard at the doors. One day two drunken Russian soldiers broke into the church attacking the women and breaking up the altarpieces. My father rushed to the nearest Russian patrol post for help. An officer with three soldiers came, arrested the two rampaging men, led them outside and shot them. There were similar stories in town with plundering Russians. In a park in the middle of the town was the Russian military cemetery with a tall, marble-imitation obelisk, on its top with a red star, around it hundreds of graves with painted tombstones. It was the heroes' cemetery, but in reality most of those buried were the victims of their own. Another sad example of the insenity of wars. Young men ripped out of their peaceful communities, put in uniform and sent to fight ended their lives as criminals rather than as heroes of their nation. Somewhere, in faraway villages in Russia mothers were praying for the return of their sons, who were buried in the heroes cemetery of my hometown, having been shot by their own comrades.

My father told me about the sad story of a German soldier, who remained back after the withdrawal of his unit, and hid in the tower of the Lutheran church. Days after the Russians' arrival he came down. He wanted to surrender. But there was no mercy. After a brutal beating he was led to the fence, was shot and buried in a shallow grave. When I came home, he was still in his grave in our garden. Just another of the millions of victims of human madness. Somewhere another mother was praying for her child, waiting for his return.

The image of the downtown with its well-kept private homes and businesses, with the tree-lined promenade, with the charm of the small Eastern-European city, lived in my memory. I was eager to see it again. The main-street promenade was no longer there. Piles of rubble stood where the coffee-house used to be, torn-down fences and trampled flower beds became the driveways for the Russian military vehicles. The county administration building with the street-level shops was just a pile of broken bricks. The attorney's office, on the ground floor with the store where as a child I admired the marvelous toys, was gone. The twin-towered Catholic Church and the old abbey were there, but the nearby building with the general store was wiped out. It was an American bombing raid that caused the destruction. Why did they do that to my hometown? Before the war I did not view the Americans as my enemies. I had to remind myself that it was their bomb that almost killed my mother, that they almost killed me when the train on which I was riding was attacked, when the fleeing crowd—I among them—was strafed with the plane's machine guns. Going by the soccer field I remembered that it was their bomb that ripped apart the playing youngsters. Deeply immersed in my thoughts, I went by the ruins.

At the entry point of the main roads to the town were wooden triumphal arches, decorated with colored ribbons, with Stalin's picture and red stars. Those were erected by the Russians for their own glory. It was a strange feeling to walk the streets where in peace times I watched the girls, where in the war years I saw Hungarian and German soldiers on guard, and now had to pass Russian patrols. It was another new reality of life for me, to live in a strained co-existence with the enemy, to see the most feared enemy in control of my town and of me. Like a movie, the memories and the images of the past were whirling in my mind, restoring the crumbled walls to what they used to be, in the empty streets seeing the familiar faces of the friendly people walking by. What happened to my town and to me, and why? Why were we targeted by the Americans for extinction? They were not our enemies. Our enemies were the Bolsheviks.

The time came to restart my life where it was interrupted by the war. After a few days of resting, wearing my German military raincoat which I bought in the prison camp for two cigarettes, and a Hungarian military cap—the only coat and cap I had—I went to my school to enroll. The director looked at me with indignation, and refused to accept my enrollment. I was wondering; was I in my home country? Was I guilty just for wearing a German military raincoat? Was I guilty in doing what the school taught me, namely to be a good patriot and defend my country? Another school accepted me, where a few months later I took the final examination and received my diploma. There was, however, little hope for enrollment at the university. Disheartened as I was, I took a job at the War Reparation Office, taking care of the paperwork for a livestock yard, shipping pigs to Russia. One of the livestock dealers with whom I had almost daily contact was a Jewish man, who came back from the concentration camp. We spent hours together talking about our wartime experiences. He was angry with us Gentiles for not helping them in the days of their deportation. But, he was also angry with his Jewish compatriots who—according to his story—in the camps stole his food, and especially with the Kapo, the Jewish police inside the camp, which—again according to him—was more brutal than the German guards were. He felt just as much betrayed by his own people, as by us Gentiles.

In 1947 I went to Budapest to begin my university studies. The ravages of the war could still be seen in the city. The Danube bridges, the beauty of which even as a young boy I admired, were in the water, blown up by the retreating Germans in 1945. The castle on top of the hill, which was the scene of fierce fighting, was in ruins. From a distance only the burned out buildings with gaping windows could be seen. Peeking through the fence I saw the evidence of the immense destruction. One afternoon climbing over the fence I went through the squares and streets, where the rusted remnants of the destroyed German military vehicles, bullet punctured steel helmets, ripped apart boots gave witness to the desperate fight of the defenders. The dome of the King's Palace went down to the ground floor, the marvelous stucco that at one time decorated the pompous building was in pieces. The walls of the rooms covered with beautiful frescos were punctured with shrapnel holes. The once precious furniture was broken to pieces. The Governor's palace was without a roof, and much of the inside structure collapsed to the first floor. Just below the castle on the severely damaged roof of an apartment building rested the wreckage of a German airplane. Many German soldiers were on the hill in the final battle, many in the underground hospital. A few were captured; most of them were killed. The narrow streets lined with the old houses bore witness to the intensity of the fighting that lasted for nearly two months. A great human tragedy of co-extinction was played out in those streets. All because of the implanted mindless loyalty and proud, blind obedience.

In the decades before the Second World War Hungary was not known as a democratic society, at least not in the sense of the western concepts, but was recognized for its relatively liberal social-political system. That was in the time when I grew up. Then came the war, which still had not changed the social structure, only added the wartime regulations and restrictions. The drastic turn came in 1944, when the Soviet enemy was on Hungarian soil, when in a desperate attempt the German troops came to stop the advancing Soviet army. Those were chaotic times. The country was under siege, the Soviet army moved rapidly forward. The American aerial bombardment virtually paralyzed the country, and the social structure was collapsing. At the time of my return in February 1946 the nation was still in a slow recovery, life was returning to an apathetic society. That was until 1948, when the Communist Party in a coup under the protection of the Russian occupation force gained control of Hungary. The party leaders who after the Bolshevik era of 1919 fled to the Soviet Union, returned in 1945, and began a ruthless campaign against their opponents. In the first election after the war, in 1946, the Communist Party received a small percent of the votes. In 1948, after jailing—or forcing out of the country the leaders of the opposition parties—in a frontal attack the communists took over the ruling. Co-existence in the social-political arena ceased to exist, replaced by a one-sided attempt for extinction. In the following elections, when only the communist candidates could be voted for, they proudly claimed to have received 99.9 per cent of the votes. Absurd as it was, they bragged that it was the victory of true Democracy. Their political and psychological strategy was to overwhelm the people with propaganda, with the constant adulation of the Soviet Union, of Stalin and of the local party heads. Stalin's large pictures were treated as altars, decorated with fresh flowers. He was called: "The dearly beloved father and wise leader." When his name was mentioned at any gathering the crowd had to stand up and clap. The media constantly bombarded the readers with glorifying reports on the great successes of the Soviet Union and of the Communist Party. The theaters and movie houses played Russian stories, all with strong political overtones. Propaganda posters depicting the heroic, liberating Russian soldier and the red-flag-carrying workingmen covered the walls. Every public building had a huge red star on the rooftop. It was a propaganda frenzy, reaching everybody from the very young to the old.

My sister's daughter who was in elementary school age one day wanted to show me what she learned in school. She dressed up nicely, tied a ribbon in her hair, made a lovely curtsey and began to recite the poem: "Stalin is our dearest father, who very much loves us children and will lead us into a bright future." Her father's face froze. She stopped, fearfully looking around to see what was wrong. Those were the roots of the problems in the society, and even in the families. Mindless loyalty and proud obedience to a brutal dictatorship was implanted in the minds of the young. The children were forced to report on their parents and on their neighbors. We never knew who was watching us. If on Sundays I went to church with my wife, next Monday I was reminded of that by the party secretary. People had to be at their work place half an hour before work time to participate in the collective reading of the party newspaper. I called it the "Atheistic bible school." There were frequent political pep talks, usually after work hours. To assure participation the exit gates were locked. In the work places the employees were constantly watched by the party agents. The economy was run on the five-year plan, and everybody had to fulfill specific work quotas. Having worked in engineering, my performance was measured in the number of drawings I produced. The size of the sheet of paper and the number of the lines were the "Accord" guides. On any party occasion we had to make pledges for extra accomplishments. To increase productivity the party called the people to challenge one another in exceeding the work quotas. It was wrapped in the bluff: "The country is yours, you are building it for yourselves." The "Reactionaries", as they were called by the party faithful, modified it to: "The forest is yours, and you are cutting the trees under yourselves." The large street demonstrations in which the participation was compulsory were frequent. The propaganda praised the exceptional accomplishments of the party and of the workers, but the stores were empty. There was virtually nothing to buy, other than the absolute essentials, simple food items, and even those in small quantities and in poor quality. The most exciting rumors covered the arrival of shoes or shirts in the stores. There was a quiet, hidden opposition to all that nonsense, but we had to be most careful.

The personal well being of the ruling Communist Party hierarchy and their cohorts was assured by the support they received from overseas, mainly from

America. They lived in the confiscated villas and homes of their deported victims, shopped at the special stores that were hidden in the back streets, not open to the public. They enjoyed the exclusive restaurants that only they could afford to visit, were treated in a hospital that was available for them only. They lived well as "Comrades" in the "People's Republic", claiming that everybody was free, but ruled with absolute terror, preached "People-Democracy", claiming that everybody was equal, but enjoyed the for themselves granted privileges. It was an evil political system, a grotesque social order that could exist only under Soviet occupation, and with the support from America. The resentment of the people who had to endure all that must not be taken as anti-Semitism, because it had little to do with racism.

Our next-door neighbor in the apartment building was a single, middle aged lady. She lived withdrawn and quietly. Our personal contact was through courtesy greetings. One night the State Security Authority came, gave her hours to pack up, and then loaded her on a truck. She was one of the many thousands who had been deported for no apparent reason. The whole city lived in fear: Who was going to be next? A military couple moved in her apartment, the man was political officer in the army; his wife was secretary at the party head-office. They were the beneficiaries of an ideological battle, as before the communist take-over he had worked in a coal mine. In those times I was careful. When I listened to the BBC I kept the radio at a low volume, and after listening moved the dial to a local station. Having had a father who was a Lutheran minister, which put him in the so-called "Black reactionary" category, I had to cover my past. In the birth certificate of our son I stated my occupation as "Factory worker," hoping that it was going to help him later in his life. The apartment building had a caretaker, a woman who showed her party membership by wearing the party badge. She most certainly was an informer for the State Security Authority. To visit my parents, who lived about 50 kilometers from the Austrian border, a special permit was needed. While all that was happening, the loud party propaganda glorified freedom and democracy, which it claimed was brought by the "Communist Party and its beloved leader Mátyás Rákosi" (He was one of the returned Bolsheviks of the 1919 terror.).

The old guard of the party returning from the Soviet Union after the Second World War brought with them the Soviet terror and propaganda technique that might have worked in Russia, but having been given in heavy doses in Hungary turned away many ideological believers. The large organized demonstrations with tens of thousands of people marching in the streets glorifying the leaders and their achievements, carrying their huge pictures, were intended as spontaneous expression of the loyalty, love and obedience of the people to the party and the leaders. But in reality those were self-indulging rituals of the ruthless dictators. They terrorized not only their opponents, but also their ideological comrades who disagreed with their brutal methods, sent them to jail, tortured and executed them. After years such tactics became much too burdensome even for the party faithful. The resentment and outright hatred was growing. The resentment was also strong against the party activists who were in the factories, in the offices and in the apartment houses, watching everybody all the time. There was a small segment of the party members that was ideologically tied, and was mindlessly loyal and proudly obedient to the party and to its leaders. They were dangerous. There was another larger segment of the opportunists who for whatever reason were willing to carry out any order of the party. They were even more dangerous. Whether it was their revenge for the Nazi persecution, was the manifestation of racial hatred, or was pure opportunism, is not clear to me. In the pre-war years they acted as the "liberals", during the communist era they were the most feared terrorists. It is an interesting irony, that the fruits of the large industrial development in the communist era are now harvested by the new capitalists, who in some cases are the same people who at one time as party members ruthlessly carried out the party programs. They can now be satisfied with their capitalist present.

Most of the fellow employees at the engineering design institute where I worked were engineers; some of them were owners of factories and shops before the communist take-over. Although on the roof of the building stood a big red star, with the exception of the party secretary and a few of the management people nobody seemed to care about the political nonsense. Having had only a few party members the party secretary did not have a separate office. He had his desk and drafting board in the same room where I had mine. We were on a first name contact level. In the pre-war years he was a jeweler. With his background he knew little about machine design. I had no reason to believe that his party affiliation was based on ideological convictions. But in his selfish interest he was loyal and obedient to the party hierarchy. Life for me was a stressful co-existence.

On October 23, 1956 an uprising broke out in Hungary. It was presented in the western news media as a "Spontaneous Anti-Soviet Revolution"; by others it was called a "Neo-Fascist Rebellion". But it was neither spontaneous, nor was it Neo-Fascist. (The selection of the "Fascist" title is in itself an interesting issue. Fascism was the political movement in Italy. The Arrowist Party in Hungary was modeled after the German Nazi Party. They had little or no contact at all with the Italian Fascists.) In 1954 after Stalin's death—and following Khruschov's denunciation of the Stalin era—a loosening in the strict control within the Communist Party began. An "underground" surfaced and held semi-secret debates, in which some of the open-minded party members, writers and intellectuals, were the leaders. The criticism of the government and of the party, which in the previous years was out of question, appeared in some of the newspapers. Even within the party itself there was an internal tension. The removal of the party hard-liners was demanded, and the reinstatement of the more liberal, jailed party members to power was openly discussed. In our institute the rumors about the coming political changes were abundant. The attorney was the principal source of the news on the latest developments. His daily visits to our group on official matters were flavored with political intrigues. In mid-October of 1956 I heard rumors about planned street demonstrations, but those rumors were taken with skepticism. On October 23, while working on my drawing board, in the noon hours the news came that a demonstration organized by the students of the Technical University was on its way. The students sent their demands to the government for fundamental reforms, with the threat that if rejected they were to start a demonstration. The government rejected the demands and prohibited the demonstration. But, it was all in vain. After the announcement of the government's rejection, the students of the universities, the workers of the factories and offices in disregard to the threats poured into the streets of Budapest. The students' initiative for the demonstration was a remarkable historic event.

One of the principal aims of the party leadership was to bring up a new, politically educated—better said indoctrinated—society. A high percentage of the university students came from industrial laborer and from poor peasant families, who in the pre-war times had little or no opportunity at all for higher education. This new generation was seen, and was prepared, by the party as the pillar of the future communist society. Political indoctrination was among the important subjects. Remarkably, these selected, and to some degree privileged, students with all the political indoctrination behind them became the initiators and torchbearers of the protest against the government. Their political education, no matter how one-sided it was, opened their minds to see the contradictions between the sloganeering and the realities. In the demonstration the government had to face the opposition of its own cadres. It could no longer blame the "notorious reactionaries" for the growing tension. The ordering of the State Security Authority, the AVH, to open fire on the student demonstrators was a much too risky issue even for the most fanatical party and government officials.

Many of us in the institute joined the students. Officially, the demonstration was held as a solidarity gesture to the Polish uprising against their communist government. We marched to the monument of the Polish general Bem, who in the 1848 Hungarian Fight For Freedom fought on our side. His statue stands on the shores of the Danube on the Buda side. There was great excitement in the air. The streets were jammed with people blocking the trolley and bus traffic. The windows of the apartment houses were open; the cheering people greeted the demonstrators. The Hungarian national flags appeared in the windows with a big hole in the middle, where the emblem with the red star had been. It was an amazing sight. There was a never before seen enthusiasm. The square around the monument was packed with chanting and singing men and women, young and old. One of the buildings facing the square was a military officer school. Standing close to the monument I watched the building with concern, as all the windows were closed. While the crowd grew and became ever louder, some of the windows opened and a few cadets appeared. The question was, what was the military going to do? There was fear that they could open fire, especially after suddenly the cadets disappeared from the windows. But, then, to our great joy and relief they joined us demonstrators, waiving at us, giving the sign that they were on our side. They were received with cheers. Writers and poets standing at the base of the monument spoke, adding to the enthusiasm of the demonstrators. The crowd kept growing to tens of thousands, and began to march across the Margaret Bridge to the Parliament building. When I was at the middle of the bridge among the spirited demonstrators, a loud argument broke out. Two young Jewish men wearing the red star party badge, in highly provocative manner called the demonstrators "Fascists." Those were tension-filled moments. The anger grew. I heard calls to throw the men in the Danube. Violence with strong racial overtones was in the making, but moderation prevailed. The marchers wanted to preserve the true spirit of the demonstration. At the end of the bridge on the Pest side stood the newly built headquarters of the State Security Authority, the much feared and hated "AVH." Critical moments came; what was the AVH going to do? I knew how powerful and brutal it was. I knew that its agents were everywhere, most likely even among us demonstrators. I also knew that the AVH was under the protection of the massive Russian occupation forces, which were in the country. In the past, whenever and wherever there was the slightest dissent or opposition, the party and the government used its power ruthlessly. Was the government going to allow this demonstration to continue, or were they leading us into a trap? I was contemplating.

We marched toward the AVH building, where the street turned to the right, leading to the Parliament Square. There was immense tension in the air, but also there was determination. The earlier enthusiastic mood of the crowd turned somber, prepared for the worst. Nothing could stop us. As I went around the building not a single AVH man could be seen. The gates and windows were closed. Not even a guard was at the entrance. I glanced up at the windows looking for the sharpshooters. Nobody was there. The streets were packed with demonstrators. An amazing sight it was! The large Parliament Square was full of people. It was bright daylight. The crowd grew with every minute, columns of people arrived from all directions. Slogans were shouted and the national anthem was sung. The crowd demanded the appearance of Imre Nagy the jailed moderate of the Communist Party, a native Hungarian, but instead other party officials appeared on the balconies of the Parliament, urging the demonstrators to go home. They were booed. The crowd did not yield. The moderating words of the leaders of student organizations and of well-known writers of the opposition could not calm the people. We stood there, over hundred thousands of us, singing, shouting, but not leaving. Cars with curtain-covered windows, and closed vans arrived driving up to the main entrance of the Parliament building. I did not know who came and who left in them. Hours passed while the crowd became more and more excited and agitated. Rumors circulated that Imre Nagy was in the Parliament building, but the government did not let him speak. I heard rumors about the government's threats made on the radio to use force against the demonstrators. The tension was high and it grew with every minute. The excitement of the events, the immensity of the power of the mass of demonstrators, had a mesmerizing effect on me. As darkness set in and the crowd refused to leave, the frightened authorities turned off the streetlights. There was total darkness. Then came the magic. Suddenly tens of thousands of hands held burning newspapers. The square was like a sea of flames, giving a magnificent yellowish glow to the Gothic walls of the Parliament. It was magnificent, an unforgettable scene, stirring up my emotions, squeezing the tears out of my eyes. While standing there, immersed in patriotic upheaval, the rumors about the army and the AVH units surrounding the square were whispered. But the crowd did not yield. In those years not having had small pocket radios I didn't know what was going on in the city and in the country. The news spread quickly that at the Radio Station Building, where the students wanted their demands broadcast, the AVH opened fire on them.

The peaceful demonstration was over. A bloody revolution began!

I stayed at the Parliament until early morning, wondering; could the demonstrators be defeated by the ruthless power of the party and the government? Was bloodshed their choice? Concerned and disheartened, wondering what was going to happen, in the darkness of the early morning hours I began my long walk home across the Danube bridge.

The first days of the Revolution, when the demonstrations continued, and when the government resorted to the use of violence, were victorious for the revolutionaries. In spite of the overwhelming force of the AVH and of the presence of the Russian occupation forces the government was forced out, the AVH was defeated. The party apparatus collapsed. The hope was high for a freer, better life. The social, political and religious organizations and the newspapers, which were prohibited in the communist era, reappeared. Hungarian soldiers stood guard in the streets, the red star removed from their caps. People brought food and drink for them, put flowers in the barrels of their rifles. The big red stars tumbled down from the rooftops of the government and party buildings. The statue of Stalin was smashed to bits. I did not know, however, that our fate was determined not in the streets of our city, but in the conference rooms of the victorious powers of the Second World War, where countries were traded like worthless commodities, ours tossed into the hands of the Soviets. The misleading, and certainly irresponsible propaganda, spread by the Voice of America and Radio Free Europe, gave strong impetus to the uprising, without telling us that no matter what was to happen, the country was to remain under Soviet control.

After the fighting quieted down, the people gathered in the streets and in the squares seeking information on the new developments. I went back to my office, as it was only two blocks from our apartment. The safe of the personnel office was opened, and in it were found the personal files, including mine, to my surprise with detailed reports by colleagues whom I trusted. The Revolutionary Committee was organized, and I was elected to it. A few hotheaded people wanted revenge on the party secretary, who stayed away during those days, and on the director who was in his office, but moderation prevailed.

A degree of normality returned. I went back to work, although not much was accomplished. The stores opened with little to sell. The peasants brought their produce to the markets, often giving it away free of charge. Some of the newspapers that were closed down by the government reappeared. Organizations, such as the boy scouts, after long years of prohibition came alive. But, regrettably, the marvelous unity of the revolutionary days was over. The in-fighting among the reemerging political and social groups and organizations began. It was disheartening!

In fear of the return of the terror-filled days many people left the country during the turmoil of the Revolution, crossing the border to Austria. I stayed, waited and hoped. There were rumors that a student delegation that wanted to deliver an appeal to the American embassy was not received because they were considered "Communists." I don't know whether this was a true story or not, but it quickly spread and caused deep anguish. One day I heard rumors that the Russian troops were withdrawing from Hungary, next day I heard that even bigger units have entered from the East. On the 4th of November, which was on Sunday, in the early morning hours heavy gunfire woke us. On the radio Imre Nagy the newly appointed prime minister spoke, announcing that the Russian troops had attacked the city and there was heavy fighting between them and the Hungarian army troops. He called for help from the Western Powers and from the United Nations. (After the defeat of the Revo-lution he was arrested and was executed). I was stunned by the events. As the day went on, the fighting became more and more intense and spread to many parts of the city. Russian tanks rolled in the streets and airplanes flew over-head, giving the sense of a siege. I saw young people on the castle hill prepar-ing for battle. Barricades made of trolleys; railroad cars and cobblestones were erected. It was a desperate fight, but the fate of the Revolution was sealed. It was defeated not in the streets of Budapest, but in the conference rooms in Washington, in New York, in London and in Moscow. As the days passed and the defeat of the Revolution became obvious, black flags and burning can-dles joined the national flags in the windows. People wore the ribbon of the red-white-green Hungarian tricolor wrapped into black ribbon. Those were sobering times.

What was it like to take part in a revolution? It was magnificent and also it was frightening. Magnificent, as I felt the immensity of my participation in a history-making event. Twelve years earlier I was a soldier in the Second World War because I thought I had to defend my country against the feared Bolshevik enemy. In October of 1956 I marched with the crowd with burning enthusiasm, protesting against the same enemy that became the ruler of the country. I heard stories, read books and saw movies about revolutions, but never before felt the true excitement that goes with it. I felt a never before experienced unity, some called it "Brotherhood". Tears were flowing, strangers hugged each other. How remarkable it was that the goods in the shop windows with broken glass remained untouched. Money was collected for the families of the freedom fighters in open boxes at the street corners, and nobody guarded the boxes. October 23, 1956 was a national revolution, not a riot. The Revolution also brought fear. What if the already experienced hate-filled fanaticism of the old party members was to return under the protection of the Russian bayonets? What if the mass-deportation that I saw in the early 1950s under the Communist regime, was to start again? Those were fearful thoughts, with which I had to live. Listening to the BBC, the Voice of America and Radio Free Europe with each day it became more and more evident that our cause was lost, nobody was going to stand up on our behalf. It was disheartening to feel betrayed by the United Nations and by the West. It was painful to accept the inevitable. Once again I had to face the fear of extinction.

The events of 1956 changed my life. It proved what mankind could become when the opportunities arrive, both in good and evil. It was a revolution against political, cultural, religious and personal oppression. It was a good example of what unarmed masses could do against heavily armed occupation forces and against a hated ruling clique. The power of the spirit with the strong desire for liberty could not be stopped by tanks and guns. Ever since those days I do not agree with any outside intervention in any internal national affair. Nations, no matter how small and weak, sooner or later can and will remove an unwanted government. No occupation force, no military might can hold them back. Regrettably, many governments interfering and occupying other countries failed to learn the same lesson.

Revolutions have been written about in many books and articles, some idealizing, others deploring the roots and the end results. For me the 1956 Revolution came as a magnificent demonstration of the human power that swept me onto the streets, kept me marching with the crowd in the belief that it could bring a better life for me. Having grown up in an almost feudalistic society, where my playmates hungered while others had all the luxuries of life, I knew that something better had to come. Having lived under totalitarianism of the Right and of the Left, both making promises, but bringing fear and suffering, I hoped for a world where hatred, violence and brutality had no place. Ideologies never attracted me, although I admired the accomplishments of the Germans, and wished to see the same progress in our country, but resented the arrogance of our Ultra Right ideologues. My environment was always overheated with patriotism, but I never could reject anybody just because of nationality, religion or race. So, when the Revolution came I tried to see its

clean, idealistic side. There were short episodes when I could see it. On the
afternoon of October 23, 1956 when hundreds of thousands of us gathered on
the Parliament Square in Budapest, I felt the beauty of unity. The threats of
the authorities were overwhelmed by the loud voice of the crowd. When the
streetlights were turned off leaving us in the dark, the flames of burning newspaper in thousands of hands lifted my spirit. It was all what I wanted to see
and feel. I was pleased to be part of this magnificent event.

In the first days when I felt free from the supervision of the feared party
agents, I was relieved. They were still there, but were no longer feared. I
despised them for what they had done. The party secretary in our institute,
who followed the party line while in office, made extra money by selling
smuggled ballpoint pens at home. Our next-door neighbor in the apartment
building was a political army officer, his wife was secretary in the party head-
office. We were afraid of them when he came over to our apartment, had to
watch where the dial of my radio stood, not to reveal that I listened to the
BBC. The officer gave me political pep talks about the might of socialist
armies, about the coming of the liberation of Europe by the Soviet Union.
When the Revolution broke out he was away from home on an assignment.
His wife was at home alone with their newborn child. Talking with them
before the Revolution they objected to our going to church. During the days
of the turmoil the party secretary wife told me that they had—in great
secrecy—their child baptized. Those were just two examples of the human
contradictions of those times; the outward willingness to be mindlessly loyal
and proudly obedient servants of a ruthless, dictatorial ruling power. In the
party secretary's case it was the inner, materialistic instinct, in the political
officer's case it was the hidden spiritual instinct. One of the feared party activists in the factory where I used to work earlier, who terrorized us, when during
the Revolution we met begged me not to give him up to the new authorities. It
was the moment when he was seeking mutual understanding and co-existence. I saw brutal beatings of men and women accused of having been the
members of the AVH. Having seen those scenes, the Revolution was no
longer what I could believe in.

What was the 1956 Revolution about? How did I see it?

As in many other events of my life, I was a keen observer of the developments in the country following the communist takeover. Having grown up in
the world of the poor village people, but also having seen the wealth of the
nobles, I felt that a better society had to come someday. After the war I did see
signs of changes that I felt were right, like the land reform, giving the land to

those whose sweat in the past went into the soil without ever owning enough of it to stand on. The industrial development under Communism giving work opportunity for those whose fate in the past was unemployment and poverty appealed to me. I was willing to participate to the best of my ability, not on political or ideological ground, but as a young man who saw in the development his future as well. It was the intolerable arrogance, the constant fear in which I had to live, and the irritating propaganda that turned me against the regime. On a national scale, in the rural and in urban areas the opposing views were evident. In the countryside where the land reform brought hope for those who could only gain from it the political and social changes were received with enthusiasm. The changes brought resentment among those who owned land before the war and became subject to government harassment. The resentment of the nobles, of the rich landlords who lost everything was there, but without any effect, their complaint was not heard. They were the pariahs of the new era. With the growing arrogance of the party and of the government, the merciless collectivization of agriculture began. Those who received the land through the land reform lost it just the same as those who owned it through inheritance or through hard work. The setting up of cooperatives or associations for the small landholders who did not have the means to cultivate their land efficiently was sensible, and I believed could also be successful. But, the collectivization was done in terrorist manner generating resentment and anger in the rural world. For them the 1956 Revolution meant a hope for a change. Although in most villages there were no demonstrations, they supported the Revolution of the city people. In the urban areas, in the cities were more sharply defined opposing viewpoints. At the time of the Revolution there were a few, and only small private enterprises, mainly locksmith and shoe repair shops and the like. The small businesses were forced into state controlled associations or collectives; the medium and large businesses were nationalized. The huge industrial development of the early 1950s produced many big industrial plants providing work for the people. There was no unemployment. The party organization was firmly in place. The propaganda machinery among the industrial workers was relentless, and gaining support. The management of the factories was in the hands of loyal, obedient and often opportunistic party members. The personnel offices staffed with trusted party members had control over the workers. I believe the party hierarchy felt quite secure by having the well-run organizations. Many of the workers at the offices and factories felt loyalty to the party and the government not necessarily on ideological grounds, but from the fact that they had secure jobs. The

people who in the past had no skill and had no work, were building machinery, were erecting giant industrial complexes. The party propaganda told them
that they, and not the "Exploiting capitalists", were the owners of what they
built. For those who lived under such political indoctrination the Revolution
meant fear of the return of the old times with unemployment and poverty.
There was fear and opposition to any change among some of the party members, especially among those who not by ideological conviction but by pure
opportunism joined the party, holding high positions in the AVH and in the
government. Before the war they were merchants and salesmen, members of
the by the party-ideology much deplored capitalistic society. There was also
great fear among those who with their arrogance provoked the resentment and
hatred of their fellow workers. They had much to lose, all the privileges, the
luxuries of living in confiscated homes.

Strong opposition to the government and the party was among the small
business operators who lost their businesses, among the educated professionals
and administrators who still had their jobs but felt insecure under the growing
take-over of their positions by the party members, among the well-to-do of
the past and among the various churches. For them the Revolution meant
hope for a better life, the regaining of the lost wealth and power. Most
remarkably there was also opposition within the party itself by the idealist
socialists, especially after Stalin's death. This was the environment in which
the seeds of the Revolution were planted, most remarkably not by the extreme
Right, not by a charismatic leader, or a group of widely respected leaders, but
by a few, mostly unknown intellectuals of the Left. For them the Revolution
meant freer expression of their thoughts. It was not their opposition to socialism; they themselves were socialists, but their opposition to the arrogance and
terror of the party leadership and its cohorts. I did participate in some of the
semi-secret panel discussions. For them revolution was not a fundamental
social-political change but a "Reform." Among the rural people, because of the
looser net of their society, in most places the Revolution was seen not as the
momentous event within their own communities, but something that was
happening in the big cities, which could also bring changes to their lives. The
Revolution meant different things to different people. The unity in which the
masses marched in the streets and demonstrated in the city squares was an
emotion-filled affair, temporarily setting aside the differences in the aims and
hopes. Once the stormy waves of the idealistic upheavals settled, the differences between the participants arose and the divisions re-emerged. Animosities among the resurrected civic, professional and religious organizations

became quite sharp. A new struggle for power began. I believe that is the psychology of all revolutions.

What was the meaning of the Revolution for me? I did participate in it by marching in the streets, did help building barricades, but was not involved in street fighting. That was against my principles. The ideologies neither of the Left nor of the Right attracted me. I resented the arrogance of those in power, also resented the idiotic propaganda. It angered me that they assumed that I was stupid enough to believe it. For me there was nothing valuable to recover through the Revolution, as my family didn't own confiscated land or other property. I did not expect the reinstatement in a lost position that the communists took away from me, because I was at the beginning of my working life. The total isolation from the outside world deprived me of knowing how young people of my age lived in other countries. All I knew was that the lives of my parents, of my relatives and friends were difficult, and could not hope for myself a better future either. I did remember the happy years of my early childhood, and also remembered the horrors of the war. The eight years of the communist terror, the fear in which our family had to live, the injustice and the suffering that my father had to endure, the destruction of what a cultured and civilized society had built for itself, the intolerable arrogance of alien rulers imposing an alien ideology drove me to deep desperation. I have felt trapped in hopelessness, and saw in the Revolution a way out of it. Disillusioned, as I was, the chaos of the Revolution appeared to me as an opportunity to leave that world in search of a better one.

Many people left Budapest in the early days of the Revolution, but as of late I talked with a few who tried to cross the Russian military ring, but gave up because it was much too dangerous. In preparation for our possible leaving, without giving any hint at the institute about my long-term plans, I visited with the director, who was a party-man, but of a better sort, whom I defended in the early days of the Revolution when some of the hot-headed people attacked him. I told him that I was going for a vacation to my parents. I assume that he knew well what I had in mind. The decision, however, was not quite in my hands. I had to leave quite hastily. While still in the building of the institute the word came that the AVH that regained its power arrived to arrest the members of the Revolutionary Committee, including me. I ran home. There was no time for long farewell, no time to pack for the journey. On November 21, 1956 we quickly put a few pieces of clothing and some food together for our son, and in the darkness of the evening with my wife and our small child we went to the railroad station, hoping to find a way to get out.

Later I heard that the following day the AVH came to my apartment, looking for me. Our long journey to the West began. It was a difficult decision with many dangers. We had to get out of the city that was surrounded by Russian troops, and had to cross a border that had its infamous barbed-wire fences, mine fields and sharp shooters. The only possibility for leaving the city was by the railroad, although the normal service had not been restored at that time. We stepped in the train not knowing how far we could go, where we could go, or even whether we could go at all. Our intended destination was my parents' town about 50 kilometers from the Austrian border. The burden was heavy on my shoulders. I was no longer alone, but two other lives, both very dear to me, were my responsibility. It was not adventurism, not ideology that drove me, but the irresistible urge to seek liberty and independence. I wanted to be alone with my family, probing my own strength, seeing what I could accomplish in life. In my past life I was pushed and tossed either by well-intentioned guidance or by ruthless brutalities of the events beyond my control. I wanted to go somewhere to find the foundations for a freer, better life.

A steam locomotive with a few cars connected to it was at the station. The dark and cold cars were full of people. The mood was somber, nobody was talking as if everybody had a great secret to hide, but from the appearance of the passengers it was clear that they were prepared for a special journey. Small suitcases, rucksacks, heavy overcoats and hiking boots revealed much. There was a long wait before the train rolled out. It was a foggy night. Rumors began to float that the Russians fired on another train on the same rail-line that left earlier. A man came to the car, telling that if we would come under fire we should lie on the floor, because the engineer was going to keep the train running at full speed. The tension grew. Mothers held their children and the men stood around them. I stood at the window anxiously looking out, saw Russian soldiers and tanks along the tracks, but they did not interfere. Each time when the train arrived to a station the concern grew; would it be held back, or would they let it go? After an all-night long journey we arrived to my parents' town. Many of the passengers stepped off the train. Russian soldiers and Hungarian police stopped everybody checking the personal papers and questioning about their intended destination. They led away those who could not show good reason for coming there. In those days many people came to the town in the hope of reaching the Austrian border. Our alibi was a visit to my parents, so we were let go. My mother's fearful question was: "Are you also leaving?" She said, that my sister with her two daughters had come a few days earlier and had already left. My father after having said farewell to his beloved daughter did not want to see us go. "Why are you leaving, why is everybody leaving the country?" The impact of the Revolution was not nearly as deep in the countryside as it was in Budapest.

My father told me that in the evenings a single-car motor train was leaving for the border. It was a mercy service by the local railroad men for the would-be escapees. Next day I made an exploratory visit at the railroad station. It was like an ant's nest. Many people gathered in groups, carrying small suitcases and backpacks, clearly revealing what they intended to do. The big question was how. I heard that the "Mercy train" was going to leave at about 10 o'clock at night. I bought two tickets for the ride, with which I wanted to secure places on it for ourselves. After an emotional farewell to my parents, on the back streets of the town we went to the railroad station. The motorcar was on the tracks behind the lines of freight cars, already full of people. We had standing room only. I was anxiously waiting for the departure. My father also told me that he had heard that in a village near the Austrian border a railroad man called "Uncle Sándor" helped people to get across the border, and he lived right at the railway station.

The journey was uneventful. The people talked freely about where and how they planned to cross the boarder. There were families with children, groups of young men, and also a few elderly. It was shortly before midnight when we arrived in the village of Fertőboz, a small station with a few buildings. Together with many others, including a group of young men, we stepped off the train. They immediately went toward the border. Most of the others stood along the rails putting on the rucksacks, bundling up the children and themselves against the bitter, foggy cold. I went to look for "Uncle Sándor". In a building next to the station office there was light. I knocked on the door. A woman opened it. When she saw my wife and my little son she invited us in. It was Uncle Sándor's home and she was his wife. She knew what we were up to. Sitting in the warm kitchen she talked about the danger along the border, because of the many Russian soldiers who had just arrived and sealed it off. The Russians were on full alert—she said—because in the previous days and nights armed Hungarian fighters went through that area. Uncle Sándor was not at home, but was expected to arrive from work. After a while he came. He also warned me about the danger of crossing the Russian lines. Not wanting to yield from my decision to go, his wife put her arms around my wife and my son and said, that I could go if I wanted to, but she would not let me take my family into certain death. The burden of the utmost responsibility for my family grew upon me. To clear my mind I went out to the yard. The night was dark. Clouds covered the sky. The border was about two miles away. The rumbling noise of the engines of the Russian tanks came from a distance. From time to time flares lit the sky, and machine-gun fire was heard. A few of the young men, who after stepping off the train went toward the border, were running back in panic. They ran into the Russians who then opened fire on them. After awhile everything quieted down. Staying out in the cold I agonized over my decision; could I bring my family into such a danger? Shouldn't we just go back and face the consequences? What if something terrible might happen? No, we cannot go back. We already came that far. There is no return from here. Thousands of others already crossed the border, why can't we? But what if we can't make it? Neither was there time, nor were there proper conditions for rational thinking. In my agony I felt that we had to go.

Inside the kitchen my wife and my son were sitting next to a stove, Uncle Sándor sat at the table finishing his late supper. His wife stood at the door. When I stepped in, my wife looked at me and quietly asked: "Do you want to go?" as if she hoped for a "No" answer. It was the moment for the final decision. Once again all the questions, the fear and the doubts rushed through my mind. "Yes my Dear, we go". The most important, and also the most fearful decision of my life had been made. There was silence in the kitchen. Outside the night was quiet, no flares lit the sky. The people who came with us on the train were gone. I looked at Uncle Sándor waiting for his reply. He stopped sipping his soup and nodded his head, giving the sign of his willingness for leading us. Not his wife, she still did not want us to go, fearing not only for my little son and my wife, but also for her husband. Mária, my wife stood up and began to bundle little Joseph in a warm sweater, in a heavy overcoat and hiking boots, put a scarf around his mouth, telling him that he could not talk or cry while we were going to be outside, because if he did, the Russian soldiers could shoot us, and he would not have a mummy and daddy. What frightful words could those be for him? What could have gone through the mind of a four year old after a long and exhausting journey, hearing about the dangers in a dark night, losing his mummy and daddy? (Quite remarkably his does not remember any of those events.) I picked him up on my back, also carried a small suitcase and a shopping bag. My wife was not feeling well in those days. She was bundled up in a warm overcoat on top of her favored fur coat, carried a small suitcase with food and clothing in it for our child. Uncle Sándor's wife stepped away from the door, shaking her head. We went out in the cold night and began a frightful journey. Uncle Sándor was leading us. After crossing the rails we went across a small wooded area that ended in a wide-open pasture.

The night was dark. Clouds covered the sky. In the distance I could hear the rumbling of the motors of the Russian vehicles. Uncle Sándor led us along a narrow trail in the pasture grass, behind him my wife, and I followed her. My son was quiet on my back. Making slow progress I was wondering how long it was going to take before reaching the border. We stopped frequently for short rests, looking and listening. Nobody was nearby, or at least I could not see anybody. As we went along in the middle of an open pasture the clouds started to break up. The moon came out shining, putting a mystical and for us frightening silvery light on the land. Stacks of corn stalks standing in the field looked like groups of people. In my hallucination they appeared moving. From a distance I heard Russian soldiers talking. A small creek was in our way without a bridge. A wooden plank was laid across by somebody who had made the same journey ahead of us. As we came closer to the Russian vehicles we bent down not to be seen. My son was still quiet on my back, wrapping his small arms around my neck. Our progress was slow. My mind was still zigzagging; "Am I doing the right thing? If I would be alone it would be well, but here is my child and my wife. Why did I bring them into such danger? Why are we here? Where are we going? Why didn't we stay at home? What would I do if the Russian soldiers would start to shoot at us? Oh, those damned terrorists, because of whom I had to drag my family away from home!" But, we kept going.

At the end of the pasture was a narrow clear-cut through a densely wooded area. The Russian soldiers were there on both sides. Uncle Sándor stopped and whisperingly told me what was ahead of us, and asked whether I still wanted to go. Nodding my head I gave the answer. The weight of the responsibility in making another decision settled upon me. Slowly and quietly we continued crawling forward, stopping, listening, as the Russian soldiers were nearby, but I could not see them. It appeared an eternity until we reached the end of the wooded area. Next was a road on which the Russian tanks and trucks were parked. We had to cross it. The lights of the vehicles were not on, and there were no soldiers around them. One by one we crawled across the road. For a short rest we stopped in a ditch. Ahead of us about 30 yards away was a high railroad embankment. As we climbed up on it a few basalt rocks rolled down making a frightening noise. From behind the embankment I could see the last, but least known obstacles; the barren, sand-covered and raked "Foot-print strip," next to it the grassy strip of the minefield, and after that the barbed-wire fences. Nearby stood a tall watchtower, but there were no guards in it. For the first time in my life I saw the real "Iron Curtain", the shameful symbol of our times, and we were about to go across it. The sandy strip had the footprints of those who before us passed across it. Uncle Sándor and I crawled ahead on the grassy strip touching the ground with our bare hands in search of the tripping wires of the mines. He said that the mines have already been removed, but neither of us wanted to risk anything at the final steps of the most important journey of my life. Those 30 or 40 feet were stressful. The coiled barbed-wire on the ground was pushed away and the fence was cut open in a narrow area. We were only yards from the freedom that I was seeking. Crawling through the opened fence we arrived on Austrian soil. Exhausted from the strenuous journey, and relieved from the fright, we hugged each other. We thanked Uncle Sándor for the courageous help, gave him the bottle of schnapps and the money that I still had in my pockets. He said farewell and began his homeward journey, disappearing in the misty darkness. For me he was a true hero, a superb human being.

My wife removed the scarf from our son's mouth and gave him the go ahead to cry. He did cry out loudly. He was quiet throughout the journey, but his loud cry was the sign of the fear and tension that he the four year old felt. Those were highly emotional moments for me. We were alone in the dark and cold night in what I perceived was the "Free World", holding my wife and my son in my arms. In the distance I saw the lights of two towns, one on the one side, the other on the other of the border, but for me those were in two different worlds. Behind me in the silvery glow of the moon was the barbed-wire fence with the guard tower, which for me were the symbols of the 20th century, the horrifying marks of my deprivation of liberty, the embodiments of human fanaticism and bigotry, the shame of the world that called itself civilized, the product of the evil of mindless loyalty and proud obedience. In an almost disbelief that I could come across that hated barrier a great relief settled upon me. Although, I was the fleeing one, I felt a deep satisfaction, almost a pride of victory over those who in their ruthless power kept me in fear and imprisoned me in my own home country. After crossing the border, leaving my birthplace and homeland behind, I stood on foreign soil, where I felt free, wondering whether I could ever forgive those who brought upon us all the horror.

In the still dark early morning hours going across plowed fields and dirt roads we arrived in the Austrian village of Deutschkreutz. In the streets we met refugees who guided us to the school building where the Maltese Order set up an aid station. It was full of women and children. Us men stayed outdoors. An Austrian rail-service man coming from work greeted me. We had a brief talk. He asked me whether I had my family with me. When I told him that my wife and small child were at the school he said; let us take them to his house. I found my wife and my child laying on the straw spread on the floor, shivering. His house was nearby. While we were sitting in their warm kitchen he went to the bedroom and asked his wife to sleep with their daughter, and give her bed for my wife and my child. After all the brutalities, living under the most immoral hoard of fanatics this episode was a reawakening of my faith in humanity. Regrettably, only for a short time.

My daily routine in Vienna was to stand in line at the American Consulate for registration for the "Green-Card," to gain entry to America. Going to America for me was a compromise. I wanted to go to New Zealand, far away from the war-torn world. My wife not wanting to be far away from her family wanted to stay in Europe. I had no false illusions about the New World. The memories of the barbaric terror bombings, the horrors of the prisoner of war camp were still much too vivid. Going to America was seen as an opportunity to continue my studies in engineering, especially in agricultural mechanization. The weather was rainy and cold. The lines at the consulate were long. Hundreds of people were milling around, passing rumors, talking about the events back in Hungary, and about the hoped-for entry to America. There was also tension and an occasional fist-fight, as among the queuing people some were recognized, who had to flee in fear for their lives not because of their role in the Revolution, but because of their role in the communist terror. I personally knew one of them. They came to the consulate by taxi, wearing fur coats, with letters of invitation in their hands from their American sponsors. Some gave interviews to American news reporters, claiming that they were the persecuted and were the fleeing "Freedom-fighters." The reality was that there were two groups of fleeing people standing in the same line, hoping for entry to America; those who fled in fear of the communist terror, and those who had to flee because of their role in the communist terror. Those were the realities of those days, of which very little was known by the Americans.

The ten years I spent at the universities in Michigan and in California, became an important period of my life. From the purely academic environment at the university in Michigan, where I experienced the transition from the refugee to the citizen status, where in full concentration on my academic and research work I was occupied with establishing a new existence, where in my social life I often had meaningful conversations with academicians who were devoted opponents to wars, I went in California. There I resided in the midst of a community that existed on militarism, relished on maintaining and flying the big B-52 bombers. My neighbors were the pilots who routinely flew those bombers loaded with nuclear bombs, whose world was centered around carrying out "Missions," whose stressful life—according to rumors—was eased by using drugs. The rumbling of the bombers, as they flew over my home, the mentality of the residents of the community which was dominated by preparation for war, that atmosphere became an alien world for me. In the beautiful, sunny California I became isolated, no longer had anyone to share my thoughts with. If I did not want to reap the scorn of my neighbors, I had to avoid talking about what concerned me the most. Living in that environment deepened my anti-war and anti-violence stand, but I had to keep it as a very private matter.

For me an awakening event was the Los Angeles riot, which happened while I lived in Riverside, California. The race issue, which existed in the societies of Europe during the war-years, and was often subject to the strong condemnation by the Americans, exploded into bloody violence in the streets of an American city. The angry words, the street fighting, the use of the military force against the civilians brought the depth of the race issues to the surface. I personally felt the affect of the racial tension when I had to change my driving route from our home to the University to avoid the stone-throwing Black youngsters. In the land of liberty I had to experience the consequences of racial belonging. For me, who as an immigrant came from a war-torn world where militarism, ideological and nationalistic fanaticism left the most devastating inheritance, where racial matters were not distant issues, but were part of my life, where in my struggle for my fundamental rights I had to join a revolution in 1956, and in direct consequence of it had to flee, the events in America took on special meaning.

Those were also the years when on the television in a series of programs the history of the Second World War was presented, in my judgment in a biased, distorted manner. Although I viewed the programs with reservation, I wanted to see how the history of that human tragedy was shown to the American viewers. Having been myself a small pawn in those events, and having seen the newsreels of the other sides during the war, by viewing the American version I wanted to find an objective, realistic picture. Quite remarkably the contradictions, which were generated in me by viewing the television stories, together with living in the social environment in California, became the fuses re-igniting the urge to gain deeper understanding of the war.

World War II having been a monumental historic event, which was beyond the comprehension of an individual, but which for me was very much a personally felt event, I was seeking all available means to broaden my understanding of it. I attended lectures at the universities given by politicians, by historians, by Americans and by foreigners, and also read the articles in the prestigious magazines. I received from none of them the objective analysis on the fundamental issues, which were the underlying causes of the war. The time of those lectures and articles was still too close to the actual events to allow objectivity. The nationalistic emotions were still too deep in the American public's mind to tolerate criticism. Most importantly there was a Vietnam War, for which the government had to arouse the nationalistic pride of the people. The military leadership could not condone the condemnation of wars when it was fighting one. The time was not right for the moral approach to the issues of wars. I found myself in a conflict with an environment in which the absolute majority saw in wars the means—many the only means—to resolve ideological, political and economic issues. They bathed in the glory of victory of the Second World War, and I lived among them with my memories and with my impressions about the same war, but as a victim of it. Following the events of the Vietnam War, which from my perspective appeared to be another senseless killing in a fatally false strategy of those who in their narrow mindedness or ignorance wanted to root out any and all ideals, which others followed, if those ideals did not serve their strategic interest and plans. To me the dynamic American social-political system's devoting its energies to stopping others in their struggles, in their own countries, in their own societies, to make progress was inconceivable. But, that was the reality.

Having been exposed to the many opinions and interpretations of the world events, I did realize that my return to Europe, the revisiting of the places where I spent the critical years, months and weeks of the Second World War, the re-living of history, the listening to the views of those whose lives were directly affected by the war, were essential in reaching a satisfactory understanding of what was a decisive phase of history, and also of my life. I could not do it on an academic level. I neither had the background, nor did I have the necessary resources for such studies. I had to seek a way to review my life by returning to my past, not by seeing it in the mirrors held by others giving me distorted images. I wanted to refresh my memories before they faded away. I wanted to build my own consensus before—under the relentless bombardment of the outside influences and without my own understanding of the events—I became a parrot, repeating the words of others without my own intellectual perception. I had little or none of the criteria to conduct what others might consider credible research. I did not have access to, and was not even interested in "Documentary evidence." I did not want to see history from the level of academia, from the viewpoint of the politicians, from the perception of the militarists. I could not think about the globalism of the war. I wanted to understand the war that was personal to me, as I had lived through it. In writing my memoirs I was striving for an explanation that satisfied my own personal intellectual needs. I did not have the factual basis on the main events of the war, but had only my own observations on the events in which I was a participant. I did not have the insight into the principal issues, but remembered only to what I was a witness. My history writing became a very personal matter. It was intended not to be a data collection, not the listing of the dates of events, not the recording of names and roles of the leading personalities. I wanted to write a "true story" as I lived through it. Writing history, no matter how much the author relies on documentary evidence is a personal interpretation of the events. There can't be absolute factuality in any account on any event in which the author was an outsider, into which he himself did not have an intimate insight. To write factually about a world war in which ideologies collided drawing millions of conviction-filled participants into confrontation, where nationalistic pride, racial antagonism and human greed prevailed, is an impossible task. I read books, listened to lectures, and viewed films on the Second World War, which covered events in most cases giving the biased views of the observers. I seldom heard rational, unbiased analyses on the deep causes, which led to the war. My intended return to Europe was for the purpose of searching for answers. In doing so I spent five year in Germany.

On the sobering trips in the Harz Mountain I often visited a small German military cemetery in the midst of a forest. Simple granite stones mark the graves. On some are engraved names, date of birth and the date of death, on many the words "Unbekannter Soldat," Unknown Soldier. They were young, 17 and 18 years old, just as I was at the time of the final weeks of the war. Walking between the graves I felt a close bond with those young dead. They all died in the very last days of the war, just as those young Germans died whom I saw in the ditches along the road on which I was led to prison in May 1945. Their blood-covered faces showed that they were beaten to death by their American captors. They all dreamed about a future and fought deeply convinced that the cause was right. They felt obligated to defend their country against those whose bombs killed their parents, relatives and friend, burned their homes, destroyed their cities. They were indoctrinated by their government just as their enemies were, to be good patriots, to love, defend and if necessary die for their country. That was what they did. Were their enemies, those young men wearing another nation's military uniform any different?

Whether those young Germans were the victims of propaganda, or were driven by pure love for their country made no difference. They were young, they wanted to live, and they did have the right to live. Why did they have to die? Why could not they also become part of my generation, to live a creative, productive life? Those responsible for their tragic fate, regardless on which side they were, must bear the moral burden. Immediately after the war ended there were hastily put-together courts of the victors, hurriedly sending their victims to the firing squads and to the gallows before the truth and realities could surface, before the guilt could reach those who were the accusers. Were those, who slaughtered hundreds of thousands of civilians in the bombing raids, or beat the captured young men to death, not guilty? How much talent and human energy was buried in those graves, and in the millions of the other graves all over the world? How much motherly tears had flowed for the young men who are resting in them? Every time when I stood at those graves I felt deep sadness and burning anger. But there were also signs of true humanity in the small cemetery in the remote forest of the Harz Mountains. There were fresh flowers on the graves.

In Germany, outside the military cemeteries I did not see monuments for the fallen soldiers of the Second World War, only small bronze plaques with a few reminding words cast in them, as if they were denied the honor that the dead of the other wars received, as if they were guilty for having fought and died for a later condemned cause. I believe that is the right way to remember those who fell victim to the arrogance and immorality, to mindless loyalty and to proud obedience. The tragic fate of the fallen should be used as a reminder about the wrongs of the past, and not as an inducement for repeating the same. During my childhood I had to make the annual pilgrimage to the "Heroes' Cemetery" outside of our village, where the patriotic speeches given by politicians preaching the honor of dying for the country echoed from the gravestones of those, who died in the hopelessness of a prisoner of war camp. Absurd!

Those young victims buried in the quiet of the Harz Mountain were my comrades. The bond between us was not an ideology, not the militaristic urge to battle with others, but the enthusiasm in building a future for ourselves. When I saw them before the war paddling their kayaks, launching their model airplanes, joyfully wandering in the high mountains, I envied them. I wanted to join them. Fate of history forced me to join them in a war, which neither I, nor they wanted. It was the immorality of the politicians, the arrogance of the militarists, together with the enthusiasm of the us young that put them in their graves. Each of my visits at the cemetery reinforced my determination to carry on my mission against militarism, against violence and wars, against mindless loyalty and proud obedience.

AT THE TOMBSTONE OF AN UNKNOWN SOLDIER.

Harz Mountain, Germany.

The rough granite tombstone has two words
"UNBEKANNTER SOLDAT",
unknown soldier, carved into it
It is not glorifying you as a hero,
not a fancy plaque with patriotic bluffs.
It is marking your grave where you
the young victim of human arrogance,
the pawn of evil minds,
are laid for eternal rest.
On the graves, including yours the nameless,
are flowers laid by someone with reverence.

Some of the tombstones bear the names,
show the age of the victims and the dates of death.
You all died in the very last days of the war,
when hastily put together groups of the young
put up the desperate battle.

In the madness of the war came the moment when you,
the living young man with a name,
with flesh and blood, with mind and soul,

became an unrecognizable human wreck,
and you became "UNBEKANNT."
The war, the ultimate of the evil of the human mind,
wiped out not only your life,
but also robbed you from your name.

You were riding on trucks when came an air attack.
Having been myself under such horror
I can imagine what it could be like.
The bullets and bombs ripped you apart,
the burning fuel incinerated you to charred bits.

I can't call you by your name my fallen friend,
but in my thoughts I see in you someone close to me.
Your tragic fate also could have been mine.
You, like all the others whose tombstone I see
were at my age, at seventeen in uniform,
dreaming about a joyful future and love,
but we all were entangled in an evil web.

Standing at your grave
I feel the true sanctity of the human life.
My anger burns toward those
whose immorality and evil mind
lead nations against each other.
As a survivor I feel a deep obligation to use all my power
to speak out against wars and violence,
to stand up against those
—no matter how powerful they are—
who incite hatred and spread horror.

For the pilots who dropped the bombs,
who opened fire at the trucks,
you did not have a name,
they saw you as the enemy.

Had they know you,
had they know your name,
had they know that you were a youngster just like them,
who dreamed about a future,
who were in love,
who wanted to paddle your kayaks,
and not to fight,
they would most likely never have dropped the bombs,
never have opened the deadly guns.
But for them, after the planting of hatred in their minds,
you had to be known as the enemy.
Otherwise the generals could not have played their evil games.

While watching on the television the replay
of the events which led to your demise,
seeing the well groomed gentlemen
insanely arguing for the use of war
as the solution to political difference,
seeing the militarists in their fancy uniforms,
eagerly waiting to live out their mindless games,
I remembered the graves with the granite stones.

Seeing all those well dressed men,
who called themselves the "Leaders,"
I was wondering;
how could they bring upon us such horror?
How could they, with their educated minds,
lead millions of human beings against each other?
How could millions of people follow them into wars?

The pictures showed Churchill, Roosevelt, Hitler and Stalin
speaking to the parliament, to the congress, to the party
    gatherings.
The huge halls were filled with those

who claimed to be the people's representatives.
When the speakers reached the climax of their speech,
calling their nations for the sacrifices in a war,
the well dressed gentlemen broke into loud applause.
They applauded the starting of a mass murder,
the killing of millions, the destruction
of what the human ingenuity had built.
They all had to know very well what wars are like,
they all had to remember the horrors of other wars.
They had to be aware that there was no conflict
that could not be resolved without violence.

But, instead of sinking into a deep silence
under the weight of what they were called upon to vote,
instead of going into a quiet meditation
over the moral issues which they were about to face
they did burst into long, enthusiastic applause.
As the speakers left the podiums they rushed to them
to shake their hands in approval of what they said.

What a tragic and frightening image
of the incompetence of those with learned minds.
In their mindless loyalty and proud obedience
they had betrayed the most fundamental moral principles.
They stood up and applauded the starting of a war.
They faithfully aligned themselves with the demagogues.

The avalanche of human immorality began its devastating run.
The small nuclei of the ideologues
pleasing the eagerness of the demagogues,
using the servility of the pity bureaucrats and of the generals,
unleashed their campaign for the war.
The germs of hatred in well phrased patriotic wraps quickly
    spread.

The people who in their ignorance did not see
that they were to be sacrificed,
in their pumped-up patriotic fervor celebrated the events.

Looking back to over sixty years those images are frightening.
How could such horrible crime be committed in the Twentieth
    Century,
when education reached a high level,
when communication was available?
Where was morality?
What happened to the noble principles?

It is frightening that in these days,
after all those tragedies,
the militarist, the politicians and the demagogues
all over the world fill the arsenals with weapons,
which can evaporate millions
putting them into the graves of the "UNBEKANNT."
It is frightening to see the enthusiastic,
blind patriotism with which educated,
intelligent people applaud and tolerate
the wasting of the nation's moral wealth.

The two words "UNBEKANNTER SOLDAT,"
carved into your tombstone my fallen friend
should be the judgment on those who started the avalanche,
whose applauding meant the approval of the horror,
who were responsible for your fate,
and for the fate of millions.
Those two words should be the condemnation
of those who are ready to repeat the same.

As a survivor, I owe it to you to let my readers know
what put you into the grave.
I owe it to you to cry out against the horrors

that made you "UNBEKANNT".
I owe it to you, and to all the other fallen young
who rest in those graves,
to stand up against all those whose evil minds sent you there,
and against those who are prepared
to send other youngster in graves.
I owe it to you my fallen friend
and to those who are still alive,
but someday may also become UNBEKANNT.

Somewhere your mother, for whom you were the beloved child,
whom she carried in her womb, whom she fed on her breasts,
whom she gave a name, for whom she prayed,
for whom she shed her tears,
whose picture she tenderly touched,
she might be waiting for your return.
For her you are not "UNBEKANNT."

Rest in peace my nameless, fallen friend!

I had visited the site of the Bergen-Belsen concentration camp, which when I saw it in December of 1944 left a deep impression on me. The camp was no longer there, no barbed-wire fences, no barracks, no piles of potatoes, no inmates wandering in mud, no guard towers. Everything was razed to the ground and was burned to ashes after the war to prevent the spreading of the deadly typhoid fever, which in the last months of the war killed thousands of the inmates. In the reception building the walls were covered with the pictures of the horror that was played out just before the war ended. Inside the camp were large mass graves with simple stonewalls listing the number of victims in them. Walking between the graves the images of the women, children and older men as they were hoarded on the road from the railroad station to the camp came back. They were the symbols of human desperation, the victims of human intolerance, of bigotry, which the war brought upon the human society. Like all of my wartime experiences their fate also reinforced my determination to use all my efforts against wars, against militarism, and against racial hatred.

On my visit to East Berlin still under Soviet occupation, I was taken to a Russian military cemetery where tens of thousands of men and women are buried. They were sent from the far corners of their country to fight the enemy. A gigantic bronze monument dominated the scene glorifying the heroism of the dead. The seemingly endless rows of the graves, the tombstones standing in perfect alignment gave the impression of orderliness, of normality, of sobriety, even of some aesthetic beauty, while in reality those who rest there were the victims of total chaos, of absolute breakdown of normality, of senseless brutality and of the ugliness of the human mind. After their ripped-apart bodies were recovered from the rubble, and their bullet pierced corpses were collected from the streets, they were buried in the graves, which in the minds of the survivors was the reward of the dead for their sacrifice. Can anything reward them for what they lost? The giant bronze monument glorifying heroism in the resting place of the dead did not impress me at all. If there is an artistic way to symbolize suffering, to show the immorality of those who sent those deceased to their graves, then such monuments should be erected in every military cemetery, and the politicians and militarists should be taken there for pilgrimages. I also saw pictures of the cemeteries in Russia where the fallen German soldiers lay silently in their graves. Now, over half a century after their demise peace prevails, their agonies and deaths are seen as totally senseless. They all could have lived out their lives, if only the immorality and incompetence of the politicians and the arrogance of the militarists could have been halted, if mindless loyalty and proud obedience could have been eradicated.

Walking along the mass graves of the concentration camp, reading the granite stones of the military cemeteries, remembering the horrible massacres of the bombing raids, recalling the desperate faces of the children and women fleeing from the brutalities of the war, I asked the question; how could it happen in the world that called itself civilized? How could societies, which have claimed to be the believers in the same God and in the same Bible, which teaches; "Thou shall not kill," bring so much suffering upon each other and upon themselves? What went wrong? What is going wrong when wars are still being planned and fought?

At the time of my return to Europe in 1966 life in Germany was almost normal. A new generation was growing up; those who lived through the tragic years of the war reached the autumn stage of their lives and lived in peace. The ruins of the bombed cities were not there anymore. Having seen the remarkable recovery, the question arose in my mind: Why did these seemingly peaceful and civilized people turn on other nations in a war, devoting all their energies and know-how to killing and destruction? Going through the crowded shopping malls, watching the elegantly dressed and well behaved people parading along the boulevards I asked myself; could these be the same people who according to the propaganda murdered others just because they were another nationality or race? During the horrible days of the war when I was among them in the bomb shelters of Nürnberg, or when in the quiet hours of the pauses in the destruction I sat with them in the movie theater in Erlangen they behaved just like I did. They were frightened, were determined to survive, were seeking momentary joy and relief from the constant fear. They despaired and hoped. They spoke with anger about the enemy that burned down their cities, but even in the worst times I had not seen any atrocities committed by them. Were those young Germans, together with whom I was trained the brutal killers, as the propaganda accused them? Did I go to Germany in 1944 to join a murderous institution? Was I trained to hate the young men who were my enemies, or were of another race? No, I was not. Could the entire German nation be an evil institution, as the propaganda attempts to make the world believe it was? Were the Germans any different from their enemies, or were they just the same? Living among them in the time of war and in the time of peace was a deeply meaningful experience for me. I keenly observed them. During both stays I met some who showed arrogance, and some who showed compassion. I did find aggressiveness in some of them, both in the crisis of the critical times and in the calm days of peace. But that was no different from what I found in the people of other nations and races. The horrors of the Second World War for which the British and Americans should also accept responsibility, and about which we seldom hear, were reminders that the true test of the character of a human being, regardless of nationality and race, comes in a crisis. I heard and read about Germans who in the depth of a crisis behaved brutally. Were all Germans collectively guilty for that, as the propaganda attempts to accuse them? In the professional and social circles I lived together with those who during the war wore military uniforms and fought in Russia, in Africa, in Norway and in France. They all were civilized, moral human beings. Could they be entirely different when they were in uniform? Could they be the murderers who under command mercilessly slaughtered women and children? Could they twenty some years after the war hide their real character? They were proud of their heritage, of their technological, scientific and cultural accomplishments, they loved their country, but they were not hateful toward others just because of their nationality or race. They had to fight in a war, which they did not want, but were compelled to become part of. Those, who by the propaganda, or by their own fanatically blinded views judge others, should go through the solemn cemeteries of the victims of wars and of hatred, and join those who want a better future for the world.

I have learned a meaningful lesson during my stay in Germany.

While the Germans lived with the physical and emotional reminders of the war, the history of that period was a national taboo. In the late 1960s only a few books, written either by German or foreign authors, were available covering those years, and those were mainly documentary records without commentary or analysis. The governments, both federal and local, the schools and the media avoided the subject. Teaching history became an overly sensitive political issue. Textbooks did not include that period. Before leaving to Germany in 1966, I had seen documentary programs on the American television in which German officials and common citizens of the wartime were interviewed, including original German newsreels. I had not seen even one such program on the German television. While in America Hitler's Mein Kampf was on the shelves of libraries, the Nazi propaganda movie "Triumph of the Will" was available from rental stores, in Germany having either of those could bring severe punishment. The memories of the war still lived in the minds of the individual Germans, but not wanting to provoke controversies they kept those memories for themselves. I don't recall any social conversation with my German friends in which the war and the Hitler era became topics. The parents not wanting to cause controversies within their families carefully avoided the subject. The children not having been exposed to the issues in the schools did not want to know about their parents' past. For me, returning to Germany from America where the events of the Second World War were frequently subject of the media—obviously from an American point of view—the absolute silence of the Germans on those issues was a remarkable phenomenon. I had taken it as a resignation rather than denial or shame. Their intelligence was too high for denial; their national pride was too strong for shame.

In the "Cold War" environment of the late 1960s the generation of the Germans, which in 1945 was defeated and humiliated, became the much-needed ally on both sides of the "Iron Curtain". The trials of the Nazi party officials and collaborators by the military courts of the occupation powers which were quite numerous, and were much publicized in the previous years, were halted under the threat of the "Cold War", bringing relief to the society. The economic recovery, called the "Wirtschaftswunder," began. The coming of hundreds of thousands of foreign workers seeking a better life in Germany restored the national pride. In their inner feelings they knew that as a great nation they had a leading role in Europe, their industrial vitality, their economic power were assets, which even the defeat in a war could not destroy. For me who saw the total destruction, observing the recovery was a memorable experience.

Attending engineering conferences in the countries behind the Iron Curtain was one of my missions. I was seeking every opportunity to visit them, believing that the personal contact on a professional level, not propaganda, was the best way to help those who were deprived of their freedom. In 1968 I was invited to give a lecture on my research at an international engineering conference in Hungary. That was my first return to my homeland since my illegal departure in 1956. The country was still under communist rule. Although, according to the official government decree all those who fled the country after the 1956 Revolution received full amnesty, and the officials of the conference assured me that my illegal departure in 1956 was not an issue, I still had some concern for my safety. In the hope of avoiding any unpleasant events at the border crossing I chose not to drive, but to fly to Budapest. At the moment when the plane entered the Hungarian airspace my heartbeat went up. I was filled with emotions and tension. Looking down I saw the landscape changing. The small plots of farmland in Austria were replaced by huge fields of cultivated land. Those were the state-owned farms and collectives. It was almost like flying over Kansas or Iowa, but I was over another world. My reception at the airport was cordial and official.

As a foreigner I had to register at the State Security Police, which was in the same ornate building where the AVH used to be before the Revolution. On the way to the site of the conference I traveled by bus with Russian, Polish, Bulgarian and East German engineers. I was the only American guest. They did not know that I was a Hungarian. The conference was held in a palace. The ornate structure stood in the middle of a well-groomed park. It was a fitting place for a scientific gathering. The program menu listed my subject, and identified me as an American university research engineer. In the evening before my presentation I walked in the large hall where the podium was set up with a microphone. There was an inner-debate in my mind; should I present my lecture in English or in Hungarian? I was listed as an American speaker, but was in my native country. In my hands I held the manuscript of my presentation in both languages. My inner debate became an identity issue. In the late night hours with the help of a Hungarian friend I went through my manuscript to make sure that I used the proper technical terminology. When I was introduced by the chairman of the program as an American speaker I decided to use English, but when the microphone was turned over to me, almost instinctively I began to speak in Hungarian. But only a few words. A never before experienced emotion set upon me. For the first time in my life I spoke about my research work in my native tongue, in my home country. My throat was grabbed by emotion, my tears began to flow. It was an eerie quiet in the hall. With my tearful eyes I could only see the blurred faces of the people in the first rows, mostly invited foreigners, who turning to each other tried to find out what was wrong with me. I drank a sip of water, took a deep breath, wiped off my tears. When I regained my composure, I apologized to the audience, telling them the weight of the emotions, which overwhelmed me. They responded with a long applause. I was relieved! That event remained a memorable episode of my emigrant life, showing how powerful emotions can be.

After returning from Germany in 1971, on the first day of attending school in an affluent suburban of Seattle, my thirteen-year-old son came home deeply upset. His classmates hearing that he came from Germany called him a "Nazi," and did not let him join in their play. This was a sad episode, which awakened me that I returned to an America that was unable to free itself from the hate-filled propaganda that poisoned the minds even of the children. It happened not in a slum, but in a successful, "schooled" upper class society. I use the word "schooled" rather than "educated", because education trains the mind to be tolerant and unbiased. I had come to America in 1956 as an immigrant from a small country that was isolated from the rest of the world by ideological and physical barriers, leaving my homeland after an exaltation-filled but defeated revolution against a tyranny, seeking my personal freedom. I felt relieved by having had my family away from the imminent dangers, and was overwhelmed by the warm and friendly welcome that I received as a "Freedom Fighter". In the assimilation process I was exposed to the views of those with whom I had social contact. There were substantial differences between our views; mine were based on my personal experience, while the Americans' on the government and the media reports. Some had shown sympathetic understanding. Others flatly rejected my views. Some welcomed my open, frank remarks, others felt discomforted. While seeing an anti-war poster on the wall of the garage of a bank I was pleased. But it was crossed out with the words: "The footprint of a chicken".

On my 1971 return from Europe I was not the celebrated "Freedom Fighter", but an obnoxious anti-war, anti-violence crusader. America was not the land of the peace-seekers, but the land of war-crusaders. In Europe the Vietnam War was seen as a terrible political blunder, a crime against humanity. For most Americans it was a patriotic war. This was quite evident to me by reading the papers, by listening to the media and talking with the people. Although, for the Europeans the fear of Bolshevism was a daily reality, there was an even greater fear of another war. While in Germany the British and American tanks broke up the pavement of the streets, tore up the farmland, the low flying airplanes frightened the animals and annoyed the people, all that in preparation for a war, the Europeans were in search of ways to normalizing the affairs between the politically divided nations. They watched in bewilderment as America pursued the war in Vietnam, and was preparing still for another war in Europe. While the Europeans, especially the Germans treated the Jewish persecution as a sad and regrettable tragedy, for which they were not willing to accept all the blame, the constant propaganda bombardment belittled their own wartime tragedies, the terror bombing of their cities. As the defeated they had to accept the realities. Not so by some of the Americans in the Seattle suburb. For them the issue was black-and-white; all Germans were bad, which they assumed by not knowing history. Not only the Germans of the Hitler era were bad, but also their descendants, not only the Germans, but anyone coming from Germany, including my thirteen year old American-born son. In their minds, in the comfort of their plush waterfront homes they were still fighting the Second World War defeating the Nazis, transplanting their bigoted views into the minds of their small children. For them waging a war somewhere far away in Vietnam, killing fellow human beings of another race was a national pastime. It was not only my young son who was subjected to the bigoted antagonism. I, the adult was also subjected to the same. I was the "Chicken" whose footprint they did not want to see. America that was the symbol of world peace for most Americans, for me became the symbol of militaristic belligerence. I wish, and I hope that some-day this image can be changed.

THE EUROPEAN
ANTI-JEWISM.

The expression "anti-Semitism" in its specificity includes all Semitic groups, Jews and Arabs, while in its common usage it is applied regarding the Jews, including racial, religious, cultural and political aspects. For clarity of the matter I use the expression "anti-Jewism."

I view the issue not as the ill of the 20th Century and of Europe alone, as it existed since the biblical times, wherever the Jews have lived. I consider anti-Jewism as I have observed it in my small village and in the cities in Hungary between the two world wars. I do not judge races or nations, do not accept the concepts of collective guilt or collective innocence. I take the position that some members of any race—including the Jewish—are burdened by horrible crimes, while the majority were victims of racial intolerance.

Race relationship can be affected by racial-genetic characteristics, exposing those with distinct racial features. In racially conscious societies such features alone can be the source for some degree of imposed or self-imposed segregation, like the Negro ghettoes, the Latino districts and the Jewish quarters in America, and the Jewish and Gypsy ghettoes in Europe.

According to the records in the late 1800s and early 1900s under the liberal immigration laws of the countries of the Austro-Hungarian Monarchy Jews in great numbers arrived in Hungary, mainly from Galicia and Russia where they had been subjected to discrimination and pogroms. The influx was organized, conducted and financed mostly by the Jews themselves, was tolerated by the Hungarian government, and was even supported by some native private individuals. It had reached the level of intensity at which the local natives—especially the merchants and traders—began to feel threatened by the fierce competition by the Jews. The immigrating Jews settled in cities forming sizable communities, opened shops, or settled in the rural towns in small groups as commodity and livestock traders. In the villages usually two or three families set up shops as bakers and merchants. Land cultivation was rarely pursued by them. They maintained their outward Orthodox traditions, making themselves distinguishably different from the natives. Among themselves they spoke Yiddish, which is like a German dialect, and spoke the Hungarian language with an accent. The tradition-burdened Orthodox Jews had to find their place in a traditional native society. Up until the end of the First World War anti-Jewism was neither a prevailing social nor a political issue. There was, however, de-facto self-imposed segregation by the Jews.

Following the First World War some of the non-Orthodox Jews became engaged in the radical Communist revolutionary movements, which was to the deep resentment of the native societies, exposing the Jews as dangerous ideological and social enemies. Communism as an ideology has far reaching historical and even religious roots. It has socially idealistic—in some respect utopian—elements, but in the 20th century it evolved into "Marxism-Leninism", and later into "Bolshevism", and became the radical branch of Socialism, propagating class struggle under proletariat dictatorship. In the traditional native societies the radicalism of the imported ideology, distorted by the Bolshevik terror, caused a deep rupture between the natives and the Jews. The seeds of anti-Jewism had been planted. After the defeat of the communist rule in 1919, and with the expulsion of the radical and criminal terrorist elements, a relative racial calm began. In the late 1920s and early 1930s as the Jews began to enter in greater numbers the educated and professional fields, some relinquishing the external Orthodoxy assimilated to the native societies. The "European Jew" evolved, who no longer was distinguishable, gained acceptance into the middle-class, educated native society. Racial intermarriages became not uncommon; in most cases Jewish men marrying Gentile women. Name changes were common, in some cases in the desire to melt into the native society, while in others to hide the Jewish identity. (Similar to what occurred in Hollywood.) This trend helped both the educated middle-class Jewish and the educated middle-class native societies to live together without racial tension. There was an anti-Jewish sentiment, which came mainly from the bias of the racial homogeneity of the lesser educated natives. Highly inflammatory rumors were planted by racially prone small, uneducated, radical anti-Jewish individuals, accusing the Jews of sacrificing Gentile children in their rituals. I had heard such rumors as a young child in my village. The secretive, isolated life style of the Orthodox Jews, together with the sacrificial rituals described in the Bible did not help in dispelling such rumors. There were no meaningful efforts from either side to reduce the tension.

The religious aspect of anti-Jewism was not a major issue. There was freedom for all religions, including Judaism. The Jews were allowed to form congregations, to build synagogues and to have their own schools. The contact between the Christian and Jewish congregations in general was minimal or non-existent. Among the Ultra-Orthodox Jews the Talmud had an equal or higher ranking than the Bible, while by those natives who were familiar with the Talmud it was considered as anti-Christian and anti-Gentile, causing tension between the relatively small groups involved in doctrinal matters. The Jewish origin of Christianity with the "Judeo-Christian" designation received special emphasis in America, while in Europe, in general, the emphasis was on the New-Testament teachings, which is not recognized by Judaism. Dogmatic anti-Jewism surfaced in some of the Christian institutions, especially on Jesus' messianic role. Although, not as an official doctrinal issue, but among the lesser educated faithful a widely spoken matter was the accusation of the Jews of murdering Jesus. Atheism, a dogmatic matter propagated by some Jewish thinkers, and as an ideological and political tool used by the Jewish Bolshevik activists, generated much resentment in the Christian institutions.

The cultural aspect of the race-relationship significantly increased in the 20th Century, when the non-Orthodox, liberal-minded Jews entered and expanded their role in the printed media and in entertainment. That involvement did not bring the traditional Jewish culture to the natives, but rather established a new liberal journalism, and brought a non-classical version of light entertainment. Another significant tool in spreading the "Jewish culture" was the motion picture with the entertainment films imported from America. It was challenged by the Germans—and to a lesser degree by the movie production of other countries. In Hungary Jewish literature did not gain a significant position, at least not in the classical field. In Germany under the Hitler regime radical anti-Jewish laws had been enacted, excluding writers, composers, books and compositions from the repertoires on racial grounds, arousing pro and anti-Jewish sentiments. As a consequence, many of the Jewish writers, composers, musicians and scientists emigrated, some of them continuing their work in America.

During and after the 1919 Red terror in Hungary, in the race relationship politics became an important issue because of the Jewish involvement. After the defeat of the communist rule the role of the Jews in politics was not significant, but gradually increased until World War II, mainly in the Labor Movement. In the propaganda the Jewish role in the Soviet Bolshevism and in the 1919 communist terror was exploited by the political Right. In 1944 under German military occupation the National Socialists gained power enacting harsh anti-Jewish laws, making the wearing of the yellow star compulsory. Strong anti-Jewish propaganda had been launched, and large numbers of Jews were deported to work in the German armament industry. Government-conducted anti-Jewism had been instigated in a war environment, when fear burdened the native population. As a principal issue, the accusation of the Jews for the outbreak of the war was planted. The terror-bombing of the cities and villages by the Americans and the British was attributed to Jewish instigation, for which they were treated as dangerous internal enemies. In a war-environment the racial-political aspect of anti-Jewism was superceded by strategic confrontation.

The denial of the existence of anti-Jewism would be the denial of the realities. At the same time the denial of the existence of "anti-Gentileism" would also be futile. The events of the Second World War, the Jewish persecution, the mainly Jewish led Bolshevik terror, caused deep rifts on all sides. Radicalism, fanaticism, bigotry, be it racial, religious, ideological or nationalistic, be it on either side, can only exacerbate the tension between the races. The current trend in the race-relations frightens me. The collisions are too deep and too frequent. Without exercising strong self-examination and self-discipline by all sides, we may find ourselves once again in violent racial-political confrontation.

"THE JEWISH QUESTION."

In the late 1930s and early 1940s in Germany and in several other European countries the issues—racial, political and economic—relating to the Jews were included in the phrase "THE JEWISH QUESTION". It was one of the—if not the principal political issue—that led to the European phase of the Second World War and to many of the events following it.

Hitler's book "Mein Kampf" had been published in 1922. In it he stated his accusatory political views on the role of the Jews in Germany's defeat in the First World War and in the social-economic chaos that followed. The Jewish issue included the role of the Jews in Bolshevism, especially in countries directly affected by it. The severe conditions in unemployment and poverty in Germany fueled the discontent, and attracted the desperate ones to two opposing camps; the Hitler-led National Socialism and the Jewish-inspired International Communism. Both gained strength, driving a wedge between the natives and the Jews. The overt counter attack of Jewry against the National Socialists began in 1933 with the article in the Daily Express: *"Judea declares war on Germany. Jews of All the World unite in Action"*. In 1934 the Zionist political leader Vladimir Jabotinsky wrote: *"Our Jewish interest call for the complete destruction of Germany."* A racial-ideological war started, spiraling into deeper and deeper belligerence, bringing the major powers into two opposing camps, and finally into the European phase of the Second World War. The racial-ideological confrontation was evident on both sides, and in every event. Germany was viewed by the Jews as a lethal threat to Judaism and to the Jewish race. Judaism and the Jewish race were seen in Nazi-Germany as an international conspiracy, an undermining element in their society, the propagator of anarchy and Bolshevism. The Communist International (COMINTERN) in 1919 stated in its program: *"...by all available means, including armed forces...the creation of an International Soviet Republic"* The events took the issues from conjecture to substantive threat.

In the economically catastrophic and politically chaotic years after the First World War, the great fear in Europe—but especially in Germany—was Bolshevism. It was the extreme branch of Socialism, a grotesquely distorted interpretation of the communist ideology, advocating terrorist class struggle and proletariat dictatorship. By the opposition it was viewed not just as an ideological trend, but rather a socially, economically and morally destructive conspiracy. Berlin was the center of the radical ideological Left. For a short period Bavaria, a province of Germany, became a Soviet Republic, while in some of the other provinces tension and uncertainty reigned. At the same time Hungary was also declared a Soviet Republic. Under the severe unemployment, poverty and runaway inflation political unrest was instigated by a highly aggressive Bolshevik leadership thus threatening the traditional social structure. The failure of the governments to solve the burning problems, the worsening economy, the growing arrogance of the Bolsheviks pushed Germany to the brink of anarchy. Only a radical social-economic policy, and the mobilization of the desperate population for a national recovery, could save not only Germany, but also the whole of Europe from Bolshevism. Had Germany not become the bulwark against Bolshevism, world history could very likely have taken an entirely different path. In Spain a civil war was brewing between the Communists and the Nationalist, with the support and direct participation of communist volunteers from America, the Soviet Union and from some European countries, while Germany and Italy provided military assistance to the Nationalists. Had the Spanish war ended with the victory of the communists, Europe would have been in a vise between the Bolshevik Soviet Union and a communist Spain, bringing unforeseeable consequences not only for Europe, but also for America.

In that dangerous political environment an American-British-German alliance could have been a rational political course. It could have become the main pillar of a peaceful, dynamic, social and economic progress for the Western World. Both the USA and Germany were recovering from the Great Depression, both were progressing in social reforms, both were in a technological upswing. Both had racial-minority problems, although fundamentally different in nature, one with the Negroes, which was purely racial, and the other with the Jewish minority, which had racial, political-ideological and economic elements. Another difference was the way they pursued their goals. Germany as a traditionally regimented society, burdened by extreme economic conditions and by the direct threat of Bolshevism, by necessity accepted a quasi-dictatorial leadership, while America as a victorious power with enormous resources, not directly threatened by Bolshevism, did proceed on a moderate course. Those facts were recognized by some politicians in both countries. It was the Jewish issue in Germany that became in America the roadblock to an alliance. The battle between the pro and contra alliance camps began. In spite of the fundamental ideological differences between Capitalism and Communism, allegedly, the Jewish American banks were the main financial supporters of the Bolsheviks in the Soviet Union. Quite remarkably, Communism as the feared ideology, and Bolshevism as the dangerous threat to the Western societies disappeared from the American political agenda. In the capitalistic West the ideological confrontation between Communism and Capitalism was sidelined by a racial-political war between International Judaism and the National Socialist Germany. The ultimate objective was defeating Nazism and Germany.

I join those who believe that an American-British-German alliance could have strengthened the moderates, and could have restrained the radicals on both sides. Thereby the war in Europe could have been prevented, and the persecution of the Jews could have been avoided. There are substantiating records on diplomatic moves by Germans, seeking peaceful avenues for the outstanding political issues. Similarly, there were efforts made by politicians in Britain and in America to find rational and peaceful solutions to the legitimate complaints of the Germans. Reports are also available on the feverish activities of American and European intellectuals, attempting to help the opposing parties to reach a compromise. Regrettably, all those efforts were to no avail.

Although, in Europe, between the two world wars was wide-spread anti-Jewish sentiment—mainly because of the Jewish role in Bolshevism—I believe that the outbreak of the Second World War was the primary—if not the sole—cause of the persecution of the Jews. In the final years of the war there was a severe labor shortage in the German armament industry, and the Jews as non-trustable for military service could fill that need. Many of the educated German Jews were allowed to emigrate before the outbreak of the war. Most of the deportees were from the German-occupied Eastern European countries and from the German-occupied Soviet territories. It was the war, which in those countries brought the ultra-right radicals to power in the otherwise moderate societies. Quite a clear example was the case of Hungary, where neither political, nor racial radicalism have been tolerated until mid-1944, when the Soviet forces were already on Hungarian territories, and the rest of the country was under German military occupation. Drawing parallels might not be appropriate, but I assume that if the violence and destruction of the war would have touched America—as it touched Germany and the Easter European countries—the fate of not only the Japanese Americans, but of the other minorities could have become the same as that was for the Eastern European Jewry. Racial violence—even at peacetime—was not an unknown element in America.

Having been the witness to some of the events in Hungary and in Germany, although not as a Jew and not as a German, but as a keen observer who spent the last months of the war in Germany, and who after the war by family relation did have close personal contact with Jews, I read and view the relevant publications with special interest. The authors, some of them academicians, on anti-Semitism in Germany raised the question; why the people did follow Hitler, when in his book "Mein Kampf" he quite clearly stated his anti-Jewish position. It is undeniable that a general resentment against the Jews, not only on racial, but rather on ideological-political grounds, was common not only in Germany, but also in some other European countries, especially where the Bolshevik terror had been experienced. It is also undeniable that the Jews in general, as a minority, in their private lives pursued rigorous, racially segregated and often hostile relations with the natives of the respective countries. Equally undeniable is the involvement of the Jews radicals in the terror of the Bolshevik era after both World Wars. When anti-Semitism as a racial matter is raised, "anti-Gentileism" should not be ignored. It was—and still is there, for some on religious grounds, for some as their traditional cultural heritage, for some on an ideological-political basis, as was shown in their active role in Communism, and for many in the post-World War II era on the grounds of the persecution. In the pre-war times for the non-political Eastern-European Orthodox Jews the racial and religious separation were the principal matters. That was manifested by their outward appearance, wearing the traditional attire, men wearing the side-curls, women shaving their heads and wearing wigs. For them there was an almost total social segregation. The educated and professional non-Orthodox Jews in many respects assimilated to the natives, but among themselves nurtured a clear self-consciousness in racial superiority over the natives. That was evidenced by the high proportion of the Jews in the professional fields, like medicine, law and banking. The non-Orthodox moderates were active in liberal politics, journalism and in entertainment, while the non-religious, social-political radicals played active roles in Bolshevism and in other extremist political movements, in some cases with regrettable consequences. The evidence of that can be found in the events of the periods after World War I, but especially after World War II, when under the Soviet occupation the Jewish radicals ruled in the Eastern European countries.

What did I as a teenager know about the roots of the fear, the resentment and mistrust toward the Jews in Hungary? First, it was the fear of the return of Bolshevism, which in its short reign in 1919 under the leadership of Béla (Kohn) Kun, a Jew, (he was later tried as a traitor and was executed by his own comrades in the Soviet Union), who together with his cohorts ruled with absolute terror. They were a threat to all the traditional social classes, from the peasantry to the nobility. Under their rule Hungary was declared a Soviet Republic. For my family the fear of Bolshevism was also a personal matter. My mother had been subjected to mistreatment. It was also the fear of the Bolsheviks' atheistic doctrines, which were seen as a threat to the Christian foundation of the nation. My father, a Lutheran minister, talked about the confrontations which he as a young chaplain had with the Jewish agents when they ruled the country. It was also the fear of the return of the economic chaos, unemployment and poverty of the Great Depression of the 1920s, which was in general attributed to Jewish speculators. After the collapse of the "Red Terror" in 1919 in which according to the records the majority of the hated commissars—25 out of 32—were Jewish, widespread rumors provided the basis for anti-Jewish sentiments, unjustly placing all the Jews in the category of agents, or at least of sympathizers of Bolshevism. They were seen as dangerous internal enemies. Both the 1919 "Red" era and the Great Depression are history to me, as I was born after those events.

The Jews in my village—all Orthodox—wearing their traditional attire were for me strange people, even the children, who did not attend our schools, and with whom I never did play. I bought candy in their store, but never was invited in their homes, as I was called in the homes of others. One of the Jewish boys said to me that his parents told him not to play with me because I was a "Goy". (Goy or Goyim in the Jewish vocabulary is a derogatory name for the Gentiles). That separation remained with me for a long time. Although, later in my teenage years, I had Jewish classmates, I never had the kind of friendship with them that I had with others. I was afraid to go to the Jewish quarters of the cities even at daytime, watched with suspicion the groups of young Jews gathering in the narrow streets, and avoided them. There was a deep mutual mistrust. My love for the little girl whose father was Jewish remained unaffected by racial difference. As the direct effect of the war intensified, and as the propaganda put the blame on the Jews, presenting them as the agents of the feared enemy, I did not know whom to believe, or what to believe. There was hysteria in a war that was being lost. The well-orchestrated propaganda constantly reminded me about the threat of the "Jewish-Bolshevik Terror" and about its alleged millions of victims in Russia. It repeatedly replayed the horrors of the "Red Terror" in Hungary after the First World War, for which also the Jews were blamed, and which touched even my family. Those events were history for me, but I was frightened by the thought of someday becoming a victim. I was young, wanted to dream about my future, wanted to be with my sweetheart, but was warned about the danger of what was to come, if I did not help the country to defend itself. Not political convictions, not racism, but fear was what guided my young mind. I was too young for ideologies, and my upbringing kept me clear of hateful propaganda. It is, nonetheless, true that the daily bombing raids, the horror pictures of the destruction of the war, the ever-growing number of victims among my fellow Hungarians did occupy my thoughts. My sympathy for the herded away Jews was equaled by the exodus of the masses of my own countrymen desperately fleeing as the front approached our area. To me they all became the victims of the terrible events. My fear was also growing about my joining them in their fate. I believe that the fear of most people was similar to mine.

In late summer of 1944 the realization of losing the war began to set in, causing emotional numbness. Trainloads of wounded soldiers arrived, filling the hospitals. Refugees crowded the streets. Military convoys moved everywhere, while the Russians were only a few hundred kilometers away. There was fear and apathy. The removal of the Jews as enemies, or as agents of the enemy, was part of the turmoil. "The friend of my enemy is my enemy," was the general attitude, and in some cases rightly, in others wrongly, the Jews were viewed as the friends of the Bolsheviks and of the Americans and British who bombed our cities. It was a war not somewhere in a faraway place, but in my homeland, destroying our homes, killing my relatives, friends and neighbors. It was a war, not made for TV movie. It was part of my everyday life. It was the ultimate of terror. It was our "9/11" that happened every day.

Between 1948 and 1956 under the Bolsheviks' reign in Hungary, when persecution on political and social-origin grounds was rampant, the Jewish radicals had a dominating role in the government, in the political institutions and in the hated AVH, the State Security Authority. My family lived in constant fear, not because of our political views, but because of my father's clergymen position as the dean of the Evangelical (Lutheran) Church. He was treated as a "Fekete Reakcios" or Black Reactionary, as the clergy of all churches were called. Others lived in fear because they were born into a noble family, had some government or administrative position before the takeover by the Red Regime, owned land or a factory, or belonged to political or social organizations. Any opposition to the communist dictated party line—even the mildest criticism—was brutally crushed. "Those who are not with us are against us" was the slogan, and that covered most of my countrymen. (Remarkably, almost the same words were used by the American President in 2003 regarding the Islamic world!) A broad section of the society, including the productive, entrepreneurial and educated elite suffered immense persecution. My father told me about a conference, which he attended as one of the representatives of the churches. It was held by Mátyás (Roth) Rákosi, the head of the Hungarian Communist Party and the de-facto head of the government. (He was Jewish, was a well known activist in the 1919 Bolshevik era, was jailed, and in the 1930s was deported to the Soviet Union. He returned to Hungary in 1945 with the Soviet occupation forces. In 1954, after Stalin's death, in a self-cleansing process of the Communist Party he was removed from his position, and was exiled to the Soviet Union. He made repeated attempts to return to Hungary. He died in exile.) The conference took place in the library of the Communist Party office, where to my father's surprise shelves were full of books on church-related subjects. Rákosi took out books, quoted from them, proving his familiarity with the issues, attacked the churches as "Reactionaries," enemies of social-political progress, as "agents of Western Capitalism." The participating church representatives argued for freedom for church activities. This caused Rákosi to turn his anger on them, threatening with severe consequences. Shortly thereafter my father received two official notices, removing him from his position in the Lutheran Church, prohibiting his ministerial services in any capacity, including celebrating sermons, thus forcing him into virtual exile. The Lutheran Bishop Lajos Ordas was put on trial and was jailed on accusation of having US dollars in his possession. The Catholic Cardinal Jozsef Mindszenty was tried, accused of treason. The same ruthless methods were used in confiscating small businesses, shops, land of small and big landholders, factories. In the middle of the night tens of thousands had been deported, confiscating their homes and giving those to the party faithful. These are the realities, which are seldom—if ever—mentioned in the American media.

The German occupation of Russia and some other European countries with large Jewish populations had a rekindling effect on the hatred of the few fanatics, and on the simmering resentment of a broader segment of the population against the Jews, accusing them of the outbreak of the war, and of the brutal terrorism under the Bolshevik rule. The reversal of the war in 1943, especially the suffering of the civil population under the American and British terror bombings, together with the activities of the Jewish underground, provoked further tension, and led to retribution. It was another war without fronts. We have to remember that in wartime in every country martial law is applied. From the news reports of those times it appeared that most of the "Retaliatory Actions" were carried out not by the Germans alone, but also by the authorities and the military of the respective countries. On that basis almost every country in Europe can be accused of anti-Semitism. During the war years, in direct consequence of the post-World War I environment not only Hitler's Germany, but also the whole of Europe was engulfed in fanatical nationalism. The threat of "International Bolshevism" was spread by the propaganda. In that environment the immigrant Jew, the visible alien without a national identity, burdened by the suspicion of being a Bolshevik agent, was viewed as the dangerous internal enemy.

What did I know about the events of the war? Only what the government and the military wanted us to know, and what I myself could actually see. At the beginning there was strong opposition in Hungary against entering the war. There were vehement debates even on the government level between those who in a wishful—by the later events proven unrealistic assumption—hoped for a strong British interference, holding back both the Nazi and the Soviet threats. Others, who had great fear of Bolshevism had felt that it was Germany, and only Germany, that could save us from the return of the Bolshevik terror. There was no war euphoria. Later as the fronts collapsed apathy set in. In 1944 American bombers flying over my head every day, destroying our cities, caused fear, but also added to the resolve to defend ourselves in whatever way we could, because we wanted to survive. The ever shrinking frontlines bringing home the realities that some day the feared enemy was to arrive led me the young teenager to entrust my future to those who were in power. There was no other alternative. People were preoccupied with gathering food reserves for a possible siege, hiding their valuables, burying their treasures. The wealthy moved in the big cities in hope of becoming less exposed. Women were in panic as reports came about raping and plundering by drunken Russian soldiers. Parents feared for their daughters, husbands feared for their wives. With every day the tension grew. Fleeing, leaving the homes behind was on the mind of many. But where to go? The roads were already crowded with refugees coming from the eastern part of the country.

The rainy grayness of the dark autumn of 1944 added to the depressing atmosphere. Trains packed with wounded soldiers, freight cars loaded with my frightened compatriots, women and children, old and crippled fleeing from the feared enemy rolled in daily to the station. At the same time the Jews the "Internal enemies" were loaded on trains to be taken to deportation camps. Under those circumstances their removal from the battered communities was seen as a legitimate defensive action by the government. The harshness with which they were treated, especially the women, children and the elderly was generally resented, but the Jews were placed by the propaganda into the category of the internal enemy, and they were blamed for the sad fate of my fleeing countrymen, and for the imminent danger in which we had to live. Those who knew better and attempted to oppose the authorities did so by risking their lives. It was "Total War" and there was no mercy for anyone who did or said anything that did not serve the war effort. I went to the church to pray for God's help, as I believed that the nation was fighting for its survival. Not ideological principles, but the survival instinct was the dominant force in my behavior.

While in the pre-World War II years in Central and Eastern Europe there was a silent, non-violent resentment against the Jews, in the days of the frightening daily terror-bombings, in the chaotic times of a brutal war there was a small minority that presumably did commit horrible atrocities. Some justified their brutality on racial, others on political grounds. Having lived through the horrors of terror bombing of the cities in Hungary and in Germany, having seen the immensity of the suffering of the victims, I also felt anger. I heard verbal abuses, read virulently anti-Jewish propaganda, but never saw any actual violent physical attacks on Jews either in Hungary or in Germany, by anyone. In our area of Hungary the removal of the Jews from the communities was carried out by the Gendarme, which was a disciplined, strong arm of the government. The anti-Jewish bigots who could have had the intention to commit physical harm, did not have access to the deportees, at least not when I was present. In December of 1944, as a Hungarian soldier coming from the war-zone I was taken to the Bergen-Belsen concentration camp for delousing and for a hot shower. There I talked with a Jewish-Hungarian physician. Hard work, cold, cramped barracks, meager food, fear and uncertainty about what was to come were what I heard. The doctor's deep fear was the outbreak of a typhoid epidemic. I heard nothing about mass killings. After the bombing raids on Nürnberg, as a Hungarian soldier I participated in the rescue operations, worked together with Jewish inmates who were brought in from the nearby camps. I witnessed no atrocities there. After the war I talked with some of the Jewish residents of my hometown, and later with my wife's relatives, among them a medical doctor, who was interned in the Dachau and Bergen-Belsen concentration camps. He talked about the meager food, the rudeness of the KAPO the inmate Jewish police, the cramped barracks, the medical experiments on twins, and the devastating typhoid epidemic in the last months of the war.

Mr. Daniel J. Goldhagen, the Jewish author of "Hitler's Willing Executioners", applying the parlance of academia attempts to argue for, and tries to prove the absurd. His self-defeating thesis—which the uninformed reader might interpret as factual proof—suggests that violent anti-Semitism was—and still is—a traditional racial, cultural characteristic of all Germans. He fails, however, to give an objective explanation for the tension between the natives and the Jews originating from the period following the First World War, when Jewish extremists as Bolsheviks ruled with brutal terror in Russia, declared Bavaria and Hungary as Soviet Republics. In his argument the target is the entire German nation. In attempting to prove his thesis he repeatedly recites the alleged atrocities committed by "Ordinary Germans". To support his claim for the collective guilt, he suggests the spreading of the blame from the trigger-pulling executioners to the railroad switch operators, whose guilt could be the setting of the tracks for the trains carrying the Jewish deportees, from the hate-spewing propagandists to the paper-shuffling clerks in the state offices. He fails to acknowledge that the alleged atrocities occurred in the climate of a vicious war, in which the Jews were viewed as the internal enemies, on the one side as Bolshevik agents, on the other as British-American spies and saboteurs. He also fails to acknowledge that the concentration camps were highly secretive and were isolated from the civil population, and that the infamous "Extermination-camps" like Auschwitz and Birkenau were not even on German soil. He also fails to acknowledge what the late investigations seem to prove that some of the alleged crimes had been committed not by the Germans, but by the local nationals of the respective countries. The uninformed reader of his book may very well conclude that the entire German nation was—and still is—a totally immoral, sadistic, murderous institution that so far has avoided being adequately punished for its crimes. His book received high praise and also condemning criticism from Jewish and non-Jewish sources. One of his strong critics was another Jewish academician Norman Finkelstein, who is a scholar of the Nazi persecution. Because of the contradictions and lack of credibility for many of the claims he called Goldhagen's book a "None-

Book". Having been in Germany in the final months of the war, and having been inside the Bergen-Belsen camp, I have reason to assume that most Germans—whether civilian or military—had no knowledge of the existence of those camps, and quite certainly not of the alleged conditions in the camps.

The tragic events of history show that neither side can claim innocence. Horrible crimes were committed by individuals and by institutions on all sides, but the application of the collective guilt concept is most inappropriate. Regrettably, Mr. Goldhagen and some other Jewish authors as academicians did not come to such a conclusion. In their highly critical books they rightfully cry out about the horrors of the concentration camps. But, as academicians they interpret the past in a non-scholastic, one-sided manner. They accuse entire nations of committing horrible crimes without examining the facts. I rightfully ask; what was their motive with publishing their books and articles? Was it to heal the wounds, or was it to open the old wounds? Was it to diminish racial hatred, or was it to rekindle it in a reversed sense, in this case in the new generations of the Jews against the Gentiles? Was it to examine a tragic period of our times, or was it to put the blame on others—and only on others—thereby diverting the attention from what burdens some in the Jewish society? It would only be fair and correct if those academicians would present those tragic times with scholarly objectivity, and treat the issues with openness, especially for their American readers, who either have no knowledge at all, or know very little about those past events.

The name Shlomo Morel is unknown to most Americans, although he was a most brutal torturer of thousands. After the Second World War in Poland more than 200,000 German nationals were taken to prison camps, out of which 80,000—the majority women and children—were killed. The commander of one of the camps was Shlomo Morel, a Jewish man, the survivor of a concentration camp. The sadism with which he tortured his victims is beyond comprehension. He stayed in Poland until the end of the communist era, when to avoid the trial which the Polish Government requested, he fled to Israel, where he lives comfortably under protection. John Sack another Jewish author in his book "AN EYE FOR AN EYE" writes about the atrocities, which were committed by Jewish extremists shortly after the Second World War, acknowledging the existence of Jewish-led extermination camps. Not much has been written however, about the involvement of the Jewish radicals in the "Red Terror" in the Eastern European countries in the late 1940s and early 1950s with countless victims, which led to the 1956 uprisings in Poland, in Hungary and in the 1968 revolution in Czechoslovakia. There are arguments that the Jewish participation in the terror organizations was justified by the fear of the return of Fascism. That argument is not a plausible one, because after a total defeat in the war, and under the Soviet military occupation no extremist "Fascist" organizations could exist. I view their actions as hateful revenge. The question can be rhetorically raised; should all the Jews be held collectively responsible for the crimes of a few? Certainly not.

In my conversations with American Jews on the subject of the role of the Jews in the Bolshevik terror they listened intensely, often apprehensively, in disbelief and denial, as if they had never heard anything regrettable committed by Jews. For them the only themes were the "incorrigible European anti-Semites", the "persecution of the innocent Jews by the Nazi natives" and the "horrors of the Holocaust". They did not want to hear that in Hungary both in the 1919 Red terror and in the post-Second World War Bolshevik era the principal persons in the governments and in the political terror organizations were Jewish. They did not want to hear that the most brutal torturer and head of the AVH, the State Security Authority, was Gábor (Auspitz) Péter, a Jew. His merciless brutality reached even his ideological comrades, for which in the post-Stalin cleansing of the Communist Party he was imprisoned. They did not want to accept that the hard-core of the feared AVH officers was mainly Jewish. These are the undeniable realities, which have to be recognized by the Jews. They have to come to grips with what their own people committed, just as we Gentiles had to face the crimes of our own radicals.

The racial-political persecution of the Jews in Europe during the Second World War was an indisputable historic fact. However, the contradictory accusations and claims about the number of the victims, about the causes of their demise generated doubts in the credibility of many of the claims, giving ammunition for the "Revisionists" who deny the validity of the accusations. As I view those tragic events it is not the actual cause of the death—whether mass murder, natural death due to epidemic, mistreatment or acts of war—it is not the actual number of the victims—whether 6 million or 3 million—but that our fellow human beings were persecuted just because of their race that should concern us all. Each and every life is sacred. Their suffering must not be allowed to be desecrated by turning it into legal matters over compensatory monetary claims nearly half a century after the events—as most regrettably the case is—but must remain preserved as deeply rooted moral matters, from which our societies, the Jews and the Gentiles, the academicians and the laymen should draw proper and measured conclusions.

The books and articles published by the Jewish authors on the issues might be respectable accomplishments, but those are also interpretations of the tragic events, in some cases with historic distortions. Treating the claims as the absolute truth would be both historically and academically wrong, especially in view of the criticism by respected Jewish and non-Jewish historians alike. The suffering of the Jews was part of the immense tragedy of the 20th century. The Jewish victims, together with those of other races and nationalities are to be treated with equal respect and dignity. Their tragic fate should be presented to the new generations not to re-ignite hatred, but to pay respect to the victims of ideological, racial, religious and nationalistic fanaticism on all sides, and to lead the still not poisoned minds of the young to tolerance, to hold back the stubborn fanatics whose only goal is continuing the wrongs of the past.

The reader may ask; why as a non-German and non-Jew, who never was, and still is not involved in politics, for whom racial belonging never was an issue, I am so occupied with the Jewish issues? The answer is; those affected my life the most. I was deprived of the carefree and joyous teenage years, which are so essential in the development of personality and character. Instead, I had to face the horrors of a war, the memories of which remained with me for my entire life. After the war I had to face terror, fear and hopelessness, putting me and my family on the sad path of the refugees. Racial belonging was not—and still is not—of concern to me. My wife was of Jewish descent. But those events, which were of dramatic consequence to my life, are and remain of deep concern, as I continue to discern truth from conjecture. Burying the memories, denying what happened and affected my life and the lives of many others is futile. We must face the past to avoid repeating the same mistakes. The Jewish society must accept the fact that they were not the only victims, but they also contributed to mankind's tragedy. They were not the only ones who were driven away from their homes and herded into concentration or labor camps, or were forced to flee. Millions of people were uprooted and deported in Eastern Europe under the terrorist rule of Jewish radicals. They were not the only ones who suffered the brutality of governments and of the racial-political bigots. They are not the only ones carrying the burden and the grief of the past. They must accept the fact that among them, just as among us Gentiles were—and still are—irresponsible groups and individuals who by blind fanaticism committed horrible crimes, brought great shame onto their society, just as the fanatics on our side brought great shame onto our society, for which those have to pay, who wanted nothing other than lead peaceful lives.

The claim by anyone that racial prejudice and racially instigated hatred were and are the moral ills of only one sole society, namely of the Gentile, and that the Jewish society is free of such ills, would be a misrepresentation of the realities. Prejudice is one of the most deeply rooted human characters, and it is found in every race, manifested in many aspects of our daily lives whether they be personal, racial, religious, ideological, political or cultural. Feeling and claiming superiority over each other on whatever grounds is not an uncommon symptom. Racial separation, preserving racial purity by institutionally opposing inter-racial marriages, enforcing race-based immigration laws, setting the criteria for racial identity were the social policies of not only the strongly condemned distant past, but are still practiced in some of the societies of today, including the Jewish. When racial consciousness, overheated nationalism, religious fanaticism and economic interest are fused together in politics, the consequences can be immeasurable. The Second World War and the events following it, are for me the frightening examples.

I don't claim that my interpretation of the events is historically accurate, or my presentation is a scholastic accomplishment. The immensity of the human tragedy that was played out on the battlefields, in the inferno of the bombed cities, in the desperate flight of mothers carrying their children from the ravages of war, in the horrors of the concentration camps, in the herding of people from their homes in the darkness of the nights after the devastating war, in fleeing from the terror across minefields and barbed-wire fences with my child on my back, all that which was brought upon us by the evil minds of the fanatics on all sides—and to which I was an eyewitness and also a victim—were beyond what I could present adequately in my writings. My sources of information were not official documents—whether authentic or questionable—were not the stories of eyewitnesses—whether objective or biased—but were my own life experiences and my own observations. I don't claim that what I saw, and what I put on paper, was the whole picture of a horrible period in our recent history. But that was how in my small world I saw it, how as a teenager I lived through it, how as a family man I faced it, and how in the autumn years of my life reflecting on the tumultuous times I understand it.

The persecution of the Jews during the Second World War, nearly sixty years later still is an almost daily subject in the American media, overshadowing all the other aspects of the war. Motion pictures and books appear, television programs are shown frequently, not to allow the fading of the memories. In some schools reading the books and viewing the films of Jewish authors on the Holocaust are compulsory. The issues are not only highly emotional, but also have legal ramifications. In Germany and in some other countries laws have been enacted (or attempts have been made to enact them) prohibiting the denying of the validity of the claims on the existence of gas chambers and on the number of victims killed in them. Legal battles have been fought between the authors of publications advocating and questioning such claims. Under such laws a British historian was sentenced to imprisonment in Austria. I view such laws as judicial absurdity.

"THE FINAL SOLUTION."

In the March 24th, 1933 issue of the Daily Express, and shortly thereafter in the New York Times the article appeared *"Judea declares war on Germany"*. In January 1939 Hitler in his speech at the Reichstag gave the foreboding warning: *"If the international Jewish financiers in and outside Europe should succeed in plunging the nations once more into a world war, then the result will not be the Bolshevization of the earth, and thus a victory of Jewry, but the annihilation of the Jewish race in Europe"*. In September of the same year the Second World War began. From those events the conclusion can be drawn, that the principal—if not the sole—cause of the outbreak of the European phase of Second World War was the ideological and racial confrontation between the international Jewry and the Hitler led anti-Semitic, National Socialistic Germany. Arguably, many other factors were involved, but throughout the war the racial and ideological aspects remained the central issues.

The subject of the Protocol of the 1942 "Wannsee Konferenz" held by the Nazi leadership was: *"Die Endlösung der Judenfrage"*, the Final Solution of the "Jewish Question". In it is stated: *"Das Aufgabenziel war, auf legale Weise den deutschen Lebensraum von Juden zu säubern"*, The task's aim was by legal means cleansing the German living space from the Jews. Remarkably, in spite of Hitler's unmistakable warning and of the outbreak of the war, the protocol speaks of "cleansing by legal means" rather than extermination. The Protocol also states, that in spite of the "high landing fees" charged by the foreign governments, of the "limited space on the ships", and of the "increased restrictions on immigration by the admitting countries", as of October 1941 the number of Jews legally emigrating from Germany and German controlled territories reached 537,000. According to the 1933 census 600,000 Jews lived in Germany. Documents show that there was almost continuous contact between governments on the Jewish emigration. If the removal of the Jews was to be conducted "by legal means", then what went wrong? Why did so many have to lose their lives? I assume not just one single cause, but a multitude of causes led to the suffering and demise of the victims, among those the executions, the war itself including the air attacks on the industrial facilities where the Jews had to work, and on the railroads on which they were transported, the harsh living and working conditions, the actions (or inaction) of the Western Powers, and in the final months of the war in some of the concentration camps the devastating epidemic. Wars are man-made catastrophes.

The question may be asked; did Germany and some other European countries have the legal and moral right to force the Jews out of their communities, and take them into labor camps, after they had been allowed to immigrate legally? Under normal circumstances they would not have had such a right. But, in wars the circumstances are anything but normal. The role of some of the Jews in the Bolshevik era in Russia, in Germany and in Hungary after the First World War caused much resentment, fear and mistrust, poisoning the relationship between the natives and the immigrated Jews. The Jews' financial success, their disproportionate presence in the business and professional fields at the time when the natives were unemployed and lived under dire circumstances added to the resentment. In 1941 in Hungary 825,000 Jews lived, representing about seven per cent of the population. According to government records they owned one third of the national wealth (not including real estate), and drew nearly one half of the national income (not including the salaries paid by the government). While the role of the Jewish radicals in the Bolshevik terror after World War I could be taken as justified grounds for antagonism, the resentfulness for their business and professional successes was politicized human greed. In most European countries the Jews were—on whatever basis—the undesirable but tolerated aliens. In peacetime neither the resentment nor the antagonism could grow into violent hatred and expulsion.

Let us start from the assumption that in spite of Hitler's warning the German plan for forced emigration rather than physical extermination was indeed genuine. There are some indications, which might give basis for making such an assumption, among those the fact that 530,000 of the 600,000 German Jews had been allowed to emigrate legally. When in 1944 the Germans wanted to gain control over Hungary's major industrial complex, in exchange for ownership they allowed the legal emigration of forty-some members of the Jewish owners, flying them to Portugal. In late 1944 when the city of Budapest was under siege, diplomats negotiated with the German SS for the safety of the Jews, sparing nearly two hundred thousands from deportation.

In late 1944 and early 1945 the Germans brought large numbers of depor- tees from Auschwitz to Bergen-Belsen, which was a transition camp in the western part of Germany. If extermination was the real aim, why did the Ger- man authorities take the steps under the most difficult circumstances of trans- ferring large numbers of deportees, among them women and children, whom they had to feed and care for (in whatever meager way)? Revealed reports sug- gest that even at that late stage of the war there were negotiations for the exchange of Jews for German prisoners of war and deportees. In early 1945, only months before the end of the war, in the most chaotic times in Germany, the German authorities including Himmler, the much-accused commander of the SS conducted negotiations with the leaders of the Jewish organizations. Reports show that in the final months of the war, when transportation came to a virtual collapse in Germany, under an agreement many Jews were trans- ported from the concentration camps to Switzerland on special, white colored busses provided by Sweden.

Viewing the issues from another point of view one may ask, why after a rel- atively small influx of Jewish immigrants the Western countries like America, Britain and some of the European countries did virtually seal their borders, not allowing more Jews to arrive? Instead of sealing their borders why didn't they vigorously encourage and help the emigration of the endangered Jews, while it was still possible? They could only gain from receiving them, as some of them were well-educated and could contribute to their economy, while oth- ers as devoted opponents of Nazism could be strategically valuable. They were not insignificant factors in a war. Was it a reasonable and morally correct stand to leave the Jews in the Nazi yoke, and at the same time wage an air war against the German civilian population, thereby exposing them to the expect- able horror of revengeful persecution? Or, was—perhaps—the strategy of the West to keep the Jews behind the front lines as a destabilizing guerrilla force? If this was the strategy, then that was highly immoral, because there were the children, the women and the old among them. A disturbing element was the attitude of the West, especially of Britain in hindering the immigration of the Jews in Palestine. America also denied entry for many of the Jews who arrived to its shores. Was—perhaps—the immigration to America on a selective basis; education, skill, wealth, health and good personal connections? Was—per- haps—the humanitarian missionary element missing? The dire situation of the Central and Eastern European Jewry under the Nazi rule had to be clear to the West. The ever-sharpening confrontation on the ideological and racial issues were the warning signs of what was to come. The political and military strategists must have seen that. In hindsight it appears that America and Britain wanted to defeat Germany at any cost, even if sacrificing the Eastern-European Jews, while the possibility was still there to avert a major tragedy. An uncontrollable element was the large Jewish population in Poland and the Soviet Union, which fell under German control in the war. The violent confrontation between the natives of those countries and the Jews, because of the role of some of the Jews in the Bolshevik reign was foreseeable. The German occupation became a liberating factor for the revengeful natives.

There are many rational anti-war arguments, which seem to substantiate the assumption that the Jewish tragedy could have been prevented by seeking compromise, instead of provoking confrontation. The terror bombing of the European cities deeply angered the civilian population, as well as the soldiers on the fronts, whose families were the victims. Rather than diminishing their resolve, it increased their determination to fight. I had seen that, and I myself felt a deep anger. The images of the Israeli mob after a Palestinian attack calling for the killing of all Arabs are reminiscent of the past. The generally unfriendly attitude of the immigrated, alien, minority Jews toward the native population, the agitating tone of the Jewish-controlled media, their alleged close association with the enemy, both to the West and East within the community of a nation at war, were all elements of the growing resentment, and in some cases of outright hatred. Another issue for some of the natives of the Eastern European countries was the exemption of the Jews from military service. While the non-Jewish men had to fight on the fronts, the Jewish men—not being trusted—served as laborers in the relative safety behind the front lines or in the home country.

Another, hardly ever asked question might be raised; namely, why the Jewish societies in the Western countries didn't do more in helping their brethren? According to the Wannsee Protokol by October of 1941 the Jews living outside Germany had contributed $9.5M to bring the well-to-do educated Jews from Germany. When the issue was freedom or suffering, or even life or death, why did they not make greater efforts, while there was still an opportunity? They had political clout both in America and in Britain, why didn't they use it to reduce the danger? Or, was there—perhaps—a feeling of indifference by the well-to-do, educated Jews in the West toward the poor, uneducated Eastern European Jews? The message was clear from the Nazis; they wanted the Jews out, and according to documents were willing to let them go. In late summer of 1944, when the Hungarian Jews were deported, I heard from them that they were to be taken to transition camps, from where they were to be shipped to Madagascar, where a Jewish state was to be established. Other Jews told me that they were to be transported to Palestine. What made these rumors believable for them and also for me, was that the families were kept together. For most people, Jews and Gentiles alike, in spite of Hitler's dire warning, it was unthinkable that the Germans intended to physically exterminate them.

Declaring war by the Jews on Germany in 1933, was a most tragic political mistake of modern history, dragging many nations—including America—into a horrible massacre, taking nearly thirty millions lives, among them a large number of Jews. It was a fatal strategic miscalculation, for which the Jews themselves paid dearly. After the failed attempts following the First World War to bring Germany under the Bolshevik reign—in which the Jews played a key role—and after Germany's rapid recovery from the devastating economic and political chaos, it should have been clear to the Jewish leadership that belligerence from their side could only bring belligerence from the other side. With the Jewish declaration of war the Nazi leadership had a strong propaganda tool to generate deep anti-Jewish sentiment. It was like pouring oil on a burning fire.

At the end there was no "Final Solution". The Nazi's aim: "Den deutschen Lebensraum von Juden zu säubern" had only been partially achieved, at an extremely high moral and political cost. The same applies to the other European countries, where the Jews were persecuted. After the tragic consequences the question is well justified: Was the 1933 declaration of war a rational political strategy, or was it a fatal blunder?

THE AFTERMATH.

After the war in my hometown several of the pre-war Jewish residents were missing. In some of the cases nobody, not even their immediate relatives and friends, seemed to know what happened to them. They vanished in the turmoil of the war. As was found out later, some chose to seek a new home somewhere else. Those who came back gradually rejoined the community and restarted their lives. In general, there was a desire for reconciliation. Not in all cases, however. A young Jewish man whose parents perished, became the police chief. Rumors were floating, that in his anger he said that he was going to line the streets with the heads of the "Goys". The threat left deep resentment, but eventually that healed as well. The case of his family was indeed one of the great injustices, as his father in the First World War served in the Hungarian army and received the highest decoration for bravery. When in the summer of 1944 the deportation orders came, the people of the town presented a petition to the authorities asking for the exemption of the family. Tragically, the petition was ignored.

The race-relationship after the war up until 1948 slowly improved, when in a coup the Bolshevik regime took control of Hungary. In the following eight years we lived in fear. There was terror on all levels, including mass-deportation, arrests, constant surveillance, harassment at the work place and at home. The same was the case in all the Soviet occupied Eastern European countries, in most instances without the Russian occupiers' involvement. The uprising of the natives against the terrorist rulers began in Poland and in Hungary in 1956, and was followed in Czechoslovakia in 1968, bringing historic changes in world-politics.

Another silent but, nevertheless, significant resentment evolved in the 1990s, when the demands by the deported Jews for monetary compensation became publicly known, which in general were considered unjustifiable and excessive. The case at issue was that all able-bodied non-Jewish men as citizens had to serve in the army, and had to go to the fronts. Jewish men as citizens, but not trusted to serve in the armed forces, had been drafted to serve in labor units. After the war Jewish organizations—mainly American—acting on behalf of the deported European Jews demanded large sums of monetary compensation, first from Germany and later from Hungary. Adding fuel to the general resentment was the surfacing of the discrepancies in the propagated claims on the number of Holocaust victims. According to news reports, on the occasion of an anniversary celebration in Auschwitz in the 1990s, on the basis of investigations, the number of victims engraved in the commemorative plaque had been changed from 4 million to 1.4 million. In protest to the change the leadership of the Hungarian Jewish community demanded the staying away of the Prime Minister from that celebration. Another contentious issue was the revision in the claims on the events in the Bergen-Belsen concentration camp, where in the last months of the war many Hungarian Jews had been interned. That camp, after the war, in the early media-reports was described as an "Extermination camp" with gas chambers and crematoriums, where allegedly tens of thousands had been murdered. The actual case was, that in the final months and weeks of the war thousands had died in an epidemic. In the worst phase of the epidemic, just before the war ended, hundreds perished daily. Due to lack of cremation facilities the corpses were gathered in the open. The arriving British forces found them there. Condemning reports with dramatic pictures were issued, describing Bergen-Belsen as one of the worst extermination camps. Years later, after thorough investigation, including the denial of such claims by some of the survivors, the camp was reclassified to "Transition Camp" without gas chambers and large crematoriums. Even the Jewish institutions admit now that there were no "Extermination camps" in German territories, contradicting their own earlier claims.

The books and articles by Jewish authors with strong accusatory claims—written primarily for the American public—generated great resentment in the Eastern European countries, especially in view of the publications by European Jewish authors, who not only did not confirm those claims, but in some cases contradicted those. The overzealous Jewish propagandists by pushing the exaggerated claims fueled the fire for the revisionists who denied the events of the persecution, and awakened the doubts in the minds of the sympathetic population. The Jewish radicals' response to the surfacing of criticism was the warning on the resurfacing of the "European Neo-Fascism" and

"Neo-Nazism". Any questioning, coming from any source, is immediately stamped as "anti-Semitism".

There are questionable and contradicting personal accounts on the events given by Jewish witnesses. A rather remarkable case is that of the Hungarian-American Elie Wiesel. He is probably the best known and much-heralded advocate and lecturer on the Holocaust, who for his work received the Nobel Peace Price. As a teenager he and his family were interned in Auschwitz. In his writings and lectures he depicted horrible scenes in dramatic words; *"mass graves expelling geysers of blood"*, a gruesome, but unrealistic claim. He also said: *"Not far from us flames were leaping from a ditch, gigantic flames. They were burning something. A lorry drew up at the pit and delivered its load, little children. Babies! Yes I saw it—saw it with my own eyes…Those children in the flames."* A horrible image, but is there any evidence for such an event? A remarkable contradiction is in Mr. Wiesel's description of the events in January 1945, when after surgery on his injured foot he was in the camp hospital. The doctor recommended two weeks of rest and good food. While—according to Mr. Wiesel—*"blood geysers were gushing"* and *"babies were thrown in the flames"*, his foot was medically treated in a hospital. Why was an inmate's injured foot treated medically in an extermination camp, where others were brutally murdered? He said, that before his foot could heal the arrival of the Soviet Army became imminent. The Germans were withdrawing from the Auschwitz area. He and his father were given the choice to stay behind and wait for the arrival of the liberating Soviet army, or be transported with other deportees to Germany. His choice was to go with the Germans, whom he repeatedly characterized as the "executioners". Why did he choose to go with them? Also noteworthy are the inconsistencies in the French and German editions of his memoirs "Night". In the French edition he repeatedly refers to "Au crématoire" the crematorium, while in the German edition of the same book published four years later, that word had been changed to "Die Gaskammer", the gas chamber. He gives plenty ground for the revisionists who seek proof, but receive only grandiloquent words.

I don't accept the views of the revisionists. However, the unrealistic, inconsistent accounts cast a shadow on Mr. Wiesel's credibility. The inhumane brutality with which, in general, the Jews were treated, cannot be denied. But the Holocaust issue should not be left in the fog of often unrealistic, over-dramatized stories of emotion-driven, overzealous authors and witnesses, who enormously profit from presenting their stories to culpable audiences. By Mr. Wiesel's own admission he charges $15,000 per lecture. Witness testimonies on the persecution, and even court documents used as "evidence", must be scrutinized, especially in view of the cases, in which death sentences were rendered upon the accused, but decades later the truth surfaced proving their innocence. Not myth, but facts should prevail. Many of the relevant documents and records on the events are available in archives, some still secretive. Thorough, unbiased, scientific investigation is essential for clearing the air on one of the tragic historic events of recent times.

The Jewish issue as a political matter appears to be far from being closed. The difference from the events in the Nazi times is that now it is on a much larger scale, involving the Muslim world. The Jews are in a bloody conflict with the Palestinians, which looks more like a territorial-political war. In the minds of the Palestinians, and of many of the Muslims, the once persecuted Jews became their persecutors. The anti-Jewish Muslim camp includes millions of antagonists on several continents, who are driven by religious-political self-consciousness—just like some of their Jewish opponents are. The rest of the world watches the events with deep anxiety. The Jews having the American support are pursuing their goals with unyielding vigor. The Arabs and Muslims are fighting back in whatever way they can. Young people in martyrdom blow themselves up in the Israeli streets. The Israelis send their airplanes with sophisticated missiles to kill the Palestinians, destroying their homes, leveling to the ground their refugee camps. In an attempt to separate themselves from the Palestinians they erected what they call the "Fence", a tall wall similar to the infamous "Berlin Wall", which was a great shame and absurdity of the 20th Century. Terrorism has become the principal issue not only in the Middle East, but also in America. America fights wars on Israel's behalf in Afghanistan and in Iraq. The threat of other wars is looming. The personal liberties of us Americans are curtailed by THE PATRIOT ACT. Where will all that lead to, when the weapons of the ultimate horror are available to all sides?

Months before the beginning of the 2003 Iraq war Mr. Simon Perez, an official in Israel, who was urging America to attack Iraq said: *"Attacking Iraq now would be quite dangerous, but postponing it would be more dangerous".* Mr. Richard Perle, one of the principal Jewish-American strategists and main advocate of the Israeli interest in America, in the days of the debates and strong opposition at the UN to the Iraq war, said: "Nobody can stop us". Similar urgent calls for the war came from the Jewish-Americans Wolfowitz, Lieberman and others. Mr. Netanyahu the then prime minister of Israel wrote in the New York Post under the headline: *"Today we are all Americans. What is at stake today is nothing less than the survival of civilization."* In 2005, a few months after the news reports that within five to ten years Iran might have nuclear weapons, Netanyahu claimed that Iran could have nuclear bombs in weeks or months. Therefore, it had to be attacked immediately. It appears to be quite clear who are behind the wars in the Middle East.

Is there an Islamic threat to the Western Civilization, against which it has to defend itself? In view of the past history with the "Crusades", the colonization, the oppressive intervention by the Western Powers, and the recent military confrontations with Israel and with America, there is a growing anti-Western sentiment with the seeds of real threat. Is there an Islamic threat to Israel and the Jews in general, against which they have to defend themselves? The threat is real, as can be seen in the escalating events. Is there a threat to the Arab and Muslim World from America, from Israel and from the Jews? That threat is real, as is evidenced by the widespread bloody hostilities. Quite remarkably these issues became the core of the politics of the last decades of the 20th Century, further culminating in the 21st Century. If not resolved, they might lead to a world-calamity.

In the early 1960s while in graduate school here in America, I had an Israeli and an Egyptian classmate. Both were well-educated engineering students with pleasant outward personalities. But they utterly hated each other. In the mid 1970s an Israeli man visited me, who in a kibbutz operated the orange picking machine that was my design. On arrival he greeted me with "Shalom", but later in our conversation said: "You Americans give us weapons and we will kill the Arabs". Anyone who believed that the Middle East could become a peaceful place, lived in an illusion. The warning signs came well before the State of Israel was established. The outbreak of violence, the battles between the Arabs and Israelis, the dispute over the occupied territories, the growing up of new generations of Palestinians in the refugee camps without hope, the increasing religious-patriotism among the Israelis, fomented the tension. The seeds were planted for what could be expected—violence and more violence—which can bring catastrophic consequences to a large part of the world, including America. The land that the Arabs call Palestine is for the Israelis Judea and Samaria, a biblical heritage, the "Gift of God to the Jews". Anyone who was naïve enough to believe that investing billions of dollars by the Israelis and by their American supporters in building the new settlement on the disputed land for the immigrating Jews was based on the assumption that someday those settlements could belong to the Palestinians, lived in an illusion. Doing it on that basis would have been totally irrational. The Jews' claim for those territories was clearly stated before the existence of their State. Unfortunately, the matter was handled by both sides not in a rational manner, but with intolerance and with brute force. The squalid conditions of the Palestinian refugee camps, the horrors of the massacres in some of the camps, the stone throwing Palestinian youngsters facing the rifle toting Israeli soldiers, the wailing women and children around the rubble of their homes wrecked by the Israeli bulldozers were images that drove the followers of Islam into a united camp, inducing the honor of martyrdom, resulting in brutality. The spiraling of the events was foreboding. Now, we are in a worldwide guerrilla or insurgency war, that will be difficult—if at all possible—to stop, and which can drag the world into an unprecedented cataclysm.

We Americans live in fear at home, and even more so abroad. Special emergency laws have been enacted curtailing the traditional civil liberties, opening the gates for suspicion and accusations. Public buildings are like fortresses with barricades and armed guards, ferry boats are escorted by vessels with mounted machine guns, airports are like Checkpoint Charlie was in East-Berlin under Communism in the worst days of the Cold War. America is at war, seemingly against the entire world, and the world is watching us in bewilderment. Do our politicians believe that a worldwide guerrilla war in which millions of fanatics, as products of the long simmering resentment against America's and Israel's Middle East policies are involved, can be stopped with our smart bombs? Do they believe that they can put together a large enough anti-terrorist force that can stop every determined fanatic? Do they believe that resorting once again—just as in the Second World War—to the horror weapon of the nuclear bomb can bring the solution to the burning problems in the Middle East? Do they believe that by pursuing the megalomaniac, militaristic tactics will not alienate even the best of America's and Israel's friends? If they do believe that, then they live in an illusion.

What was—or better said—what were the real issues in the dangerous Middle East tension? Was it Saddam Hussein the dictator, who not long ago—when in war against Iran the perceived ardent enemy of America—was America's trusted man? Was it the weapons of mass-destruction that allegedly Iraq had, that never had been used, and no proof of their existence had ever been found? Was it the oil that Iraq possesses, which quite paradoxically powered part of America's industry? Or, was it the Intafada, the Palestinians' struggle against the Israeli occupation, which Israel couldn't stop? Why can it not be said what appears to be the real issue behind America's willingness to fight wars in the Middle East, not just against Iraq, but against other countries? Why can't the advocates of wars admit that the real issue is America's imposed—or self-imposed—obligation to Israel's defense? The weapons of mass-destruction have been in the past—and are again—in the pro-war arguments. Oil is also an often mentioned issue, especially in the foreign media, because of the close association and the personal interest of some of the top American government officials in the oil industry. While both the weapons of mass-destruction and the oil issues are propagated, the real issue in this crisis appears to be much deeper. It is "Bellum Judeorum", the war of the Jews for the domination in the Middle East, and—perhaps—eventually in the entire world. It is their war that they want America to fight and win for them. The Israeli government officials together with the pro-Israeli Jewish-Americans repeatedly demanded wars against Iraq, Afghanistan, Iran and Syria and some other Arab and Islamic nations, and they repeatedly attacked those European countries which—based on their painful war experience—want to resolve the disputes by peaceful means.

World peace is now endangered by two fanatical camps; one in the Muslim World, the other in the world of Judaism, one grown out of desperation, the other out of conceitedness. Quite remarkably both claim peaceful, religious convictions, but both have shown deep, hateful fanaticism. Neither of these camps are isolated small groups, but are highly influential organizations actively pursuing their goals worldwide. Not all Muslims, and not all Jews are involved, but there are many radicals among them. Denying that would be the denial of the tragic events which did occur. The American-born Israeli doctor Baruch Goldstein who slaughtered scores of praying Muslims in their mosque, and was lynched and killed by a Muslim mob, is now the revered hero of some of the Jews. The young Palestinians who blew themselves up in the Israeli streets killing scores of Israelis are the revered heroes of some of the Muslims. It was a Jew who assassinated the Prime Minister of Israel for having pursued a peace serving effort with the Arabs. Arabs assassinated the President of Egypt for pursuing peace with Israel. The Palestinians live in their homeland like refugees and prisoners. The Israelis live in their country like frightened conquerors. The desire of the Jews to have a homeland became their nightmare—they have to live behind a tall fence. For the American supporters of the Jewish cause came the unattainable worldwide confrontation that frightens the nations which strive for peace. The dispute between the Palestinians and the Israelis has grown into a global religious-political collision—Islam against the Infidels, Judaism against Islam, the American Evangelical Judeo-Christianity against Islam. And the world is irreversibly drawn into it. It also evolved into a potential crisis between America and its allies. Once again, just as in the case of the Second World War the institutions, which were established to preserve peace, became "irrelevant". Once again, nations, which through their own painful experience have seen the futility of wars, and refused to participate in wars, are subjected to the wrath of the warmongers.

Israel does have the right to exist, and the Israelis are entitled to live in peace. So are the other nations on earth. The United Nations—not a perfect institution, but the one established to prevent wars—cannot be treated as irrelevant. Not unilateral American power politics, not the fanaticism in the Islamic World, not the religious-patriotic fervor of the Jewish fanatics, but the sober and unbiased leadership of the world community should conduct this extremely dangerous case. To drag the world into wars, which according to the bragging militarists "will be nothing like what your father had seen", using thousands of the most destructive missiles and bombs, killing tens of thousands, is totally immoral, and is a crime against humanity. Political wisdom, morality, humanitarianism and tolerance are the means by which a world leader must conduct itself. If it fails to do so, history's judgment will be harsh. The consequences are immeasurable, and the responsibility is enormous.

The definition "Bellum Judeorum" cannot be found in the speeches of officials, or anywhere in the media. For some it sounds provocative, biased. However, my intention is not to arouse such reactions, but rather to direct the attention to those issues which in my subjective opinion—based on the available information—led me to view the current crisis from a broader perspective. Reviewing the events of the recent past, I did find the connection between the statements by the Israeli government officials and by the Jewish members of the American political institutions and the rapidly growing belligerence in American politics. The calls were repeated, each time with greater urgency. Accusation of individuals, organizations and governments, which opposed the Middle-Eastern wars without prior unquestionable evidence of wrongdoing, was harsh and included charges of anti-Semitism. These facts cannot be denied.

It is understandable that America supports Israel, guaranteeing its security. It was America that helped to establish Israel, and it has a large and powerful Jewish constituency. Therefore, the ties are strong. The questions can be raised; however, why does the Israeli government want America to wage wars that can drag that region into chaos? Why does America want to fight wars that can spill over to Israel? Why don't they pursue efforts to somehow settle the Palestine conflict, which is the root of the crisis? For the cost of the wars America could help the Palestinians to live a decent life, not to sacrifice themselves in suicide bombings, allowing the Israelis to live in peace. Once the bombs fall hatred and brutality reigns, the Israelis might face unprecedented horrors, a never before experienced anti-Jewish sentiment might arise everywhere, threatening those who want to live in peace, in mutual respect and tolerance. Let us not forget what happened in the Second World War. On what ground can the Israeli officials expect that the countries of Europe that watched with the deepest dismay the endless hostilities between the Israelis and the Palestinians, had seen the destruction of the homes of the Palestinian refugees and the community centers which they have helped to build, and whose delegations were not allowed by the Israelis to investigate the cases, to participate in wars on Israel's behalf? On what grounds can the American government expect that the European countries become involved in a war—or in wars—in the Middle East that have been led for years by America and Britain without acceptable justification?

There is one common threat that touches many nations. That is terrorism, against which most are ready to stand up united. But even that threat is burdened by controversies, specifically by the portrayed causes. According to those who claimed responsibility for the destruction of the World Trade Center, it was viewed by them as the symbol of the exploiting and oppressive American-Jewish Capitalism. The Pentagon was seen as the center of the American military aggression against the Arab and Muslim world. From the American and Israeli sides the attacks are seen as against the free world. Both arguments are fundamentally wrong, because both ignore the underlying causes. Terrorism—the struggle of the oppressed weak against the powerful oppressor—must be a deep concern for all of us. Especially now when the tools of terror can be devastating and can reach most everyone. Terrorism that we face is not the act of tiny cells, but of determined fanatics across the globe. It is supported not by a few, but by large numbers of the sympathizers. Listening to them, talking with them, negotiating with them might be the only way to prevent a world catastrophe.

The unfolding events, the ever-sharpening rhetoric on all sides bear the signs of the coming of another world war. The American, British and Israeli politicians in their uncontrolled frustration attack everybody who is not willing to succumb to their belligerent policies, calling for boycotting, not refraining from insulting nations and their governments. They attempt to drive wedges between allies and friends, between the peoples and their governments, and they try to frighten them. The symptoms are foreboding, breaking up friendships, pushing nations into opposing camps. Not an unfamiliar strategy. "Divide et impera" had been used quite successfully in history. But there have never been times like what we live in. All the participants in this insane rush have the devastating weapons, and all are ready and willing to use them. Nobody enjoys invulnerability, not the Israelis, not the Americans, not the Europeans. With "9/11" America lost its illusionary invulnerability. Anything can trigger chaos, in which the fanatics, the frightened, the militaristic maniacs, the believers and the criminals will be ready—or will become compelled—to go for battle, without caring what the consequences might be.

Ignoring the lessons of history was—and still is—the fatal fallacy of the human society. The end result was that just in my lifetime alone millions of people, Gentiles and Jews, perished in senseless wars, which could have been prevented by reasoning. But one-sidedness prevailed on all sides. Propaganda poisons the minds, hatred spread by the politicians and the media turns people against each other. Another propaganda war is being waged now, tearing apart societies and institutions. Insults are the tunes of communication, calls for boycotting are the battle cries. History is repeating itself. Another world war is in the making. Before it will be too late, the Jews in Israel and in America, should stop the advocates of wars, and should call for "Pax Judeorum".

ROADMAP TO DISASTER.

(My article from 1996)

Following the unfolding world-events in which America is a principal partici-pant, and in which I can sense the systematic buildup of antagonism and out-right hatred, I ask the question: America, why are you doing this? When demonizing of countries and their leader becomes a daily routine, their names appearing on the radio waves and on the television screen in an almost con-stant barrage of accusations, when I can see the seeds of violent hostilities, even of wars, then the question arises in my mind: America, where are you going? It is my instinctive reaction, which is induced by the re-emerging of my memories of the past, especially of those, which dramatically affected my life.

Truthful and objective reporting by governments on confrontational issues is a non-existing practice. Propaganda as the form of manipulated reporting is directed to serve the confrontational efforts by strengthening the resolve of one of the sides, and by undermining the resolve of the other. The definition for propaganda in the Webster Dictionary is: "Any systematic, widespread dissemination or promotion of particular ideas, doctrines, practices to further one's own cause or to damage an opposing one". In another definition it is: "Ideas, doctrines, or allegations so spread; now often used disparagingly to connote deception or distortion." The issues are subjected to manipulated information, often ending with tragic consequences. Dr. Goebbels the propa-ganda minister of the Hitler regime stated in one of his speeches: *"There can be no good government without good propaganda, and there can be no good propa-ganda without good government."* But, what is good propaganda?

For me, a young, keenly observing teenager, the Second World War had different faces; one was presented by the Hungarian and the German govern-ment propaganda, another received through the secretly listened-to enemy radio propaganda, and still another that I myself could see in my daily life. Out of these came the behind closed doors talked-about rumors.

Way back then in the early 1940s, I saw photos and newsreels, some of which nowadays are shown on the documentary television programs here in America. The events were the same, and the images are the same. The difference is in the commentaries. In one—way back then—those were directed at the war-weary viewers, with the intent to generate pride and enthusiasm, to show the glory of victory, to prove the superiority of our side and the inferiority of the enemy. In the documentaries shown here in America the same events and the same images were presented to the armchair audience, but under different commentaries, to prove just the opposite. While way back then the visual images alone could generate a sympathetic reaction of the viewers toward the vanquished, the verbal commentaries turned the attention away from the human elements. Not an uncommon propaganda tactic even in these days, as was the case in showing the events of the Vietnam War. Way back then, the images of the newsreels showing the German tanks roaming the Russian steppes, the scenes of the ruined and burning Russian cities, the images of the captured Russian soldiers were spiriting evidence of the invincibility of German armies, and of the weakness of the enemy. The commentaries with which those images were presented directed the attention away from the brutalities of the events. I assume that the viewing of the newsreels here in America, showing the burning and crumbling German cities had a similar pride-generating emotional effect. The viewers under the influence of the propagandistic commentaries saw in the smoke and flames the destruction of Nazism, but not the suffering of the children and women, who were losing not only their homes, but also their lives. Images of similar kind showing the burning of bamboo huts of the Vietnamese by the American soldiers, with commentaries attracting the viewers' attention away from the human suffering aspect to the guilt and punishing of the Vietcong, were much the same immoral propaganda tactics.

A lasting impression for me was a Russian propaganda film, which I saw shortly after the war. In it self-sacrifice as the ultimate of heroism, and the horrors of wars were portrayed in a scene of a soldier laying under the barbed-wire fence of a German fortification, mortally wounded, holding together in his mouth the ends of the broken wires of a detonator, blowing up the Germans. It could well be a true case, and in its propagandistic presentation to the audience it was to achieve the impressions of heroism in self-sacrifice, and the horrors of wars. In an American war propaganda film the bombing of German cities was shown. It was totally impersonalized, machines against structures. Neither the airmen flying the planes, nor the residents of the burning buildings were shown. In another film, that from the Vietnam War, American soldiers could be seen carrying the torches from one bamboo hut to another, burning them down. The people screaming and fleeing were visible. In that case no commentary could divert the attention of the viewers from the human suffering. It was a documentary of the horror of human brutality. One fundamental difference between the war propaganda of the Second World War and the Vietnam War was, that with the new communication technology the news media in dramatic images could bring home the brutality and futility of wars. The government and the military no longer could keep for themselves the monopoly of propagandistic information. The power of uncensored information became clear. If I can find one single element of hope for holding back the hands of the immoral politicians and militarists, keeping them from repeating the horrors of the past, it is the technology that provides freely flowing information.

One of the most important experiences of my life was my extensive exposure to the multitude of single-sided propaganda. After long years of those exposures I gained the ability to view the events critically, developed the basis for drawing my own conclusions on events, which each side presented for its own propaganda purposes. The end result was a decisive change, leading me to a highly critical reception of any and all government-presented propagandistic information. Based on my observations on the development in my own concepts and attitude, which I attribute not to the wisdom of age, but rather to my exposure to multiple perspectives, I feel that I can serve those who in lack of such exposure still view the world from a single-sided point of view. I am thoroughly convinced about the immeasurable significance of multi-sided information and understanding on all human relationships, whether personal or international, as the most powerful—if not the only—means for preventing violence, especially wars. In that respect I consider the Internet as a powerful tool in the hands of those of us, who are against violence and wars. While I am writing these lines the Internet is still an open communication channel, but I sense the eagerness of the government officials to control it.

One of my highly respected critics expressed his displeasure over my "unpalatable" skepticism and criticism of the policies of the US governments, especially on the issue of using war as a political tool. In my reply to him I wrote: *"You may rightly be irritated by my seemingly endless criticism of the American government's policies toward some of the nations. You may rightly feel, that I as a foreigner, who personally benefited from such policies by having been allowed to immigrate as a refugee to this country during the Cold War, I am wrong by pointedly attacking the policies and the politicians.... Had I been spared from the agonies of a defeat, had the world events been different, would I be the member of a victorious nation, would I read your memoirs in which you point out the failures of my victorious government, my reaction would quite likely be no different from yours.... If in my book I would want to please my readers, rather than to shake them up to see the brutal realities of wars, I would have failed in my mission. What can be more unpalatable than wars? Let us not suffocate the brutal truth in the mirage of unreality. Victory intoxicates, propaganda blindfolds, defeat sobers. I believe this applies not only to me."*

Having been myself subjected to a variety of indoctrination, I view the indoctrination of others with deep concern. Some of the young men and women in military uniform, under single-sided indoctrinational propaganda are being shaped into mindlessly loyal and proudly obedient servants of the government, just as I was when I was young. Some are trained (as I heard on a documentary television program) to become "Blood-thirsty killing-machines," and are sent to the lands of others thousands of miles away to carry out so-called "Missions," as if those would be holy acts. They are the tools of the government. They are sent out to other countries in the name of "Democracy" and "Liberty", but in reality they bring death and destruction. I remember the images of our troops landing in Somalia. The government propaganda told us that the young men were sent there to feed the starving people. But, that event was preceded by tension-filled reports on the television screen, as if it would have been a major conflict with a mighty military power, not on the land of feuding tribes. The young American soldiers went ashore in camouflaged fatigues, with blackened faces, armed to their teeth. Their unspoken "mission" was to fulfill the ambitions of a few obsessed politicians and militarists to capture a by the propaganda demonized tribal leader. In that "Mission" instead of feeding the hungry, hundreds of women and children were reportedly killed. Many lives were lost just because of the ill-guided ambitions of those in power. The whole Somalia episode is now forgotten, we don't care anymore about feeding its people. The government, after having lost its propaganda war at the cost of many human lives, switched to silence on that case. I can never forget the television pictures of the armada of ships and airplanes in the Persian Gulf, which—we were told—were there to keep the peace. But instead, an Iranian civilian passenger plane was shot down, killing hundreds of our fellow human beings. The evening television news showed the Chief of

Staff standing in front of fancy charts with the usual military arrogance, telling us that the Iranian passenger plane flew on a "hostile course threatening our navy vessels". It was not true. As another proof, he told us that "the plane's radio operated on military frequency", which was not true either. All those false reports came from the over-eager young sailors who wanted to prove their fulfilling of patriotic-military duties. I had the opportunity to speak with one of the young men who was there. Years later he was still proud of "taking out an enemy plane". He also learned well the military jargon. For him the bodies of the plane's passengers floating in the water were "collateral casualties". While I listened to those propaganda lies the outrage of the civilized world grew, but our officials did not want us to hear about it! At the end it became another defeat of a bloody propaganda war, which after several years of denials the government wanted to rectify by quietly paying millions of dollars to the families of the victims, as if the value of human life—the most sacred—could be expressed in money. In one of the shamefully tragic episodes of the 1991 Gulf War thousands of the retreating Iraqis—who were granted safe passage by our military commanders—were slaughtered on the Basra highway. In a television interview one of the officers called it a "Turkey-hunt." Only a few and short scenes of that horrible atrocity were shown on the television screen, never mentioning the magnitude of that human tragedy. The civilized world cried out, but our officials did not want us to hear about it. When hundreds of women and children were killed in a civilian air-raid shelter in Baghdad with bombs specially made for that attack, we were told by the officials that the shelter was a military command post. It was not. Our government propaganda attempted to divert the viewers' attention from the human tragedy to the success of the "pin-point accuracy and penetrating ability of our smart bombs." When in Iraq hundreds of soldiers of the foe were buried alive by our troops in their desert bunkers, and the International Red Cross protested, the spokesman of the Pentagon in answer to the questions on the televised news conference replied: "War is about killing and it makes no difference how." I can never forget the heated words of our politicians arguing for the capture of the Panamanian ruler. In their obsession our officials unleashed a military attack against the shantytown of Panama City, testing the sophisticated new "Stealth-planes," killing scores of the poorest of that country. They were proud of the "excellent performance" of the planes. To remove the signs of that tragedy, the burned-out remains were reportedly quickly bulldozed, and the survivors were locked up in a military base. The civilized world protested, but our officials did not want us to hear about it!

Where are we today? (In 1996)

The government buildings became like fortresses. Uniformed, and I assume also not uniformed guards are everywhere, metal-detectors are at the entrances, television cameras are mounted on the rooftops, barricades are set up in the streets. Why? Who are they afraid of? Why are they afraid? What is happening? Are—perhaps—many angry men in our country who at one time in military uniform were trained to become "blood-thirsty killing machines" and "demolishing experts," were sent to the jungles of the Far East and to the deserts of the Near East to fight futile wars, killing our fellow human beings, and destroying their homes? When they came back wounded, physically and psychologically crippled, poisoned, they awakened to the horrors of wars, but could not find anybody to take responsibility for what happened to them. Are—perhaps—the mourners of the victims and the survivors of our cluster bombs too numerous and too angry? Is it—perhaps—that people of other nations had enough of the ever-present military and economic threats by our government against those who do not want to surrender to its will, or to the will of its local agents? Is it—perhaps—that people of other nations living under our occupation, whether under the terms of treaties or business contracts, whether under our own flag, or under the flags of organization which our government imposes upon them, whether in the Far East, Near East or in Europe, want to live in independence? Is it—perhaps—that nations, which learned from the horrors of wars and militarism, seeking peace, resent the presence of our military? Why was our much-celebrated hero and general of the Gulf War booed-out from the lecture rooms in Europe? Why aren't we Americans welcome anymore in many parts of the world?

I also find it most repugnant, when our high government officials surrendering to the demagogues call not only the leaders but also entire nations "Outlaws" and "Rogue." The Webster dictionary gives the description for outlaw as: "A habitual notorious criminal who is a fugitive from the law." Are the millions of people in a nation criminals? The description for "Rogue" is: "Wandering beggar, rascal, scoundrel, an individual varying markedly from the standards, esp. an inferior one." Are the decent, hardworking men and women of nations rascals and scoundrels? The use of such language by the American government officials—including the President—is utterly repulsive and impertinent, disqualifying them to any role in the affairs of the world. Where is the decency of the civilized American society? Why do the God-fearing Americans allow their officials—including their President—to drag this nation to the bottom of the cesspool of the human society? Why are those nations "Outlaws"? Just because they are determined to defend themselves against any planned aggressions by us, or by our allies? Are they "Outlaws" just because they attack those military installations, which are maintained by us close to their borders, for bombing them? Are they "Rogue" just because they want to live by the principles of their traditional religion and culture? Are they "Rogue" just because they build factories to produce fertilizer—which our government tells us is an explosive—to turn their dessert into productive land? Are they "Rogue" because they drain swamps—which our government tells us is genocide, depriving the tribes from living their traditional way of life—to grow crops for feeding the people who are condemned to starvation by our embargo? It was our government that threatened them with nuclear bombs to destroy their fertilizer factory, and to stop draining the swamps. If those are the political principles of our government toward other nations, we have all the reasons to be afraid. If those are the moral principles of the policy makers, we have all the reasons to be ashamed. If that is the course this country wants to take, we have to build more and more fortresses, not only around government buildings, but everywhere, because we will have plenty reasons to be afraid. If we have to be afraid of somebody or something, we better find the roots of the problems. No armed guards around buildings, no television cameras on rooftops and no barricades in the streets can protect us. (The recent events were proofs to that!) Where do our politicians live, when instead of seeking disarmament, they plan the extension of military bases? They argue; "We live in a dangerous world, and we have to defend ourselves." But what makes this world so dangerous? The world does not need military bases; it needs open societies without boundaries, open communications without secret deals between governments, open exchange of ideas without the threat of nuclear weapons, peaceful social and economic changes to improve the lives of the people. We don't need million dollar missiles aimed at cities. The profiteers, the manufacturers and marketers of weapons, who enrich themselves from the phobia of the governments, should be stopped, and their wealth and power should be used for the well being of the people.

My outrage is directed at the politicians, who in their arrogance cannot or don't want to listen. I heard enough of their bluffs and lies from the Right to the Left, under the symbols of the Arrow-Cross, the Swastika, Hammer and Sickle, Red star and White star, cheating nations into horrible wars, causing immense suffering, but not solving any of the burning problems of mankind. I grew up in a world where I had to live in fear, where the national borders were reinforced with concrete bunkers, with barbed-wire fences and mine fields, where the government's will was ruthlessly enforced, where armed guards stood on every street corner. Are we going to follow the same ugly path? If so, our fate and our country's fate will not be different from the fate of the failed.

I watched on television one of the presidential inauguration celebration. The commentator emphasized that it was a demonstration of the American democracy. The President talked about going across the bridge to a brighter future, but what I saw was the glorification of old fashioned militarism. Young, and not so young, men in uniform acting like robots marched in the avenue. Polished cannons, attended by smartly dressed soldiers, were fired in saluting him. What an anachronism! Are we still living in the dark ages when the military was the best of a nation's pride? I would like to walk across a bridge on the other side of which there are no cannons, no indoctrinated, bewildered young men in uniform. I had seen enough of that in the past in different countries, under different rulers. Can't we just break away from such outdated circuses? Can't we find noble ways to celebrate?

I heard many times that my ideas are "Simplistic," "Naive," some even said "Stupid." But what are the alternatives? Regrettably, I had to live my entire life in the world of the "Alternatives"; wars, injustice, hatred, economic and social disasters. The joy of my youth was stolen from me by a war, in my early adult years I had to struggle for my fundamental rights, in search of a better life I had to cross mine fields and barbed-wire fences risking the lives of my wife and my small child. Is this what we want the future to be for our children? Regrettably, I had to live much of my life in "Hot wars" and in "Cold wars," but had only short periods of what could be called "Peace." The governments in all countries, wherever I was in those years, were preparing for another war, or as they liked to call it, for another "Conflict," each blaming the other side. The huge armies faced each other along the fronts in Europe, each preparing for the destruction of the other, each ignoring the fact that the victims of those conflicts could be the civilian population. Each was building more and more, bigger and bigger missiles aimed at the cities of the other side. Public buildings were assigned as shelters; children in the schools were trained how to act in case of a nuclear attack. It was insane, but we kept marching along the fateful path, believing what the governments were telling us. There appeared to be no way out of another disaster.

In that seemingly hopeless quagmire came a ray of hope when Russia, the feared and deplored foe, changed the course of history. In a courageous, but quite risky act they unilaterally reversed the insane trend. While our politicians were still talking about maintaining Europe's military occupation—which lasted for nearly 45 years—and projected its ending sometimes decades later, the foe in 1990 opened the sealed walls, which divided Europe. They began to withdraw their military forces. Our politicians were stunned. They scrambled, but could not hold back the events. Suddenly, countries, which were under the foe's military occupation became free. History was made by the foe. Regrettably, all that was not initiated by our politicians, they wanted to continue confrontation; they wanted to play the dangerous game. They missed an historic opportunity, when in its courageous transition they treated the giant foe as a dwarf, an invalid, subjected it to the propaganda, presenting it as a beggar nation, rather than treating it as a peace-making partner. They did hurt the foe's national pride, the consequences of which will come someday. (!)My views on these issues might be treated by the reader as those of a man, who through his own life-experience suffers in negativism, who in his confusion and misunderstanding of the events targets those who in his false judgment see distorted realities.

On the following pages I include my son's essay. He was four years old, when in a cold November night of 1956 I carried him on my back crossing barbed-wire fences and mine field, in search of a better, a peaceful life. He became a professor, member of the academic world, shaping the minds of the new generation Americans. Although, he is member of a younger generation, grew up in a different world, in many respect not agreeing with my concepts, and not accepting my conclusions, we do have a common paths in our thoughts. My son was the next generation of the young Americans to be sacrificed in the Vietnam War. I am pleased that I could save him from the agonies, which I had to go through as a young man in uniform. For what I had to do to save him I was called by some a coward, a traitor. But I would rather be a morally right coward than someone, who under false pretense of patriotism sacrificed his own son. I don't have to join in the sadness of those fathers whose only place to be near their sons is in the military cemetery. His name is not engraved on the marble wall of the victims of an immoral war. I had seen the names of too many young people carved into tombstones everywhere in the world. I had seen too many flags on the graves of the dead young. I had seen too many good patriots marching in the streets in memory of the fallen. In those forests of flags, in those parades I saw the betrayal and not the honoring of those who with their bodies pierced by bullets or torn to pieces by shrapnel are silent forever in their graves. I heard too many loud speeches by politicians in the military cemeteries talking about the "fallen heroes," calling the new generation to follow the example of those who "made the ultimate sacrifice." But I never heard a speech on the tragic death of the victims of the failures of the governments. Was anybody ever called to answer for the tragedies they brought upon this nation? The strategists well paid by the nation quietly retired into a comfortable life, wrote their memoirs, gathered fortunes by giving lectures to culpable audiences, explaining why all the wrongs they did were right. The generals, who demanded the loyalty and obedience of the young just to sacrifice them in senseless battles, rewarded themselves and each other with medals to be stuck on their chests, gave interviews in which they blamed everything and everybody for what has happened, except themselves. I see in the fallen young their victims.

AMERICANS AND THE "NEW WORLD ORDER."

An essay by my son
Joseph Molitorisz Jr. Ph.D.
1998

Recently I attended a banquet in Austin honoring some of this nation's best and brightest in the news media. The list of their accomplishments was indeed long. There were the usual speeches and anecdotes, mostly good-humored stuff. The pitiful conclusion to this otherwise socially-redeeming event came when all were asked to stand and join in the singing of the "Star Spangled Banner" to a videotape recording projected onto a large screen featuring a renowned pop singer opening for what looked to be a football game.

As I stood there lip-synching, I felt deep discomfort setting in. I studied the surroundings. In the room with the "best and brightest," I sensed an air of self-delusion mixed with self-satisfaction. My thoughts turned to why it is that we Americans feel so misunderstood in the world, about why we perceive the recurrent tides of anti-Americanism as such disdainful phenomena. I reflected on encounters with Europeans on a recent study tour of Germany. Above all, I reflected on media coverage of the Gulf War.

Just two weeks earlier I was with American colleagues in Berlin. On the final day of our stay we visited the city of Dresden long inaccessible to Westerners. There, while photographing a pile of rubble, a monument to the horrors of war, we witnessed quite by chance the beginning of a demonstration. The crowd quickly swelled. Later we heard that there were 35,000 participants involved. There were babies in strollers, young couples, retired people, i.e.

what looked to be the entire spectrum of the population. In fact, to some of us it looked like the entire population. The procession was quiet and friendly with the occasional banner reading NO WAR IN THE GULF, NO INTERVENTION IN LITHUANIA. I don't believe this event ever made the news in our country. When inquiring of a nearby organizer as to how long it took to plan for such massive turnout, he replied: "Oh, about a week." One week? We were astonished. "We have had some practice at this as of late," he continued with a gleam in his eye, referring to the marches which culminated last year in the fall of the hated Communist Government. Then he took his turn to inquire "You Americans, why do you want war?" The powerful symbolism of being in Dresden, which at the very end of the World War II took some of the heaviest allied bombings, did not escape us and made our response a true burden.

A small crowd was gathering for the novelty of experiencing Americans. I replied that in our country there was a breadth of public opinion from ardent support for, to genuine opposition to the war. All the while, I sensed the total engagement of the people who surrounded us. They were relishing this opportunity for dialogue. Referring to the CNN coverage they are able to view in their city, an onlooker pressed me: "I watch the live coverage of the war. Why do Americans glorify war?" I could not respond. "You should send your people over here to see this monument just as you have come to see it. This may change their minds about war. It certainly forced us Germans to do so." she continued. Again I came up with nothing to retort. I could only focus on us Americans conceiving of war as something on TV. "over there" without the benefit of anything challenging our intellect and moral fiber. I realized at a gut level just how ill prepared we are to engage in real dialogue. Yet, it became amply clear to me that this ability is precisely what is called for as soon as the shooting war stops. The much-touted "New World Order" does not only put our government in the center of attention. It also puts Americans and their attitudes squarely in the context of global dialogue. This is not good news, I would submit, for us. We, as people, do not know how to meet the demands of global citizenship. We don't even have the necessary tools. Not enough of us speak anything but English. We lack any capacity for putting current events into historical context. Indeed, we don't know the most pedestrian ideas with which to initiate a minimum of public discourse with our global counterparts. We do not read foreign newspapers to educate ourselves about world events. So goes the familiar litany of shortcomings.

What is proving to be most dramatic is that others know these things about us. We can't fool them about our ignorance. What Americans seem to know in the opinion of their interlocutors is what they are fed by television. Period.

This brings me back to news media personalities. It seems to me that first and foremost among their duties should be the inducement of the American populace to get some perspective on those who are participants in the "New World Order." Not only do we not know what their views might be, but we have not even been able to initiate interesting a global dialogue. We simply, sadly and shallowly wallow in our self-reflection. "Contemplating ones navel" is an apt metaphor for describing the service rendered us by our media. Indeed, we get the media we deserve. This is what is so disconcerting about the way in which the processed, pre-digested "Star-Spangled Banner" incident affected me in that audience. To an unprecedented extent, Americans are challenged to act in order to not be relegated to second-class citizenship in the "New World Order." Yet, we fail to realize in any meaningful way what responsibilities and burdens are implicit in the act of engaging ourselves with the world out there. Without the benefit of a broader intellectual context, this very notion of "New World Order" read off the President's lips cannot mean anything more to us than a mere cliché: "America is Back." You don't have to be a starry-eyed idealist to imagine the daunting challenges that lie ahead for Americans if we want to make a contribution above and beyond providing military muscle for the current war. We have engaged our brawn for now on the world scene. This is making an impact. Our brains and ideas are thus far disengaged. Unfortunately, those in the media who could affect change and liberate us from self-delusion are, it seems, too busy honoring one another on their accomplishments."

ECHOES OF THE PAST.

(My article from 2001)

Viewing with today's eyes the 1934 Nazi propaganda film "Triumph of the Will", was depressing. Thousands of goose-stepping uniformed men marched in the streets like robots, their faces frozen in pride, radiating discipline and devotion to the "Führer". The people standing on the sidewalks and leaning from the windows in near ecstasy greeted the marchers. The film gave the impression that the whole German nation was one big unity. The image that the film projected was that there was no power in the world that could stop the will of united people. Hitler stood in his car, with pride and satisfaction on his face, greeted the marchers with raised arm. His Deputy in a frenzy shouted in the microphone: "Hitler ist Deutschland! Deutschland ist Hitler." The crowd responded with enthusiasm. After viewing the film I asked myself: How could educated, intelligent people become so absorbed by propaganda bluffs, that they could feel that their leader embodied the nation? It was propaganda to the ultimate. It raised the enthusiasm of the spirited, and frightened the faint-hearted. That was the purpose of the film. That was in 1934, more than a half-century ago, when the propaganda tools and the mentality of the people were supposedly different.

During the years of the Second World War as a young man I saw the newsreels in Hungary, showing the German and Hungarian soldiers triumphantly chasing the enemy, their tanks roaming the Russian steppes, the burning Russian cities "liberated," the "Asiatic barbarians" surrendering. We were shown a clean war, where if anything ugly happened it was invariably committed by the enemy. After the war the images of the victorious German and Hungarian armies disappeared from the movie screens, replaced by the images of the heroic Russians. I saw the Russian newsreels, which depicted the Soviet armies as the warriors of liberty, the Russian soldiers as liberators, and the Germans as the guilty who committed all the crimes

With the end of the war the defeated armies were eliminated by taking the soldiers in the isolation of the prisoner-of-war camps. The breaking of their military morale was achieved by disarming them, stripping off their rank-showing insignia, taking away their military decorations, putting them behind barbed-wire fences, subjecting them to humiliation. There was no need for political propaganda to influence their minds. The morale was already crushed by the defeat. I myself was in an American prisoner-of-war camp and went through the psycho-process. It was quite remarkable that in the camp—where I was among mostly German prisoners—never was there any argument over political matters. I never heard anybody blaming others for their fate. It was a defeat that was total and was accepted. While it is common, when veterans of wars come together, to talk about their war stories, in the prison camp there was none of that. For the war-weary prisoners the war was over, they did not want to hear about it anymore. It was also interesting that the Americans did not use any propaganda means in the camp. The guards stood at the gates and along the fences, they watched us from behind the machine guns on the guard towers, but never showed any signs of propaganda. There was no need for it. The targets of the propaganda campaign, which started soon after the guns became silent, were the civilians. Although they also were among the defeated, they were not incarcerated, they stayed in their homes. They could not be controlled directly like the captured soldiers were. The tactics of the occupiers was the bombardment of the civilians with propaganda..

When returning to the Russian occupied Hungary from American prison, the first impression was the intense propaganda with which the Soviet occupation forces and the new political powers—the returned Bolsheviks—targeted the civilian population. The posters glorifying the victorious Soviet Union, adulating the heroic proletariat and the Communist Party, covered the walls. On the Communists' posters was the image of the Hungarian flag to impress the viewer that the party was a national institution not a political power imposed upon the nation by the occupation force. The dogmas of a distorted internationalism were wrapped in the national flag. The propaganda aim was to eradicate the past, when only a few months earlier there was a desperate battle defending the country against Bolshevism. The souls and minds of those who were not silenced in prison camps were targeted by propaganda. That was over 60 years ago.

I lived through the years of the Korean War in the communist world, and later came to America. That was a revealing experience for me. On the pages of the newspapers and on the movie screens the victorious North Korean soldiers liberating the South Korean towns and villages were glorified. The wrecks of the shot-down American airplanes, the captured, weary, bloody faced, trembling pilots were presented as proof of the defeated America, and of the heroic superiority of the victorious North Koreans. After my arrival in America I saw entirely different images of that war. It was the defeated North Korean soldiers in the hands of the victorious Americans, proving their superiority. Those were two opposing perspectives of the same events, both were real, but each had a different propaganda purpose.

In the first years of the Vietnam War I watched the reports here in America, while in the later years I viewed the events in Germany, on both the West and the East German televisions. That was still another eye-opening experience for me. On the American television I saw the pictures of the sweating marines battling the "Gooks," the big bombers dropping bombs, helicopters hunting the Vietcong fighters. It was presented with the commentaries claiming the righteousness of that war. Nothing was said about the brutal killing of civilians. The generals were winning the battles, and America was winning the war. The news announcers listed the daily successes by giving the numbers of the killed "enemy," never mentioning that those were also human beings. They failed to mention the American casualties. The West German television presented the events with cautious criticism, occasionally inserting comments reminding the viewers about the futility of the war, warning that before America's entering the war the French also battled the Vietnamese, and were defeated. Dramatically different was the reporting on the East German television. It showed the burned and ripped-apart bodies of children and women, all victims of the American napalm bombs, projected the grotesque faces of Vietnamese whose bodies were riddled with bullets. The long caravans of the Vietcong fighters carrying their supplies through the dense jungle, the determined faces of the young men and women fighting for their freedom and independence against the "Imperialist America" were all proof of their heroism. The "enemy" was shown in the images of the captured American airmen led from the wreckage of their airplanes by young Vietcong soldiers. Those pictures were projected as proof of the evil character of the American enemy. Night after night I saw the same shocking pictures, read the numbers of the American airplanes shot down by the "brave Vietcong fighters." While the American propaganda claimed victories, the East German television reported the defeat of the Americans. The American propaganda gave the number of the Vietnamese casualties, and the East German propaganda listed the number of the killed Americans. The truth was somewhere between the two.

I followed the 1991 Iraq war through the American and also through the overseas media. The propaganda technique was much the same as it was in the other wars. To find the truth, or something close to it, I gathered information from both sides with the help of the computer. It was not the kind of war that our propaganda attempted to show. Our "Smart bombs" were not as smart as the generals told us. The targets of our missiles and bombs were not just the Iraqi soldiers, but were also the "collateral" civilians. There was, however, one major difference in the propaganda war. The communication technology allowed me to see and hear the reports directly and almost simultaneously from the opposite sources. There was no way to hide the truth anymore.

We are battling once again against "International terrorism." The propaganda machinery of the government accuses countries, religious and political groups, of waging "terrorism" against us the righteous. The news media doesn't say why those "Criminals" attack our embassies, why they attacked the World Trade Center's towers. They don't search for the cause of the self-sacrifices of the "terrorists." They simply search for the accused, offer bounties and promise retaliation and punishment. For them dropping bombs on civilians by uniformed military men is morally and legally right, but if the bombs wrapped around their bodies are delivered by desperate individuals, or by a group of fanatics, it is immoral and illegal, it is terrorism. In my view dropping bombs, whether by military man in uniform or by a "terrorist" in rags, is a crime, and it constitutes terrorism. Our political strategists, the well-educated and well-informed elite seem to ignore the lessons of the past. Instead of communicating with the "terrorists," questioning them why they are willing to sacrifice themselves, what would stop them in carrying out their senseless violence, they fight them, without knowing who they really are, and what they fight for. If all the resources which are spent on converting the public buildings into fortresses, if all the intelligence and police work directed to finding the "terrorists" would be spent on seeking contact with them, giving them the opportunity to express their views without resorting to violence, there would be no need to fight them. As long as our strategists view them as terrorists, they also view us as legitimate targets. Having been myself in a revolution, having been called by the Bolsheviks a "Terrorist", and at the same time celebrated by Americans as a "Freedom-fighter," I have a good basis to view terrorism from another point of view. I ask the question; what can turn a decent human being into a terrorist? Is it just plain senseless brutality? Is it blind fanaticism? Is it the urge for revenge? Or, is it desperation and hopelessness? I believe those are all elements of the psyche of terrorism. I was a "Terrorist" in a revolution, which came about because the government officials in their narrow-minded arrogance did not want to listen to those who had well justified grievances. I am deeply worried about the present trend here in America. Our officials wage wars, send bombers, launch missiles, but they call all those acts justified, legal and moral. If somebody else does the same, they call it "Terrorism."

How little the propaganda technique has changed since my younger times is shown by the images we see and hear in these days. In this case I am thinking about our official government propaganda, which is directed against the foe, identifying nations by their leaders, projecting their pictures on the television screens as if they were the embodiments of those nations. Our political strategists identify Iraq with Saddam, Cuba with Castro, Iran with the Ayatollah, as if there would not be millions of other people, children, women, young and old, peaceful, decent people living in those countries. Our government officials demonize the leaders and insult their nations calling them "Rogue" and "Outlaw." That is the way they want to turn the public against the "enemy," that is the propaganda method with which they want to poison the minds of the people. The government told us that we fought against Saddam, but we killed Iraqi people, we embargoed Saddam but starved Iraqi children. We harassed the Ayatollah, but shot down an airliner killing hundreds of Iranian civilians. We chased Noriega but our "Stealth-bombers" dropped the bombs on the poorest people of Panama City.

How could intelligent, God-fearing people of this country tolerate the spreading of such hateful war propaganda? We are not writing 1934, we live in the communication age of the 21st century. The undue glorification of the victorious, and the unjust condemnation of the defeated were and still are the principal pitfalls in history-writing's credibility. I cannot believe that the leaders of the foes were and are pure "evil," and our leaders are all righteous men. Had the Second World War ended differently, we would see much different propaganda images. The world would celebrate Hitler and Mussolini as the saviors of Western Civilization from the threat of the atheistic Bolshevism. Monuments would immortalize them. We would read and hear about the war crimes of the British, American and Russian politicians and generals. We would listen to stories about the horrors of the deportation camps in the Soviet Union and in the deserts of Utah, but would know nothing about Auschwitz and Birkenau. We would talk about the racial discrimination in America, about the deportation of the "Japs," but would never hear about the persecution of the Jews. We would have altogether different images of ourselves and of our foes. I believe these are the realities.

Regrettably not much has changed since the times of my youth. The propaganda—even in the civilized West—is still using the powerful tool of distorted, manipulated images of the foe. We are still the captives of the official lies. The true measure of the civility and morality of a government is in its ability and willingness to remain truthful and objective in critical matters, in refraining from truth-distorting propaganda, in avoiding using threat against others, in showing understanding and tolerance. Ill-intended propaganda will produce hatred and violence. That was true throughout the human history and it is still true today. The more accusatory and hate-filled the rhetoric of our strategists becomes, the more reasons I find for fear of retaliations by the accused. Hateful propaganda was and still is the most serious threat to mankind. It is the birth-bed of militarism and of terrorism. No peace can be expected when truth-distorting propaganda is allowed to prevail. The only way to stop political violence is by silencing the hate-mongers, whether they are government officials or "terrorists," by eradicating the truth-distorting, agitating propaganda, and by listening to each other.

A few years ago the principal architects of the Vietnam War were in Hanoi to meet their ex-enemies, to examine the roots and the causes that led to the demise of three millions Vietnamese and fifty thousand Americans. In a television interview during that visit the chief architect of that horror, who served during the war as Secretary of Defense admitted, that he did not know at that time—and he still does not know—how and what actually happened in the incident that was used by the American government as reason for starting the war. He, as Secretary of Defense who advised the president and the congress, who laid out the official policies of our government, admitted that he did not know the facts. The President swallowed his words without examination, acted upon them, and mobilized the nation for a war, bringing three million people to their graves. It happened not in another century, not in the "Evil Empire" but decades ago here in America. They unleashed the tremendous destructive power of the American war machinery against the "Gooks," as they called the Vietnamese, sent the brainwashed young men to slaughter men, women, children, burn the primitive bamboo huts of the poor. They sprayed them with poisonous chemicals to defoliate their forests, dumped millions of tons of bombs on their cities, villages and forests. They did all that without knowing the facts. The "War architects" were gloating over the successes in the numbers of the casualties of the enemy. The, at that time admired young "Whiz-kid" conducted a war that he did not understand what it was all about! Now, he cries "Mea culpa." He dared to say that the war was a "Mistake." After murdering three million human beings he dared to use the word "Mistake," as if that immense tragedy would have been just a minor incident. He, who together with all the senators and congressmen, with the powerful members of the so called "Security Council," with all the well educated and informed presidential advisors dragged this nation into a human tragedy, into a crime against humanity, now lives comfortably. They are washing their hands of all the guilt that burden them, and try to explain that it was only a "Mistake." They were willing and eager to send the young men—including my son—to die for a "Mistake." Millions of Vietnamese and fifty thousand American families have to mourn their mothers, children, fathers and sons just because of a "Mistake" by our politicians! Millions of men in Vietnam and in this country have to bear the consequences of the irresponsibility and immorality of the "Whiz-kid" and of his followers who in the war years gleefully led the nation into a tragedy. Now, aging and with deep wrinkles on his face he said: "It was a mistake!"

Will, perhaps someday the horrors of Dresden, Hiroshima and Nagasaki also turn up in the official government records as "Mistakes"? Will, perhaps someday our officials and the nation come to the recognition that all wars were—and still are—not just "Mistakes" but are crimes against humanity?

A few years ago the Government of the United States warned Germany not to vote for the enacting of the International Criminal Court, which was to try soldiers and officials for crimes they commit while in service anywhere in the world. The issue is the jurisdiction over war crimes and crimes against humanity, regardless of the nationality of the accused. Why does the American government oppose the empowerment of such a court? Is its opposition an admission of guilt? Is it—perhaps—that those who might be called to answer for the massacres in Hiroshima, in Nagasaki, in Dresden, in My Lai, on the Basra highway, in Somalia, in Panama, or wherever else, are still among us? Is it—perhaps—that facing an international court might reveal much of what our government doesn't want us to know?

The world is stunned by the actions of the American foreign policy makers, and there is growing opposition everywhere. None of the major international organizations support hostile military action. But our officials ignoring the outrage, zigzag the world spreading the warning of a disaster if their policies are not followed by the other nations. The horror of another major war is looming in the air, but our politicians relentlessly pursue the disastrous course, speak with total disregard about the human victims who for them are "Collateral casualties." How would our leading politicians answer the Iraqi mother who during the Gulf war brought her nine children to the air raid shelter in Baghdad for a safe night sleep, while she went home to clean their house, and our "Smart bombs" hitting the shelter killed all nine of her children, together with four hundred other children and women? How would they tell that grief-stricken mother that it was the "Mistake" of our intelligence to target the shelter as a communication center, rather than what it really was, a civilian air shelter? How would the American public react to such horror if that mother would have been American, and her children would have been American youngsters?

In the ornate hall of a Chinese official building filled with dignitaries and news reporters, the Presidents of America and China stood behind microphones talking and listening to each other. The television camera swept across the magnificent hall, bringing in focus the foreign policy makers. They sat in the first rows, listening intensely to the heads of states whether they would say anything that was not in line with the pre-prescribed official policies. They could be satisfied, for nothing has changed. One of the issues on the presidents' agenda was "De-targeting" the deadly missiles from each other's cities. Sitting behind at my desk, looking out to the seemingly peaceful city of Seattle, I had to realize that in the minds of the policy makers that city—and I in it—are the targets of the monstrous weapons. So are the cities and the people in China the targets of the American missiles. One of the discussed points was the avoiding of "accidental" launching of those horrible tools of death and destruction. Yes, accidental launching! I heard not one word from either of the presidents about disarming, only de-targeting the missiles. The requests by the Chinese in return for their de-targeting was our policy-makers' commitment not to be the first to use nuclear weapons. Regrettably, America does not even have the moral right to make such commitments, because it already has the tragic legacy of having been the first—and so far the only—country in human history to use nuclear bombs. Our policy makers refused once again to make such a commitment. The presidents representing one and one half billion people did not want to talk about disarming their missiles. I have to keep living under the frightening inheritance of the past fifty years.

Living in the computer age I often see the three letters "www." I wish to invite all, especially the young for whom the computer is the future, to use the power of the computer, add still another, a deeper meaning to those three letters, plug in the minds of every computer user around the world

www = World Without Wars.

AMERICA AND THE WORLD COMMUNITY.

America's dangerously arrogant foreign policy forces the member states of the European Union to distance themselves from the alliance, which initially was intended to secure peace. Their attitude should not be considered as anti-American, but as anti-war and pro-peace. NATO was a defensive military institution against the once powerful Soviet Union. There is no more Soviet threat. NATO lost its true purpose, but the American government uses manipulative means to change the NATO Charter from a defensive to an offensive posture, with the intent to drag it into the Middle-East wars. This became clear during and after the debates on the Iraq war at the United Nations.

The European media recently reported with resentment America's setting up military bases in Rumania, Bulgaria and Poland. The question they raise is why there, and for what purpose? Is it—perhaps—in a strategic planning against the European Union, more specifically against France and Germany? There are indications, such as the outburst of calls by American politicians for boycotting European products, the frequently mentioned "European anti-Semitism", together with the *"France stinks"*, *"Germany stinks"* slogans on the Internet, substantiating such an assumption. Are—perhaps—those military bases in preparation for a future war against Russia? The tense relationship, the negative propaganda, the accusatory claims on anti-Semitism propagating the urgency for bringing the threatened Jews out of Russia are pointing in that direction. Is—perhaps—the aim with setting up the bases to split Europe into strategic regions? The geographical location of those countries clearly shows the probability of such a strategic consideration.

The indignation of the Europeans over America's secret use of their air-space for transporting political prisoners, and the alleged existence of secret prisons on their soil, where political prisoners are subjected to torture, added to the tension. The European Union strives for ideological and military inde-pendence from belligerent policies. They want to achieve political, economic and strategic balance. For that they want to expand the EU. This trend is clear, and from the American point of view is concerning. But that is the real-ity.

World peace or world calamity, co-existence or co-extinction hinge more than ever on the American governmental behavior. It is deeply disturbing when American government officials instead of seeking peaceful solution to conflicts, openly argue for the use of the ultimate tool of terror—war. America as the self-proclaimed leader of the world should follow a rational foreign pol-icy, and as one of the founders of the United Nations—which is seated on its soil—should adhere to the peace serving principles of that organization. If not, no matter how many nuclear bombs America has, irrespective of how many countries American troops are stationed in, regardless of the flag-waving enthusiasm with which people proclaim their patriotism, and in spite of the sacrifices that the young and misled men and women in uniform are willing to make, some day history can make America irrelevant. History's mills are working, and if the government officials do not see that, we the people, who have to bear the burdens of their wrong-doings, have to tell them. Mighty powers rose and fell, disappeared from the stage of history. Nobody can pre-dict the events that may change the course of the world. The choice is ours; co-existence or co-extinction.

America's relationship with the European countries and with the European Union should have utmost importance in the American foreign policy. The historic ethnic and cultural ties are strong, and the economic interest is mutual. Regrettably, the Second World War brought a deep rupture in the relationship. The collapse of the Soviet Union and the evolving of a united Europe presented new opportunities. The realities are, however, quite differ-ent. There is a growing confrontational tendency in some political circles in America.

In the Eastern European countries after the collapse of the communist ter-ror regimes, racial-political tension erupted. Outside and also inside agitation aroused the radically inclined young generation of Jews, for whom the perse-cution and the Holocaust was history. It was not just a racial issue, but also was political agitating. A propaganda campaign was started as a counter attack against the growing criticism of the Jewish role in the communist era. At the same time a highly aggressive legal battle began—led mainly by American Jewish organizations—demanding large sums of compensatory payments for the Jewish deportees. It happened over half a century after the events, generating resentment among the natives of the respective countries, who also suffered, lost their possessions and died in the war. These are the realities that the Americans have to understand. If minorities want to live in a harmonious relationship with the natives, they must conduct themselves accordingly. The American patrons have to understand that the European Jews were not only the victims, but are also burdened by the guilt of their own radical fanatics. Reproach, re-awakening the racial tension, agitating, are not the roads to reconciliation and co-existence, but to co-extinction.

It would be illusionary to view the present living-together between the Jews and the natives in the Eastern European countries as true reconciliation. Meaningful reconciliation cannot come from a few idealists, or from small segments of the societies, but has to be exercised by the people as well. My observations indicate that it did not happen. Not yet. Quite to the contrary, there is now a mutual resentment between the Jews and the natives, which is deeper than has ever been at peace times in my lifetime. It is not uncommon to have hostile confrontations when over-zealous Jewish radicals carrying the Israeli flag disrupt the celebrations of the natives provoking incidents. *"I would exterminate all Christians"* were the words of the program manager of one of Hungary's radio stations in a program on Christmas Eve 2003 in a "chat", in which in the most vulgar and obscene tone the Christian traditions were attacked. To an objecting telephone call he revealed their identity: *"We* (at the radio station) *are all Jewish"*. In its outrage one of the moderate national daily newspaper printed the entire text of the chat, which is a shocking reading full of vulgarity and obscenity. It was not the first incidence when the same radio station launched highly impertinent and provocative programs. In one instance it called the ancient crown of Saint Steven, the most revered historic treasures of the Hungarians *"A Big Shit"*. In another case they called for chopping down the crosses as symbols of Christianity into firewood, or use them as billboards. There were also cases when prominent Hungarian Jews broke the rules of decent conduct. In one incident a high-ranking Jewish religious leader deeply insulted the Hungarians by saying in an interview, that without the Jewish cultural contribution the Hungarians would still be *"primitive horde, tenderizing the meat under saddle, wearing peasant drawers"*. Such a statement was not only inappropriate, but also was baseless, causing deep resentment. In another incident on a Hungarian national holiday, when the Hungarians traditionally wear on the coat-lapel a bow of ribbon with the national colors, a Jewish man ripped the ribbon from the coat of a little girl. Another act of impertinence and provocation which caused deep resentment and uproar, and received great publicity in Hungary.

Nobody denies the Jewish cultural and scientific contributions, but to claim that the rich, centuries old Hungarian artistic, literary and scientific culture did not exist without them is ridiculous. Such provocation are frequent and ever-more bold, resurrecting the times, when under the Bolshevik era the radio programmer's parents' generation reigned, and—some of them—terrorized the nation. Such incidents are also the warning signs of what might come if they could ever regain the controlling power.

There is a desire by the native population for preserving a culture, and that is presented by the American media as anti-Semitism. Even the moderate Hungarian newspapers were alarmed by the events. They view such events not as isolated incidents, not as misspoken words of a few fanatics, but as a campaign, one paper characterizing it as "Anti-Christian, anti-religious, filthy hate-mongering." which is instigated and supported by subversives from outside and from within the country. The outrage of the natives is growing, the media in general calls for restraint, but the anger is deep. The Jewish-controlled media either ignored the event, or attempted to whitewash the incidents calling those "Unfortunate slip-of-the tongue", and argued: "For some people such opinions are acceptable". No matter how it is interpreted, such impertinence cannot be ignored. Such cases are not only the signs of insensitivity, but are harmful acts of arrogance. Regrettably, some American politicians publicly responded by claiming that in Hungary "Neo-Fascism" is growing. A minority should consider seriously its minority status. Whether Jewish or any another minority that wishes to live harmoniously in a society, the practicing of self-control over objectionably provocative, disruptive exhibition of racial, religious, political or nationalistic attitude is essential. This is especially important in countries, where the natives, in general, adhere to traditions. A minority also has to accept that it is viewed by the native majority with scrutiny. This is true in any and all societies.

The American Jewish community—or at least those whose voice is heard—seems to view the European Jewish issue in an entirely different light. For them it begins with the *"persecution of the innocent Jews"* and with the Holocaust, which is often viewed through distorting magnifying glass, and ends in a god-fatherly role acting as the care-taker of all Jewish matters. They either do not know, or don't want to recognize the fundamental differences between the cases of the American Jewry and of those living in Europe. In America there is a Jewish political and economic dominance in a non-traditional society that has not been directly subjected to the horrors of wars. Those were the European Jews who had to exist in tradition-respecting native societies, they were the deportees who had to work in the factories. They had to do it to survive. It was the European Jewry that had to return to the communities, which in the turmoil of the war rejected them. Many of the survivors did just that, they returned in the hope that there was going to be a reconciliation. Those who did not believe in a peaceful co-existence found new homes somewhere else. The Eastern European Jews have to live with the shameful heritage of their Bolshevik radicals. The Bolshevik terror following the two World Wars, and the persecution of the Jews during the Second World War left deep scars and resentment in the Eastern European societies. Those Jews who have been accused of committing crimes in the Bolshevik era, suffered during World War II in the hands of the revengeful natives. After the return of the Soviet era those natives who were found guilty, or were accused of mistreating the Jews, received harsh punishment. Hatred and violence rather than reconciliation was the rule. After Stalin's death programs had been initiated by Jewish organizations to bring the Jews out from the Soviet Union, and recently from Russia and from other countries, in a rescue operation to save them from the growing anti-Jewism. Such programs are still active, including those promoted here in America in magazines and on television, seeking donations for flying the endangered Russian Jews to Israel, giving the indication that not only reconciliation is not in sight, but violent confrontation—even wars—might occur. Those are not the signs of peaceful co-existence, but of the coming of co-extinction.

The 21st Century might become a critical turning point in history, leading either to a general reconciliation and equilibrium in racial and religious matters, or to a global cataclysm, to co-extinction. I believe the Jewish issue will remain a crucial element of world-politics, splitting the world community into an American-Israeli military alliance against a worldwide Islamic camp and against Europe. Europe most likely will try to stay neutral—as was during the 2003 Iraq War—or, as the American and Israeli officials described it; "irrelevant". However, behind "irrelevancy" can still be animosity, which clearly surfaced during the Iraq War, when accusations of anti-Semitism were made, and calls for boycotting nations were propagated. Joe Lieberman the Jewish American Senator sent out an e-mail: *"All Americans with integrity of character must boycott France"*. An unmistakable and dangerous warning, bordering on the declaration of an economic war on anyone who is in his way. The self-proclaimed religious and pious Senator in a television interview said: *"I may speak softly, but carry a big stick and use it too"*. His words are sobering and frightening, as he has aspirations for the post of the presidency of the United States. Some called for sending the Statue of Liberty back to France, and for flushing the French wines, perfumes and cheeses. There was a hate-filled propaganda campaign by American and Jewish politicians against the European countries, which opposed the war in Iraq and wanted a peaceful solution. Those were not the elements of reconciliation and co-existence, but were the dangerous symptoms of a broad, hateful tendency. We heard about "Oslo Agreement", "Madrid Agreement", "Camp David Agreement", "Peace Process" and "Road Map To Peace", awakening hope for peace, but the likelihood of co-extinction is growing.

We are again in 1933, when "Judea declared war on Germany". But at this time Judea seems to have declared war on the world. Can the world community live in constant fear, giving up liberties? That is where we are today, waging wars to secure peace, (Absurd), breaking up the world community into armed camps, alienating friends, making enemies. My Gentile generation in Europe did show courage with which it faced its failures and its crimes committed against each other and against the Jews during the Second World War. Over half a century after the tragic events, and in spite of the significant corrective efforts, the incrimination of the Europeans by the American media is still an almost daily recurrence. But guilt also burdens the Jewish society for the horror that their radicals brought upon the Gentiles. Not only the communist ideology, but also the Bolshevik terror with which it was imposed upon the many millions in Eastern Europe are inseparable from Jewish history, for which never came an admission of guilt. There is a moral and ethical inequity that is resulting in a continued racial tension. Over half century after the tragic events the highly emotional treating of the issues should be changed to unbiased, objective examination. My generation that lived through those times and was the witness is now dying out. What will be left behind us are the innumerable documentary evidences still hidden on the shelves of the secretive archives, stories written in books or played on the silver screen. There will be no more witnesses—whether driven by emotions and skewed memories, or by the desire to be objective. Maybe it will be necessary to rewrite the history of the 20th century. I think it has to be rewritten. There is much distortion, biased interpretation and outright lies on all sides which blanket it, which cannot be removed until the emotional human element is prevailing, until either side is unwilling to subject its claims to scrutiny, until laws are in force preventing the questioning of claims. The truth cannot be denied forever, whatever it might be. This highly dangerous trend must be stopped.

Writing openly—and where due also critically—about the burning issues of our times is a risk-filled undertaking, exposing myself to the wrath of those who view the events of the past—and also of the present—from a narrow point of view, not seeing, or not wanting to see what the roots of the great human tragedies are, how and why civilized nations and races could turn against each other, committing the most horrible crimes. Avoiding the subject, or discussing it in distorted one-sided manner would be the betrayal of intelligence, a disservice to the reader. The choice is ours; co-existence or co-extinction.

I ask my Jewish readers to receive my thoughts not in the light of bias, but of the fear with which I follow the growing tension, for which the radicals on both sides are responsible. There is—there must be—a way for our co-existence, or seeing in a dramatic way—for our mutual survival—which has to be built on tolerance, but most importantly on mutual respect. The other alternative is co-extinction. My generation, Jews and Gentiles alike, had seen what it could be like. The Jewish society, just as the Gentiles must exercise the moral-intellectual control over the individuals and groups, who on whatever ground—be it race, religion, social-ideology or politics—drag us to the brink of mutual annihilation. We live in highly dangerous times, when technology provides the most horrible tools of destruction, and those tools are available to most anyone who wants them. Some among the Jews nurture a deep hatred derived from biblical times, presenting the Jewish history as an unending persecution. There is some truth to it, but not the whole truth. Collective innocence and collective guilt—as often applied in historical judgment—are fundamentally faulty concepts, with which much of the moral failures of individuals or groups—Gentile and Jewish—can be camouflaged.

Critical examination of the old concepts—religious or social—is an integral part of the human social-cultural evolution. The injection of new concepts—even the controversial ones—is also part of the evolution, without which there would be stagnation. Among all the social-cultural issues religion is the most ancient, the most deeply rooted and the most meaningful for many people. It is more than just cultural; it is also a spiritual matter. Treating it with profanity and vulgarity, like the Jewish programmers of the Hungarian radio station did, is most repugnant. If it would have been an isolated incident one could accept the alibis. But it was not. It is a well-conducted, systematic indoctrination of the young generation.

I am not practicing any religion, don't accept the doctrinal teachings and don't follow ideologies. But that is my private, personal matter, which doesn't entitle me to ridicule others' beliefs. I am critical of the religious institutions, but at the same time recognize and accept everyone's right to seek spiritual satisfaction in whatever way they can find it. That is one key part of co-exist-ence. Respectful and reasonable argumentation on the radio waves is accept-able, but not vulgar and profane attacks on others' faith and traditions. Most regrettably we are witnessing the biggest religious war of human history, although, it is not propagated as such. But the opposing camps are in the Islamic, the Judeo and in the American Judeo-Christian world. The Hungar-ian radio station joined the war with broadcasting the programmer's words: "I would exterminate all Christians"

Judge me as you please for writing about the sensitive issues. Condemn me for placing the blame to where I think it belongs. With sharing my thoughts I want to help you the reader to consider the world events of our times from a broader viewpoint. I do not claim that my interpretation is the correct one, as it is subjective and personal. My intention was to remain unbiased on the sensitive issues. I tried to avoid the danger of falling into the trap of well-sounding, sin-gle-sided arguments on matters which were—and still are—undermining the desire that most of us have; to live in mutual respect, tolerance and peace.

TERRORISM AND THE TERRORISTS.

I have experienced two variants of terrorism; air-war against civilians and racial-political radicalism wrapped in ideological camouflage.

AIR-WAR.

The terror of air-war came in my life in the Second World War. It was conducted by the strategists not only to disrupt the enemy's industrial production and transportation, but also as psychological warfare against the civilian population, causing constant state of fear and panic. In my view air-war is the ultimate of terror.

The loss of the family home in a fire is a devastating experience. Such events on massive scale, extending into years, in the absence of the men of the family, women and the old bearing all the burdens, dramatizes the suffering. Such was the case in the air-war against the European cities. Men of the families as soldiers were away from home, women and the elderly were left alone with the children, while entire city districts were in flames, rows of city blocks were crumbling. Air-war is the most barbaric warfare, targeting the defenseless and the vulnerable, destroying their homes and the basic essentials for existence. The howling of the sirens, often days and nights, frightened them, wearing down the nerves, disrupting the normal life functions. Living for years in constant fear brought the survival instinct to culmination, broke down the essential social structure of the communities. The terrifying sound of huge explosions, the sight of burning homes, the thunder of collapsing structures, the darkness and musty air of the bomb-shelters undermined the strength even of the strongest. For anyone who did not personally experience the horror of air-war, it is unimaginable.

Was air-war strategy against the civilians the game of a few evil-minded? No it was not. On all sides, American, British and German a large portion of the population held it right, some with reservation, others with enthusiasm. The opposition was small and powerless. The governments and strategists advocated it through propaganda. The local authorities prepared the people. Air-raid shelters were built, gas masks were distributed and drills were conducted. Insane, as it was, it gained momentum. The front pages of newspapers carried the reports on the successes in the destruction of the enemy cities.

On March 16, 1945, seven weeks before the Second World War ended, after a heavy night-time air-raid, with a group of Hungarian soldiers on a rescue assignment I entered the burning city of Nürnberg. This was the second time when I was there on such an assignment. With a steel helmet on my head, and with a shovel on my shoulder, under the smoke blanketed sky I marched to the burning city. Fire engines, ambulances, trucks and cars were running to and from the city carrying the dead and the injured. The closer we went to the city-center the more the devastation was. In the district where we were taken everything was on fire, debris, collapsed walls covered the streets, flames were shooting out of the gaping windows, the air was hot and heavy. Firefighters feverishly tried to extinguish the flames. People in long lines passed buckets from water filled bomb craters. The underground water system was destroyed. The rescuers cleared the rubble searching for survivors. We joined them. The magnesium bars, which did not ignite, were menacingly sticking out of the ground. While struggling with the difficult task of clearing debris and extinguishing fires, another wave of bombers was arriving. The rooftop sirens were silent. Most had been destroyed. For the others there was no electricity to drive them. Hand-cranked small sirens howled, but in the loud noise could barely be heard. As the bombs were falling nearby I ran to the closest bomb-shelter that was open. It was hell on earth. People wrapped in blankets, holding small packages on their laps were sitting along the walls. For them, after the night raid, it was another frightening event, of which they already had experienced many. The commander of the shelter closed the heavy steel door, turned the big latches, locking us inside. It was dark, and the air was heavy with musty smell, like in a crypt. The thunder of the exploding bombs, the tremor of the ground grew as the carpet-bombing came closer. The people were sitting slumped and, some were looking up to the ceiling. Were they praying, or were watching whether the concrete walls could hold? I didn't know. We all were at the mercy of somebody or something. Crouching, I was holding my shovel. The whole shelter was moving when the building was hit by a bomb. There was a terrifying thump. A deep rumbling noise followed from above, dust was falling, the concrete walls of the shelter were cracking. Screaming and crying the panicking people rushed to the door. Staying in the shelters was certain death, as the walls were cracking, and the heat was increasing. The door could not be opened, the latches were stuck, they did not move. The other exit was behind the cracking walls. I thought that was the end. Under dim flashlight the commander kicked and pushed the desperate women and elderly men away from the door to make room for himself to use a pickax, with which he could pry the latches and open the door. The stairway to the street was blocked by debris. While clearing those away hot and heavy smoke poured down. Outside there was an awesome sight, flames engulfing everything, the asphalt was burning, walls were crumbling, piles of rubbles were smoldering. I had seen corpses covered with horrible open burn-wounds, their clothing burned away, some still were holding a water bucket. They were the firefighters who could not reach the bomb-shelter in time. The sight of the grotesquely burned faces, the smell of the burned flesh terrified me. I was dazed. The smoke was choking, the heat was scorching, glowing embers floated in the air. To keep my military overcoat from catching fire I threw it in a puddle of water soaking it. My hands were bleeding from digging bricks and pieces of concrete. My eyes were burning from the smoke. It was hard to inhale the hot, dust and smoke filled air. Wherever I looked it was the same; fire, debris, crumbling walls. The people emerging from the shelters covered their faces with wet cloth, jumped over the burning asphalt, and ran to open spaces away from the burning and crumbling walls. Small rescue teams were formed, went from shelter to shelter, searching for survivors. There were no ambulances to treat the injured, as the streets were impassable. Fire-trucks could not come to fight the fires. It was total abandonment of helpless people. I was in Dante's inferno.

Late afternoon, when another rescue team had arrived, exhausted and depressed I left the place with my comrades. Going from city block to city block the picture was the same, total destruction. Looking back I thought that the city could never be rebuilt. During the war nearly 40,000 tons of bombs were dropped on Nürnberg, killing over 6000 civilians, and turning much of the city into burned-out rubble. After having lived through two terror bombings in that city, it was hard to imagine how the people could cope with the horror of the many air raids they had to endure.

Winston Churchill in 1919 already talked about an air attack on Berlin with thousands of airplanes. He projected, that in the next war the main objective was going to be the killing of civilians, women and children. On May 11, 1940, the British Cabinet under Churchill's leadership lifted the laws protecting the civilian population. For him the Germans were in two categories: "Some are curable, and others killable". On the next day the air-war against the German cities began. Charles Portal, one of the principal advocates of Churchill's war policies, in a parliamentary statement outlined the program as; in 1943 and 1944 1,250,000 tons of bomb were to be dropped on German cities, destroying 6,000,000 homes, making 25,000,000 homeless, killing 900,000, and injuring 1,000,000. Air-war against civilians became an important strategic element, with the aim to demoralize the population. By the strategists it was called "moral bombing". This was the strategy followed by the leaders of nations claiming civility, God-fearing Christians. The British bombardment was not the first attack on cities. The Germans bombed Warsaw in 1939.

The 1942 "Area Bombing Directive" of the British government stated that the main targets of the bombardment were to be the densely populated cities. Lists of German cities were prepared by size, by structural characteristics, by street layouts and by the size of the population. Research had been conducted on the effectiveness of explosive and firebombs on the mainly wood-framed old structures. Tests had been carried out on spreading fire by the generated air turbulence in narrow streets. Replicas of cities had been erected and burned. The results were clear; firebombs were more effective than the explosive bombs. The combination of the two was the solution to wipe off cities and towns. Of an early version of the napalm bomb 3,000,000 were dropped on Germany. Later came the magnesium bar, of which 80,000,000 were dropped on German cities. It burned for about eight minutes at extremely high temperature, and was virtually inextinguishable. I had seen them and the devastation they caused in Dresden and in Nürnberg. On February 13–14, 1945 in the air raids on Dresden 650,000 firebombs have been dropped. The number of victims in the German reports was 200,000, almost all refugees, women and children who arrived there fleeing from the advancing Russians. They had no place to hide from the bombs. The firestorm swept them, the extreme heat baked them. They were burned alive in the streets and parks. It was pure terror, a horrible war crime. On March 17, 1945, only weeks before the end of the war, 1100 tons of explosive bombs and 300,000 firebombs hit the city of Würzburg, totally destroying it. The technique of mass killing and destruction of cities had been perfected. Airplanes and bombs had been produced in enormous numbers, people to fly the planes and drop the bombs were trained and indoctrinated. During the war 2,700,000 tons of bombs exploded over Europe, of which nearly one half were dropped over Germany. On March 23, 1945 the small town of Dinslaken was severely bombed by Americans, dropping phosphorous and explosive bombs, killing 700 people, mostly women and children, almost the entire population. The low flying fighter-bombers strafed those who were fleeing to the nearby forest. This was just one of the thousands of tragic cases. In the bombing campaign on German cities nearly 600,000 were killed, millions became homeless. Hundreds of cities and towns were destroyed, burned, turning irreplaceable cultural and historic treasures into rubble.

The German air-war against Britain was also terrorism, as it was directed against the civilian population. The firing of the V2 and V1 missiles (The letter V stands for the word "Vergeltungswaffe" or retaliatory weapon.) fired on large cities, intended to be Germany's "moral bombing", killing and wounding thousands. The German leadership was gloating over their successes, reporting: "London burns", "Death and destruction in London", "The city will be erased."

Some of the pilots and airmen who after the war saw what devastation bombing did on the German cities, were shocked. Some said that they did not know that they were bombing civilians. They thought that they were bombing ammunition and weapon factories. Some argued: "Where could we go to express our doubts? Had we considered it immoral, and said so to our commander, and refused to do it, what would have been the consequence? Court marshal." I can accept such an argument, as it was the case on all sides. But I have to add the question mark to the excuses that they did not know that the targets were cities, not just the industrial or military areas, but also the residential city centers and the large outskirts where the laborers lived. There could be an alibi in the nightly attacks, when only the light of the dropped flares illuminated the targets, but not in the daylight attacks.

My small hometown in Hungary, which had no military installations, was the target of three terror bombings. In August of 1944, at bright daylight, a low flying American bomber dropped bombs on a soccer field, where boys were playing a game. I had seen body-parts of the boys hanging on trees. In October of 1944 several bombs with time-delay ignition were dropped on the center of the town. One bomb bore in the ground in front of the soup kitchen for refugees and wounded soldiers where my mother as volunteer was working. Hours later came huge explosions causing much destruction. In January 1945, at daylight the entire downtown was leveled by American bombs, killing many. It was terrorism. On December 6, 1944 the passenger train on which I was riding was attacked by American fighter-bombers, repeatedly strafing the fleeing passengers, I among them. It was a massacre. The planes were flying at treetop level, they could see who the targets were.

Terror bombing did reach the French as well, who as ally of the Allies under German occupation—and the one to be liberated—suffered immensely under the British and American bombardment. Cities and towns were destroyed, tens of thousands French women and children were killed. During my stays in France twenty years after the war—not revealing my American identity—I heard endless outbursts of resentment, claiming that they suffered more casualties and more destruction by the American and British bombing than by the occupying Germans. I heard stories that bombings came after the Germans withdrew from the cities and towns. They called the airmen "Bastards". Having heard the horror stories, I could understand why many Frenchmen refuse to use the English language, even if they could speak it.

The British Air-marshal Arthur Harris—the much-praised hero—was the principal architect of the European air-war. In the last months of the war, when the allied victory was certain, he ordered another wave of terror bombing on the already devastated German cities. He wrote that he wanted to destroy once again the already destroyed cities, just to punish the people. Most everything burnable was already in ashes, and only heavy explosive bombs could be effective on the rubble, of which, for this purpose he had made plenty available. According to recently released reports, since 1943 existed a British designed and American manufactured Anthrax bomb. It was filled with the deadly chemical, which could kill all living creatures in a 2.5 square kilometer area. Reports state that Churchill was enthusiastic about it. What prevented its use was the planned invasion of the German land.

In the summer of 1944, I was among the first to arrive to the crash-site of an American bomber. Not far from the burning pile of the wreckage on the ground sat the only surviving airman. He jumped with his parachute just before the plane nose-dived. He was a good-looking young man with shiny, curly hair, trembling and shaking. The other members of the crew were in the burning wreckage. After terror bombing a city somewhere in Germany they were on the way to their home base. The angry villagers gathering at the site called him an "Air-bandit", and wanted to kill him. During the nightly raids millions of small phosphor-coated sheets have been dropped by the planes, which by daylight ignited, burning down barns and homes, igniting the wheat and rye fields. There were grounds for hatred.

What was the role of this young American in a brutal war? Was he a terrorist, or was he the stooge of the terrorists? Most certainly he did not view himself as either. He was a soldier—whether volunteer or drafted—after thorough
indoctrination believing that he was fulfilling his patriotic duty by serving on a
bomber. He was led to believe that killing the enemy—whether civilian or
military—was morally right, and was strategically necessary. Although on his
last flight at daylight he could see the city below, he may have thought that it
was a huge military compound or an industrial plant. But even if he realized
that the target was a city with hundreds of thousands of residents, it was still
the enemy. Was he a combatant facing another combatant? For some a debatable issue. He was a member of the crew on a heavily armed airplane, carrying
tons of bombs to kill unarmed civilians. Quite likely he was not the commander of the plane, therefore, it was not his role to order the releasing of the
bombs. But, even if he was the one who pulled the lever, he followed command. What was the jeopardy that he faced? There were two; the German
fighter planes and the anti-aircraft guns. If he was a gunner, and fired at a
German fighter plane, he faced another combatant. One might say it was a
"fair game". Actually that was what brought him down to the ground. For targeting the anti-aircraft batteries—but not the city sectors—the fair game issue
could still be applied. The reality was, however, that in most cases the anti-aircraft batteries were not the primary target, only the residential and industrial
sectors were. There are also arguments claiming that in Germany during the
war almost everybody was in some sort of military service, therefore, almost
everybody could be viewed as combatant. The argument might be subject
among the strategists around a conference table, but in reality it cannot stand.
Traditionally wars have been fought by soldiers facing each other on battlefields. Technology changed that by the introduction of airplanes and missiles.
Air-war brought the horror from the foxholes to the homes of the combatants,
attacking and killing their families. In the Second World War nearly twice as
many civilians perished behind the fronts than soldiers on the fronts. Inarguably, air-war became the strategic tool of international terrorism, and the
strategists who applied it were international terrorists.

While those tragedies were happening, in the secret laboratories in America, in Britain and in Germany the best brains were working on the nuclear
bomb. It was a mad rush for an even more devastating weapon. The technique
of air-war as a strategic element in international affairs had nearly been perfected. The sophisticated airplanes can deliver the deadly blow anywhere in
the world. Missiles loaded with the devastating nuclear warheads can erase any

cities. And that is not a monopoly for anyone anymore. There are several countries, which have sophisticated airplanes and nuclear warhead carrying missiles. America the once assumed safe place became vulnerable, its cities—just like the German cities were—can be turned into flaming ruins, can be wiped off the ground. Co-extinction as an act of international terrorism became technically possible.

RACIAL-POLITICAL TERROR.

Racial-political terror came in my life in three stages. The first was under the Bolshevik rule in 1919 in Hungary, which I have experienced indirectly through my parents, as I was born after it. The second came under the Nazi's reign in the chaotic last months of the Second World War. The third reigned under Bolshevism between 1948 and 1956. I use the term "Bolshevism" rather than "Communism", with which I am differentiating the ideology from the ruthless application of its grotesquely distorted social-political concepts. Bolshevik and Nazi terror applied psychological bombardment, targeting the mind of the masses.

I experienced Nazi terrorism in Hungary in the last year of the Second World War, when part of the country was already under Soviet occupation, the rest was under German military control, when the daily bombing raids on cities and villages frightened the people, when the streets and roads were crowded by fleeing refugees. In that chaotic and desperate environment, under tight military control, reigned the terror. The political opposition was liquidated, and any disobedience was mercilessly crushed. In a racial-political confrontation the Jews—including women and children—as non-trustable aliens—were removed from the communities and were shipped to concentration camps. Forcefully taking them from their homes, subjecting them to rude treatment was terrorism. I had seen freight car trains side-by-side, one loaded with fleeing refugees, the other with deported Jews. Both were the victims of war terror. That was from mid-1944 to early 1945.

Between 1948 and 1956 came another wave of race-motivated terror wrapped in the camouflage of Communist ideology. The eight years of living in constant fear had its effect on our soul, mind and body. The terrorist rulers came to power in 1948, barely three years after the war ended. They were a clique that arrived in 1945 with the Soviet occupation forces, prepared for a take-over, but in the first post-war election in 1946 the Communist Party—which they claimed to represent—received a very small percentage of the votes, not giving the legitimacy for ruling. Undermining the social political structure began, in what was called the "salami tactics". First came the liquidation of the remnants of the wartime regime. That was quick and easy. Then came the neutralization of the upper social-class. It was also easy, as they were powerless. They were deported to the countryside, where they had to do manual work in agriculture. Their homes were given to the newly arising Bolshevik party elite. The churches having been influential on the public became targets. The respected leaders were accused of treason, or of other fabricated crimes, were subjected to show-trials, and were jailed. The clergy was infiltrated by agents, who in service of the ruling clique controlled the affairs from within. The ground had been prepared for a take-over. In a coup d'état the key political leaders of the opposition either were arrested, or had to flee. The next step was nationalization—better said confiscation—of industry, commerce and private properties. To assure that no counter action could arise, the State Security Authority as a terror institute was extended on the pattern of the Soviet KGB. The party organization from the highest to the ground level was set up. Every factory, office or residential block had a party watchdog. The party secretaries were the key trusties, for they controlled the communities. As it has been found during the 1956 Revolution, extensive reporting on people went to the State Security Agency, myself included. Men who had military or civilian medals for bravery threw those in the Danube. Documents showing recognition for service in the pre-war years had been burned. Papers showing family nobility had been destroyed by the owners. The entire nation was in the grip of the clique. We lived in panic. Uncovered conspiracies, capturing foreign agents, prevented capitalist sabotages dominated the daily news. Not only the "class aliens" but also party insiders were under watch. Many of the ideological faithful fell victim, including those who for long years had served the Communist Party, just because they opposed the methods of the clique. Their show-trials were publicized as warnings to others. This was the pattern in all of the Eastern European countries.

Who were the principle terrorists? Mainly fanatical Jewish radicals. They recruited their cadres, put them in charge of the cells of the society. Recruited the sub-agents, gave them titles and power, with which their loyalty or obedience was gained. Was their system based on ideological principles, or was it conspiratorial opportunism? I believe the latter was the case, which was proved by the sudden collapse of the seemingly invincible organization during the 1956 Revolution. Within hours and days the thoroughly controlled party institution disintegrated, and the party leadership disappeared. Not even the presence of the huge Soviet army could prevent it. It took nearly four decades and major political changes to allow the surfacing of the ugly matters. Many of those whose guilt was obvious, hurriedly changed colors, became "Democrats", or left the country. Their political activities were concentrated on preventing investigations of their past, and on blocking the releasing of the evidence of their committed crimes. When it became obvious that the revelation process could not be stopped, they used unusual means to force the new regimes not to conduct any investigations against them. Immunity had been granted for the terrorists. Some of the evidence is now exhibited in a museum called "The House of Terror" in Budapest.

What was it that led some of the Jews to become the leaders—or accomplices—in a terrorist organization? Was it the attraction of an ideology? It is true that Communism, as an ideology was the thesis of mainly Jewish thinkers. Was it a biblical missionary self-consciousness of "God's chosen people" to become the rulers of the world? Based on the events of the past, racial self-consciousness as a factor cannot be ruled out. Was it a revengeful response to their wartime persecution? I did hear such arguments from Jews.

Terrorism as a major warfare with extremely dangerous consequences is practiced on all sides, paving the way to co-extinction. Government officials conducting terrorism from plush offices, generals in fancy military uniforms conducting wars are just as much terrorists as the ragtag fighters with their faces covered with a kerchief. The strategists and politicians—be those German, British, American or whatever else—who plan and conduct wars or terrorism are all war criminals.

After what I had seen and experienced, that is my judgement.

THE MISPLACED
RECRIMINATION.

"Truth is the first victim of wars"—is an often-quoted phrase. It is not an abstract thesis but a reality, as its validity had been well proved in recent history. If truth could have prevailed, there would quite likely not have been a Second World War, a Korean War, a Vietnam War, an Iraq War, nor any other wars. But, truth fell victim to arrogance, lies became the "truth" and millions had to suffer and perish because of it.

Much had been written about the shameful fallacies of governments and societies leading nations into wars, but regrettably those have not been—and still are not—mentioned in the text books of history in the sense of national self-examination. The lies as causes of wars are always found on the other side, the crimes are always committed by the foe. The victorious do not want to blemish their self-glorified, righteous image, do not want to allow the diminishing of the fervor of patriotism, do not want to weaken the resolve of the people in supporting the government. For them self-adulation is the course. Their lies enter history as the truth. For the vanquished the painful realization of the defeat and recrimination is the ordeal. Their lies, and also the lies of the victors are entered as indictments to be used against them. Lies start wars, lies keep the warrior's fighting spirit, and lies prevail in condemning the defeated. That is the reality.

Are wars the play-fields of gangs of gung-ho mercenaries killing each other? Are wars the outpouring patriotism of conscience-driven young men and women in fear for their own or for their countrymen's freedom and security? No, wars are premeditated mass-murders, the culmination of systematically implanted lies in agitating propaganda by governments against other nations, injecting the notion in the minds that killing and destruction can be acts of patriotism. Wars are crimes against humanity committed by the high-est-ranking government officials. That is the reality!

At the beginning of the 21st Century once again history was repeating itself, lies were poisoning the minds, a horrible war was in the making. The strategy had been set in motion by governments with the help of the immoral propagandists and the unscrupulous media, systematically feeding misinfor-mation to the culpable public, demonizing the leaders of the targeted nations, stirring up hatred toward anyone who was not willing to follow their course. The institutions behind the strategy were the same, and the tactics were the same as those were in the Second World War and in all of the other recent wars. Lies and distortions—whatever those might be—were presented to the public by highest level government officials, even if those were proved wrong by contradicting evidence, or were debatable because of the absence of sup-porting evidence. But, nevertheless, the well-working old strategy of repeating the same lies until they become believable was being applied.

The American public was bombarded with well-orchestrated propaganda, claiming frightening consequences if Iraq was not attacked. The American Secretary of State in a speech at the United Nations presented—what he called—"indisputable evidence" of the imminent threat that Iraq represented to America. One has to ask; was it a realistic argument that Iraq, that since 1991 had been under constant surveillance by satellites, by reconnaissance flights and on the ground by the UN inspectors, could amass the military-technological advances to represent a threat to America? Was it conceivable that with roaming their country by the UN inspectors the Iraqis could hide the rather sizable projects necessary to build complex weaponry? Was the aerial photo of an allegedly existing terrorist training camp somewhere in that part of Iraq, which was not under Saddam's control a convincing evidence of Iraq's involvement in the terrorist war? Was the alleged medical treatment of an alleged Al-Quaida member in an Iraqi hospital—presumably guarded by his fellow fighters—a clear proof of Iraq's alliance with them? Not even the Secre-tary of State could claim that Iraq had supported Al-Quaida. Was an alleged, secretly recorded telephone conversation between two Iraqi military men a provable evidence of hidden chemical and biological weapons? Were the pic-tures of a well exposed missile launching structure and a few empty shells of an outdated Soviet-era short-range rocket launcher the real proof of the Iraqi threat to America, as was claimed by the Secretary of State? "Convincing evi-dence" can be fabricated for serving the cause of the belligerent. Meaningless "findings" can be exaggerated—as was the case in the Secretary of State's accusatory claims—some of which allegedly came from a doctoral dissertation of a student from the 1980s. The letter that was presented as proof of Iraq's purchase of uranium for weapon production was proved to be a forgery. For anyone with a minimal sense of objectivity the purported "evidence "was not only unbelievable, but was laughable. That is how the representatives of most member-states of the UN saw the claims. Nevertheless, the American government officials presented those on every forum, and on that basis dragged this nation into a horrible war. Where did all the "intelligence reports" come from that the government used in justification of a war against Iraq? Some came from British sources, like the "45 minutes" story, which eventually became discredited. Most of the member states of the UN Security Council did not accept the "evidence" as provable facts. They had good reasons for that. They wanted to avoid a war, and wanted the continuation of the peaceful disarmament. Since the early urgent calls for the war came from Israeli officials and from Jewish-American activists, could—perhaps—they be the suppliers of those false reports?

Let us assume that some of the allegations made by the American Secretary of State were real. He did show photos taken by spy-satellites of certain objects, therefore, their locations had to be known. It is claimed that our spy-satellites and spy-planes are equipped with cameras that can take extremely sharp pictures. I saw on computer screen a Russian satellite photo of Seattle, zooming in on it I could see my house and my car parked in the driveway. I assume our reconnaissance techniques are as good, if not better than what the Russians have, therefore, the Iraqis could not hide anything from the CIA. Would it not have been logical to send the UN inspectors to examine each case right on the spot? If those installations did exist—and if they did violate the UN resolutions and represented a threat to America or to Israel—would it not have been reasonable to destroy them without killing thousands, and without destroying anything else? Iraq was not a closed country; the UN inspectors could go wherever they wanted. The means of investigating Iraq's military arsenal by the UN were in place, and could be expanded. Nobody could make a plausible argument for a war. Following the war, the best investigating teams were sent to Iraq to find the much propagated weapons of mass destruction. None have been found.

The opposition to the war was broad, tens of thousands marched in protest in the streets of Europe and America, I among them. But, for the warmongers interviewed on the radio and television the world-opinion was irrelevant. One can ask why Richard Perle did go on the television in the evening of the UN session where the Secretary of State presented his speech, to instigate for the war? He said that nobody could stop "us" in waging a war against Saddam. On whose behalf was he speaking? At that time he was not a government official. Who was he referring to? Who were those "us"? Why did he attack all those nations that wanted to avoid the war. Why were the opponents of the war called "Anti-Semites"? Whose war was it? Mr. Perle acknowledged that the speech of Secretary of State could not change the positions of the nations, which opposed the war, but for him those nations were "irrelevant". Mr. Wolfowitz, another ardent promoter and planner of the war, who was often called the "Brain of the Pentagon", made enticing predictions that the war was going to be easy, the Iraqi people were going to receive the Americans as liberators, and it was going to be cheap because the Iraqi oil will pay for it. His academic wisdom was dead wrong. (Or, was it an element of a great conspiracy?) While I am writing these lines years after the starting of the war, young American soldiers still are dying in Iraq, and there is no end in sight for the battle. In some political circles the recurrence of another Vietnam War is on the agenda.

In the months and weeks leading to the war Perle, Wolfowitz, Lieberman and their peers were frequently on the television screen arrogantly agitating. They dominated the daily news as if they were the principal policy makers. (It appears now that they really were). After the great fiasco in not winning the hearts of the "liberated" Iraqis, after the continued loss of young American soldiers, and after the surfacing of the lies and of the horrors committed by Americans to their captives, Perle, Wolfowitz and the other warmongers disappeared from the television. Most likely they are working behind closed doors on the strategy of how and whom to blame for their lies and their fiasco, and how to avert any responsibility for this great human tragedy. I find it almost inconceivable that the American public tolerates such dishonorable behavior.

The undeniable cause of the tension in the Middle East is the Israeli-Palestinian conflict. Iraq was the most industrious and militarily the most advanced Arab country that stood behind the Palestinians in their uprising against the Israeli occupation. Iraq was viewed by the propagators for the war as the enemy of Israel. Iraq was presented to the American public as a threat not only to Israel, but also a direct threat to America. Remarkably, not long earlier, when in war against Iran the ardent enemy of America, Iraq enjoyed the military favors received from America, sending none other than Rumsfeld to Saddam for negotiating on military assistance. That was the case of the "The enemy of my enemy is my friend". But there was another case; "The enemy of my friend is also my enemy." On the insistence of the Israeli government and of its American allies the American government was compelled—and seemingly also was willing—to change course and conduct a hostile propaganda campaign and a war against Iraq. For the American public a "Casus Belli" had to be presented. The propaganda machinery was set in motion, and the flow of the lies began, first at a moderate tempo, but later at an intensified rate. Some of the stated claims were self-contradictory, some have been contradicted by government agencies, some ended in the junkyard of absurdities. The more insupportable the claims became, the more intense the introduction of new claims was. In an attempted cover-up for the obvious lies, just before the outbreak of the war an ultimatum had been issued to the Iraqis, wanting them to publicly acknowledge that they were the ones who lied. It didn't work.

Under the American military occupation of Iraq thousands of American inspectors under the leadership of experts were sent to search for the prohibited weapons. The government officials, including the President, assured the public that the weapons of mass destruction—the claimed reasons for the war—were to be found. After several months of intensive search the leader of the investigation team reported that they could not find any trace of weapons of mass destruction. He concluded that, although Iraq at earlier times might have had programs for the development of such weapons, in the years preceding the 2003 war no such programs have been actively pursued. His final report clearly contradicted the government's claims. The media in defense—and most likely under the urging of the government—flashed the news on finding a few pieces of rusty projectiles, adding the claim that those "could have been loaded with chemical substance". Some of the officials quickly proclaimed those projectiles as clear proof of Iraq's guilt and of the correctness of the government's claims, only to be contradicted by the media, admitting that those were just old, conventional ammunition. In rapid succession all the claims used for the justification of the war collapsed. The American government as the "World Leader" lost its credibility. But, instead of admitting the horrible blunder for which thousands of Iraqis and young Americans had to lose their lives, for which millions of Iraqis had to endure humiliation and suffering, the American government officials are trying to avoid any responsibility. They claim now that they were misled by the false intelligence they received. But, in fact it was the CIA that questioned—or even denied—some of the claims used by the Secretary of State in his infamous speech at the UN. If the CIA was not the source of the false information, if the British intelligence was admittedly severely erroneous, if the worldwide media consistently contradicted the American claims, then what or who was the source of intelligence on which the President and the government based their waging the war?

Both the President and the Vice President continued to claim that Iraq was an imminent danger to America, therefore, had to be attacked. In fact it was the President who repeatedly misled the American public, among others claiming that Iraq was defiant by not allowing the entry of the UN inspectors. The truth is that the inspectors were allowed to search for the prohibited weapons, and it was the President who ordered them out just before the Iraq invasion. Lies upon lies were piled by the highest level of the government. Now, after the great tragedy of the war, after the horrible destruction, and under the still ongoing bloody hostilities, the President argues that waging the war against Iraq was right, and the world is a better place without Saddam. But, there is a long list of those without whom the world could be an even better place. That list includes those who don't hesitate to resort to war, even when there are peaceful solutions available.

The doubts, the disbelief, the questioning of the government's actions by us ordinary citizens are often rebuffed by the officials as coming from the uninformed and the ignorant. It is inarguably true that we don't receive the secrets briefings by the CIA, we do not have an insight into the coded reports of the murky diplomacy, which leaves us at the mercy of the news releases by the government and by the often censured—or at least "massaged" media. So, if our opinions with which among ourselves, and from time-to-time also publicly, we express our views are based on the available information are proved wrong, that is forgivable. If in the interpretation of the news we add our personal thoughts and feelings, which might be speculative, we are not violating a trust that is granted by our listeners. Those are matters of negligible significance without any consequences. The official statements and words of the President and of the government officials are entirely different matters. Those are not insignificant personal opinions aired in casual conversations, but are highly consequential policy matters. A complex array of institutions serve them constantly with the latest secret reports, acquired with the most sophisticated technology by trained specialists. The incoming reports are analyzed, screened and evaluated before being delivered to the desk of the President. That is not a haphazard process conducted by amateurs. There is no room left for personal interpretation, or for personal opinions and feelings. Supposedly, only the proven facts reach the highest officials. If—as the case seems to be—the President claims that he was misled by the received reports, then we the uninformed and ignorant might raise questions: Who misled him and why? What was the source whose influence prevailed? Why were the warnings by our well-meaning allies not considered? Why did the President—and also the other officials—relegate our allies to "irrelevance"?

The recent revelations about the arguments leading to the war give us a frightening picture of how this nation's and the world's affairs are conducted by our government. This is one of the rare cases when the officials are caught in lying while the war is still being fought. Usually it takes half a century after a war when slowly the facts emerge. Not this time. Even before the outbreak of the war there were many critics who—based on well-proved facts—questioned its justification. The official in charge of national security with reference to the September 11, 2001 attack stated that there was a clear connection between al-Qaida and Saddam. So far nothing has been found that would substantiate that. At the UN Security Council Meeting the Secretary of State presented the "evidence" on the existence of weapons of mass destruction possessed by Iraq, which represented the direct threat to America. After months and years of search by thousands of inspectors none of such weapons have been found. The Vice-President in March of 2003 claimed to have had proven facts for the existence of weapons of mass-destruction in the hands of the Iraqis. Now, he talks about "possible programs" for the development of such weapons. The President in February of 2003 warned the Americans about the Iraqi's drones with which Saddam could spray the deadly biological and chemical agents. The inspectors found the "deadly drone"; a small model plane made of balsa wood that could carry for a short distance a video camera for reconnaissance. Then came the official statement from the British Prime Minister on the "45 minute readiness" of the Iraqi missiles to deliver the chemical and biological weapons. The President and government officials quickly grabbed the "indisputable evidence", which turned out to be totally false. The US government officials still claimed to have knowledge of the existence of the weapons of mass destruction. New inspection teams with thousands of experts were sent to search, but returned empty-handed. The head of the inspection program in his report concluded "We were all wrong". Now, there is another phase of the blames and counter-claims, this time targeting the intelligence agencies. If the CIA, the most important intelligence institution contradicts, or declines to substantiate claims, then not that agency, but the White House and the government have to be investigated.

The diversionary tactics of the warmongers in clearing themselves from any responsibility for the great tragedy of killing thousands of Iraqis and Americans, for the suffering of millions on several continents, for the fear in which we have to live every day, began. A new theater had been set up to attract the attention of the public away from the real issues. The CIA, the FBI, the White House, the ex- and present government officials were dragged to the "9/11 Investigating Committee". The accusations were flying, the confrontation between the government agencies and their officials became a public spectacle. But where were the principal agitators? Were Perle, Wolfowitz, Lieberman, Rumsfeld or any of the other warmongers called to the Committee to reveal publicly, under oath, their roles in the war? No, they could not be questioned, they can hide behind an invisible shield.

The stew of the lies is boiling, bringing newer and newer revelations. The accusations are broadening first on departmental and agency levels, which quite likely can grow into a personal battle. Our allies and also our foes are watching that with bewilderment. The Middle-Eastern turmoil is not subsiding, young Americans and Iraqis are still dying, and at home we are still living in constant fear of terror. But the people are praising the officials who lied to them, celebrate a non existing victory, not seeing the tragedy that was brought upon them by their own government and by the immoral agents of a great conspiracy.

Quo vadis America?

THE USA PATRIOT ACT.

"The (...) can ask the secret court for a warrant to monitor activities of anyone sus-pected of terrorism, and is given new authority for searches.

Using secret warrant the (...) can break into offices or homes to conduct secret searches. Agents don't need probable cause, just a suspicion of involvement in a crime. There would be no notification of what was found in the secret search."

What is left out between the brackets? Nazi "GESTAPO", or Bolshevik "NKVD"? No, neither, although both would fit well. What is the date of the Act? Is it the dark years of the 1940s? No, it is 2001. Is the place of issuing Hitler's Germany or Stalin's Soviet Union? No, it is the United States of America. The empowered authority is the FBI, the document is "THE USA PATRIOT ACT", the issuer is the Attorney General of the United States. It defines domestic terrorism as "an attempt to intimidate or coerce the civilian population or change the policy of the government by intimidation or coer-cion." Those are frightening words, on the basis of which even the most mor-alistic criticism can be construed as domestic terrorism.

I was shocked by the events of September 11, and I am also concerned about what might happen in the future. I am also frightened by the President's words: "Either with us or with the terrorists." Where do those of us belong who neither feel with those who committed the attack, nor want to be sub-jected to break-ins by government agents just on suspicion, with the approval of "secret courts"?

"No notification of what was found in the secret search" sounds to me like the replay of the secret searches of the AVH—the terror arm of the Bolshevik regime in Hungary in the worst days of the Stalin era—when the "evidence" discovered in the drawers was often planted by the searchers themselves. Agents are agents, no matter under what government they serve. They are eager to perform, to deliver result. That is their duty, and that is what brings

recognition and promotion. We heard about such cases here in America even at peacetime. What about in a crisis, in a national emergency?

I frequently drive by the building of the Immigration and Naturalization Service in Seattle. This is the place where hundreds of people are being held under THE PATRIOT ACT, on the basis of being reported by over-zealous patriots who see terrorists in everyone who does not wave the flag, or by angry neighbors who did not like to have Arab-looking people next to their place, or by someone who did not like to hear the angry words of those whose friends or relatives were being killed by American bombs in their own home country, or by someone who believed that those not agreeing to their views are involved in terrorism no matter how minor it is, or were reported by someone on reading unpatriotic books, or were sent there by secret courts that nobody knows what it is. There could also be terrorists among them, who in their desperation were driven to violence. I believe there is one thing certain; all those locked up became our ardent enemies.

Governments, although democratically elected, but exercising their power without transparency, using secret courts, secret warrants and secret searches, spying on the citizens through listening to their telephone calls, collecting information on what books they buy and read, treating open and valid criticism, descent, intimidation and coercion on political issues as "domestic terrorism", are just as totalitarian as any of the much deplored dictatorships. Bolshevism, the worst terrorism of our times called itself "People Democracy", and practiced all the above horrifying tactics, which are parts of the U.S. PATRIOT ACT.

In a bookstore I saw the following sign:

"WARNING.

What does the USA PATRIOT ACT mean for the bookstore and library patrons:
Under Section 215 of the FEDERAL US PATRIOT ACT (Public Law 107-56),
records of books and other materials you purchase from bookstore or borrow from a
library may be obtained by federal agents. The Federal Law prohibits booksellers
and librarians from informing you if records about you have been obtained by federal
agents. Questions about this policy should be directed to: Attorney General John Ash-

*croft, Department of Justice, Washington, DC 20530-0001, (202) 352-1555,
askdoj@usdoj.gov."*

Most of the bookstores obediently obliged, without warning the customers.

FAREWELL TO LIBERTY.
(A reflection on the PATRIOT ACT)

You, magnificent but elusive ideal,
that touches the human soul and inspires the human mind,
for which mankind yearned and cried out in revolts,
I am saying farewell to you.

Not that I really knew you,
not that other than in my burning enthusiasm
while marching in the 1956 Hungarian Revolt
I have felt your wonderful presence.
But now, when once again
dictatorial laws are curtailing my rights,
when for writing or reading a book
my freedom might be lost,
fear is settling upon my soul for losing the hope
that someday I could enjoy your embrace.

I sense the return of the dark times which were part of my life,
when you have been accused as the subversive,
when you were shown as the evil of mankind,
when you and those who followed your principles
have been treated as social enemies,
when the government officials and the demagogues claimed
that your noble principles were dangerous,

therefore, had to be erased,
when instead of treating the causes of the social ills
with rationality, compassion, in peace,
the governments empowered their agents
to extinguish your ideals with brutal force.

Remarkably, they had an easy task.
The mindlessly loyal and proudly obedient patriots
willfully followed the evil laws,
like parrots repeated the bluffs,
enthusiastically waved the flags.
While spreading hatred and waging wars
they soothed their troubled souls
piously reading their holy books.

Yes, I had seen that myself.

Now, history once again repeats itself,
and for me, who had seen much hatred,
feverish patriotism, flaming terror,
the current events are frightening.

Why do I have to lose you yearned friend?
Why do I have to live in fear again?
The answer is much the same
as it was in the deplorable past;
mindless loyalty and proud obedience
implanted and nurtured in the minds
to assure the reign of arrogance.

Cherished Liberty,
I watch your vanishing with pain.
I wish I could save you, hold you back,
embrace you, enjoy your magnificence.
But you are pushed aside,

your principles are overwhelmed
by the loud voice of the demagogues.
You have to vanish, because you are in the way of those
who claim to be your savior,
but in their arrogance
cannot tolerate your noble principles.

Farewell to you beloved Liberty!
I mourn you yearned friend!

THE REAL ISSUES OF THE 21st CENTURY.

The current state of world-affairs casts a dark shadow on the future. The dreams for a united world are shattered, the division of mankind into opposing power-groups is rapidly developing. This division is not on the basis of ideological principles, at least not as it was in the 20th Century in Europe, when after the First World War in the chaotic political environment fundamental changes in the social order came under dictatorships in the form of Communism and National Socialism. With the defeat of Germany and its allies two major powers remained; America and the Soviet Union. The division of the world was between two ideologies; the Western Democracies and Communism, geographically concentrated in the war-torn Europe. Although, the threat of Bolshevism—which was the terrorist imposition of the grotesquely distorted communist ideology—did exist after the Second World War, the military stand-off between the major powers—both in possession of nuclear weapons—remained under control. The possibility of "Mutually Assured Destruction" compelled the strategists on both sides to refrain from major hostilities. It was the small nations' rebellion, like in Poland and Hungary in 1956, and in Czechoslovakia in 1968 against the terrorist rulers that changed the course of history. The inconclusive end of the Korean War, the less than victorious end of America's military intervention in Vietnam were other examples of the historic roles of small nations. With the disintegration of the Soviet Union the only major military power is America. In the new role it is exercising its economic and military domination.

In the 1960s the confrontation between the Arabs and the Jews has intensified. At the same time a major strategic change in the American foreign policy was enacted. The Far-East engagement, especially in Vietnam, was no longer considered as essential strategy, and a withdrawal even if it appeared as a military defeat had been concluded. As part of the same strategic move in secretive deals an accommodation with China had been arranged. The changes in the Soviet leadership resulted in decreased tension in Europe. Although for the public there were no apparent reasons given for the political changes, the shifting of the political and strategic emphasis from Europe and Asia to the Middle East became America's principal foreign policy. Under those circumstances the Israelis gained confidence and encouragement to the extent that they bombed the nuclear facilities of Iraq, with that opening the gates to ever widening hostilities, including wars. The 20th Century ended with a war, the 21st Century opened with another war against Iraq, both fought by the United States on behalf of Israel. At the same time under the American protective military umbrella for Israel, the open, bloody hostilities between the Palestinians and Israelis widened. Those were the conditions under which we entered the 21st Century, not showing any sign of reconciliation on either side. The division was based on historically ancient issues with biblical backing, mixed with racial, religious and power-political elements. The division is between the Muslim World, the Judeo-American alliance, and the new Europe. Although, Asia and especially China with its huge population and explosive industrial development is likely to become a principal political and strategic power, at the present time it is not part of the growing tension.

In the Middle-East religion as ancient human spiritual institutions became a key element of politics. The Arab-World and the worldwide followers of Islam became united by their religion against Israel and its American protector. Although the religious aspect of the conflict is denied by all sides, the realities clearly show it. The common racial-roots of the Jews and Arabs—both Semitic—exclude the racial aspect of the conflict. The roots of the confrontation between them are territorial, namely the claims by both sides for the same land, the Israelis deriving their right on biblical grounds, while the Arabs claiming it on historic and ethnographic evidence. The denial of the religious aspect of the conflict appears to be quite difficult by the fact that it expands from the Middle East to Asia and Africa, involving the Muslim population. On the Israeli side religion is only part of the issue, as the majority of both the religious and non-religious groups actively support the "Greater Israel" concept and thus the confrontational expansionist policies.

The growing division between America and Europe is rooted in America's belligerent attitude in the international matters. One example was the Balkan War, which was seen by the Europeans as an American intervention in a clearly European matter. The tension between the ethnic-religious groups of the Balkans was judged by the Europeans as a European internal affair, but not a threat to anyone outside the immediate area. America viewed—or at least argued—the case on the ground that it was the defender of the Muslim population against the Serb oppression. But, in reality the case was much more complex. It was a long ethnic-religious rivalry with nationalistic elements. On the one side the Muslim leadership wanted to establish a strictly religious society, imposing their rule on the others, or force them to move out. The Serbs as strongly nationalistic and as Eastern-Orthodox, with equal vigor wanted to preserve their controlling role. The atrocities committed by both sides were horrible, but were no justification for an equally horrible American air-war. There were also political elements, namely the Yugoslav leadership's opposition to an American domination in that region, and the possibility of the growing Russian influence in the Balkans. The Europeans wanted the entering of the United Nations in the dispute without outside military intervention. America blocked the UN involvement, and drawing the NATO into the conflict resorted to military action. The echoes of that episode are still strong in Europe, strengthening the position of those who seek a unified and peaceful Europe free of American domination. The European Union is becoming a reality, not as an anti-American power, but as an independent political, economic and strategic entity. Its expansion is underway, eventually reaching Russia and the other ex-Soviet states. Once that is accomplished, the political, economic and strategic balance could be achieved, adding to the potential of a less belligerent world.

NATO, the American controlled remnant of the Cold War set up for the defense of Europe against the Soviet threat lost its purpose. Quite rightfully the Europeans were reluctant to extend its existence without redefining its future role, especially after the Balkan War. On the American side NATO is seen as an important military strategic reserve to be used—if necessary—in the Middle-Eastern conflict. For that purpose the maneuvering to convert it from a purely European defensive to an international offensive character that can be used in any conflict, on whatever continent—as it was attempted in the case of the 2003 Iraq War—began. It became a contentious issue. The EU in a counter-move established the concept of its own, separate and independent strategic defense force. The American response was the relocating of some of the military bases from Western Europe, mainly from Germany, to Poland, Rumania and Bulgaria. Such maneuvers opened the suspicion about the ultimate intent, which might include the splitting of Europe into strategic spheres, and the building of a strategic military position against both the French-German alliance and Russia. From the American point of view relocating the military bases to countries, which after the World War were under Soviet occupation, made sense. While in some of the Central European countries the American military presence became a divisive political issue, the people in the Eastern European countries viewed the American military presence as protection against Russia, which after the Second World War occupied them, and as shield against a French-German domination. The short term effect might be rather insignificant. However, as a long term strategic move it might foreshadow the possibility—and even probability—of future confrontations.

One key issue of the 21st Century will be the world-leadership, which up-until now was in the hands of America. It was achieved and was sustained since the Second World War by America's overwhelming military power over the politically divided Europe, over the politically and economically unstable Russia, over the de-militarized Japan, and over the self-isolated China. With the turn of the Century that situation is no longer as it was. Europe is regaining its political, economic and also strategic independence. Russia grew out of the transition from the Soviet system into a self-conscious nationalistic power with an immense nuclear arsenal. Japan although still an insignificant military power, has the economic potential to restore its strategic position. China is becoming a powerful country in Asia with immense military power, including nuclear weapons. Another, up-until the turn of the Century insignificant Islamic World is also entering the stage of world events. At this time its main power is the large numbers of followers spread across continents, but the potential is there to become a major political and strategic factor. Although numerically not a significant power, but with its close alliance and decisive influence on America's politics and strategies, and with its nuclear arsenal, Israel became the key element in international matters, and might very well determine the course of events in the 21st Century.

The 2003 Iraq War, especially the events preceding it, had major impact on world politics, bringing a drastic decline in America's world-leadership position. The unprecedented war-propaganda campaign with distortions and exaggeration on the highest level, from the President to the Secretary of State at the international forums and in the media, destroyed the American leadership's credibility. The arguments for the military intervention in Iraq—instead of maintaining the UN's close surveillance and search for the alleged weapons of mass destruction—became a major irritant to many countries. The mindless and seemingly endless switching from one unsubstantiated accusation to another made America's position unsustainable. Not having found the claimed weapons of mass destruction proved the correctness of the war-opponents, and shattered the credibility of the American leadership. The general consensus of the world-opinion was that America under Jewish pressure wanted to have the war, irrespective of whether there was or was not any proof of a threat by Iraq. America's response to the cautionary attitude of many nations was intolerable arrogance, calling the world-community "Irrelevant". With such impertinence and disrespect for the world-community, together with the loss of the essential credibility, America's world-leadership role diminished, and will be difficult to restore in the 21st Century. That can bring the world to the brink of a cataclysm. A mighty and arrogant military power that is losing credibility can take only one course; become a tyrannous dictatorship. That is the present course on which America's relationship with the nations of the world is evolving. Can we Americans sustain our existence in the illusion that under the utopia of a non-existent "Star-Wars" umbrella we are safe? This is what the leadership is telling us. The reality is that we are vulnerable, that we also can be destroyed while we try to destroy others. This is a dire prediction, but not an impossibility. It is not too late to reverse the course, but it has to be done soon. The world-community cannot tolerate the impertinent arrogance with which it is treated, cannot accept the ruling of blind fanatics, and cannot exist under constant threats.

The real issues of the 21st Century will quite likely be the same as were in the 20th Century, namely, the confrontation of the Jewish-controlled interest groups as political, economic racial powers, with the by them not controlled, or not influenced racial and political entities, including the Arab and Muslim World, and also the newly emerging Europe. The confrontations are likely to continue. With the Second World War the Jewish power in America grew to the point, where it is now virtually controls America's foreign policy and its military strategies. This is clearly evidenced by the events in the Middle East and by the tense relationship with some of the European countries, mainly on issues regarding the Middle East. There are signs of fundamental changes in the American and European relationship, which are caused by the pro-Israel and anti-Islam policies of America. The close geographical location of Europe to the Middle East and North Africa with the natural resources, the huge markets for the European industrial products are incentives for maintaining normal, peaceful contact. Politically and socially it is in the interest of the European countries with large Muslim population to keep the racial, political and cultural affairs in balance. It is only logical that they oppose any action that could jeopardize the given conditions. Europe is regaining its rightful place in the world affairs politically and economically, which brings with itself the determination to establish a strategic position as well. It is not in an anti-American sense, but is intended to provide the means for independent decision-making. These changes are viewed by some Jewish groups as dangerously undermining the monopolistic American power position in world affairs, especially in view of America's critical role in the defense of the Jewish interest. The European political and economic power-block at this time is the French-German alliance, which pursues the goals of an integrated Europe. The expansion of the European Union to the other countries, eventually including Russia, could form an enormous economic, political and military-strategic entity that could on an equal power base influence the world-politics of the future. Political and strategic maneuvers had been made and are being made by America to offset the French-German power position by establishing special strategic relationships.

I assume that many of the Jewish politicians and their American supporters see the possibilities of the future in somewhat the same light as I outlined it, therefore, are determined to achieve their goals while America still is the sole dominant military power. Their actions show a high-degree of urgency on the issues. On Jewish insistence Iraq had to be attacked. Iran, Syria and some other Arab and Muslim countries are on the enemy-list and most likely will be attacked. The Muslim institutions are targeted worldwide. While the Middle-Eastern tension is brewing, the diplomatic games in the Far East are in a dynamic state. China as a world power eventually will enter world-politics in a forceful manner. It is a nuclear power, and under the dangerous developments in the world it will be compelled to increase its arsenals. The Asiatic countries being fearful of major upheavals take a position similar to the European countries. They consider their own quarrels as their internal affairs, not allowing outside intervention.

The immediate real issue for the first decades of the 21st Century will most likely be the Middle-East crisis and its worldwide repercussions, which might lead to serious confrontations and even catastrophic wars with the Muslim World. Consequently, the relationship between Europe and America might deteriorate to the point where the normal economic and strategic cooperation could turn into confrontation, not excluding highly dangerous hostilities. The "Nuclear card" which since the Second World War has not been played, in a final showdown might be used.

THE IMAGES OF CO-EXTINCTION.

(My essay from 2003)

The television screen changed. In one scene I saw a clean-shaven young man wearing a sophisticated coverall-like outfit with attached gadgets and wires hanging from it, under his arm a high-tech helmet. He was an American pilot climbing in the cockpit of a multi-million dollar warplane, ready for a "Mission" against an already war-devastated, backward Afghanistan. The other scene was a bearded young man wearing a—by American standard—primitive garb, a turban-like twisted rag covering his head, on his shoulder a rifle, climbing onto a seemingly old tank. Those were the images of two battlers, and also of two societies—the modern American and the backward Taliban—both pumped up with "missionary" convictions, both believing that they are the saviors of sacred human institutions. One was convinced—or was led to believe—that he was fighting for the Western Civilization, defending it against the menace of the hateful religious fanatics of Taliban. The other in his religious fanaticism was ready to sacrifice himself in the struggle against the "Infidels". Both were heroes for their own people, and were the terrorists for their opponents.

The American propaganda carefully avoiding any direct reference to the religious aspect of the conflict—not calling it anymore a "Crusade", as it was called in the early days of the war—in a hidden way, but by all means attempted to divert the attention from the real issues, systematically injecting the religious aspect. Religious extremism is not new to America, where cults, sects and even main-line churches have not only spiritual, but also political clout. Religiosity became politicking, and politicking became religiosity. That is probably true in the Islamic world as well. Taliban is in general considered as the extremism in Islam. In reality the issues in the "America Strikes Back" war in Afghanistan were rooted in the deep conflict between two "Religious-Political Nationalism"; the Islamic-Arab and the Judeo-Zionist, extending the conflict to their respective benefactors; the global Islamic world, and the Judeo-Christian America. The description "Religious-Political Nationalism" characterizes the nature of the conflict—deep religiosity intertwined with politics and nationalism, or politics and nationalism intertwined with religiosity, making religion and politics inseparable, forming vehemently opposing cultures—Islam vs. Judaism and Christianity—all fanatically pursuing their respective political-nationalistic interests and religious aspirations. This is not a new historic phenomenon, as most wars and conflicts had all three elements—nationalism, politics and religion. While the war against the Soviet Union was viewed in the West as purely ideological—Bolshevism vs. Nazism—for the Europeans it also had a religious aspect; defending western Christianity against atheistic Bolshevism. With the religious aspect of the war, even the ideologically and politically indifferent population could be drawn into the war efforts. The recent events have the frightening prospective of spiraling into a global confrontation between the major powers of the Northern Hemispheres and the immensely large Islamic world, unleashing the most devastating weapons.

The unrelenting bloody hostilities between the Palestinians and the Israelis over land and water, the massacres in the refugee camps achieved what the Western Powers—especially Britain—after World War I by all means wanted to prevent; unifying the disunited Arab world. By drawing new maps they split them administratively, creating new kingdoms and sheikdoms. Religion remained the connecting link. The unending American bombing of some of the Islamic countries, (a cowardly and uncivilized act), the inhumane embargo depriving the very young and the sick of the essential food and medication (a highly immoral act), drove the Muslims into one "Religious-Political" camp. Reading the Arab news media one can sense the evolving of Arab nationalism and the emerging of Islam as the unifying religious and political power not only within the Arab world, but also for all the followers of Islam, from the Middle-East to Asia, to Africa. Nationalism and religious fanaticism joined in violence-prone movements on both the Arab and the Jewish sides, driving both into deeper and deeper conflict. America the melting pot of nationalities and the haven for all religious beliefs became the main supporting pillar for the aspirations of the Religious-Political Nationalistic Zionism. The intention was right, giving a homeland for the Jews. The consequences are tragic; hostility and hatred between the Semitic people, dragging the world into immeasurable danger.

The towers of the World Trade Center viewed and repeatedly targeted by the extremists of the Islamic Religious-Political Nationalists as the symbols of America, which is the ultimate benefactor of Zionism, crumbled, burying thousands under the rubble. America retaliated by bombing the cities and villages of Afghanistan, which only a few years earlier in another religious war of Islam against the atheistic Soviet Union had been devastated. More and more threats were being made by both sides. The "coalition" in the war against terrorism—which could extend to Iran, Syria, Yemen, Indonesia and possibly to other Islamic countries accused of harboring or helping the terrorists—appears to be more-and-more like a coalition in a war against Islam. These are the realities.

Was the turban-wearing, primitively-clad, rifle-carrying Taliban man thousands of miles away the real threat to America? Were the terrorists on the airplanes crashing into the WTC towers and into the walls of Pentagon members of the Taliban? As far as we know they were not. Were the already ruined cities and villages in Afghanistan the legitimate targets for our sophisticated bombs? No, they were not! Killing the poorest and the most backward, destroying their modest homes was an easy way for our politicians to divert the attention from the real issues. Those were the easy, risk-free targets over which our generals glorifying themselves could claim cheap victory. The realities are different. America's war in Afghanistan has much the same mark as what the Soviet's war had, namely that of a quagmire.

Is Osama Bin Laden the real enemy? Only a few years earlier he was the "freedom-fighter" in Afghanistan against the atheistic Soviet intruders, receiving support from none other than the American CIA. His heroism was praised by the American news media. Is he a fanatical representative of the Muslim cause? Yes, he most likely is. Is he behind any and all terrorist acts, which are committed against America? Possibly. Could he be the powerful man who wants to destroy the Western Civilization—which our politicians attempt to tell us he is? Hardly. Would his killing by our bombs or bullets bring terrorism to an end? Not likely. There was terrorism before bin Laden, there will be terrorism after bin Laden. His martyrdom in the war of Islam against the Infidels would in the eyes of his followers elevate him to sainthood. Would it not be better to listen to him and to his followers? They strongly objected to the American military bases in his homeland Saudi-Arabia, from where our planes flew to drop the bombs on their fellow Muslims. Was the price of the thousands dead in the WTC towers right for keeping our bombers in Saudi-Arabia? Is it a good deal to live in constant fear just for maintaining our military presence in the Muslim world? Would it not be better to talk with them, to listen to them and with that prevent another WTC disaster, saving many-many lives? They are also humans—although our propaganda treats them as demons. Is talking with terrorists demeaning for our officials? Menachem Begin the much heralded prime minister of Israel was at one time called by the British a terrorist, who in Jerusalem blew up the British military headquarters killing scores of officers, and was on the most wanted list. Terrorists are not born, but instead are the products of extreme circumstances. Then who is the real enemy? Could it—perhaps—be our very own attitude toward others? Can't our politicians and militarists set aside their pride and arrogance, and pursue reasoning? Words don't kill, only weapons do. Bombs can't reason, only rational minds can.

The cost of the "America Strikes Back" war is already measured in billions, and that is just the beginning. The tragic demise of the thousands of victims is not the end. It might very well be just a start. Do we want to repeat the horrors of Dresden, Hiroshima and Nagasaki? Do we want to see another Holocaust? It might not be an exaggeration to draw such dark predictions. Would it not be better to invest in peace? America gave a ten billion dollar loan guaranty to Israel to build homes for the immigrating Jews—on Arab land. Would it not be better to build homes for the Palestinians as well, who driven away from their homes spent nearly a lifetime in the squalid refugee camps? Would it not be better to deliver food for the Afghan people instead of showering them with cluster bombs? What cause for terrorism could extremists like Bin Laden find if the Western World would show understanding for the grievances of the oppressed? Who would follow them in terrorism if there would be a pleasant and peaceful life for his fellow Muslims to enjoy? These are not irrational questions.

If the makers of the American foreign-policy in their militaristic illusions believe that by devastating Afghanistan—and perhaps scores of other Islamic countries—they can stop terrorism, they should be reminded that terrorism is not a frontal enemy that can be bombed to pieces. It is like cancer, hidden in small cells, attacking wherever there is a vulnerable spot. The struggle of the Vietnamese people for independence, fighting a long and bloody guerrilla war, and at the end forcing the mighty America to withdraw should be a good lesson to learn from. In the propaganda during the Vietnam War the Vietcong was the evil, the hated enemy. Millions of tons of bombs were dropped on their land, their fighters and the unarmed civilians were hunted like animals, over three millions of them have been killed. Thousands of young Americans died, tens of thousands came home bodily and psychologically crippled. Today American businesses are seeking commercial deals with the old enemy, and American tourists roam their countryside admiring the historic treasures. All that horror could have been prevented by listening to Ho Chi Minh, who was a well educated man and was a devoted nationalist leader of Vietnam, but who had been viewed by our policy-makers as a terrorist, the real Satan. The Islamic world extends to continents, its members are counted in many millions, and their devotion is deep. They cannot be ignored. They cannot be bombed to oblivion. They can hit us whenever they want. We are vulnerable. That is the reality.

What is the real issue? It is religious fanaticism entangled in politics, in greed, in nationalistic bigotry, turning the Israelis and the Arabs, the Jews and the Muslims against each other, dragging the Judeo-Christian America into the conflict. Anyone arguing against such a thesis should pay attention to the images we saw on the television; the praying Israeli soldiers, the praying Palestinian fighters, the praying Taliban men and the praying Americans. All praying while killing each other. In one scene American Special-Forces soldiers were shown, mumbling "God be merciful to your soul", while practicing the stabbing of a Muslim enemy. That is the reality. Waging wars is the most deplorable crime that any society can commit. We, in the Bible-reading Christian World should be aware of that, but regrettably never follow the most elementary moral principle. Attacking the defenseless, the unarmed, women and children is terrorism, no matter who does it under whatever justification. Counter-terrorism is an uncivilized response to an uncivilized act. If the American policy-makers can't see that—as it appears to be the case—then those who call themselves "allies" and "friends", and especially those who themselves experienced the horrors of wars, should warn them against committing the same crime.

In the horrible days of the Bolshevik terror in Hungary after World War II, the government's slogan was: "If you are not with us, you are against us." Those were frightening words, terrorizing an entire nation. There was no room left for rational thinking, there was no place for dialogue, but there was fear. And then, in 1956 came a Revolution, with which the disintegration of the Soviet Empire began. The words of the President in 2003: "Either with us, or with the terrorists" are equally frightening, leaving no room for dialogue. Does opposing the bombing of villages and cities and the killing of the uninvolved people in Iraq and Afghanistan mean being with the terrorists? Does crying out against wars and violence mean being un-American? In my case it was an angry and desperate outburst of frustration after long years of failed hope to have deeply rooted grievances cured. The same is heard over and over again from those against whom America wages war. Terrorism can take on a form of aggressive self-defense of individuals, or of societies, against overwhelming military or police power behind an oppressive government or occupier. Terrorists are not born. They are the products of circumstances, in most cases of oppression, injustice and foreign occupation. They are not immoral criminals—or at least not all of them—quite to the contrary, in some cases they are morally superior. This may be hard to accept by those who view terrorism from our government's perspectives. The worst form of terror is war. It is premeditated mass-murder instigated and conducted by government. The American government is fighting terrorism without examining the causes, without understanding its very fundamental human elements, without seeing that often its own—or its ally's—conduct sets the ground for terrorism.

In a television interview one of the Russian commanders who led his forces in crushing the 1956 Hungarian Revolution said that he had received the reports from their intelligence sources that in Budapest was a "Fascist revolt, blood-shed was in the making, people were slaughtered in the streets." He said that he was convinced of the validity of the report and of the correctness of his action, believed that Fascist, counter-revolutionary terror ruled in Hungary. What he did not know—and those who provided the report and gave the orders did not want him to know—was, that it was the AVH, the State Security Authority, the government's agency that opened fire on the unarmed demonstrators. The era of "Glasnost" became the eye-opener for the commander, which allowed the emerging of truthful accounts of the events. In the interview he regretted what he did. Hence, every society, including ours needs a "Glasnost."

There are many tragic examples in our recent history when misinformation, or intentionally distorted information, served as the basis for violence on both sides, not only in the "terrorist", but also in the Western Democratic societies. During the 1991 Gulf War as justification for the war we heard about the terror of the Iraqi soldiers in Kuwait, throwing babies out of incubators. Not only a not credible story, but also one that was also proven false. In 2003 the Secretary of Defense on a hearing—once again justifying another war—spoke of liberating the Iraqis from "the fear of having their tongue cut out, or their ears chopped off by Saddam's death squads." There is a good expression for such propaganda tricks that applies to both cases: Cheap shot.

In a news report on the television a group of American soldiers was shown kicking open the door of an Iraqi home, aiming their guns and shouting, calling the people to come out. First a man appeared with raised hands, signaling to the soldiers that others, his family, were inside eating, and turned to call them out. His young wife came dressed in a colorful robe-like outfit, with three small children clinging to her, one maybe two years old boy, a little girl probably four, and another young boy. They were frightened, their tears running, their small hands raised and trembling. Three small children and their mother with raised hand facing the gun touting American soldiers, who followed them with aimed weapons. Not having found anything, the soldiers left in a shameful retreat. The faces of the children and of their mother are forever carved in my memory as the symbols of the victims of military terror.

THE WRONG COORDINATES.

The scene, as was described by the British reporter, was total devastation. Not a standing wall remained of the small village in the mountainous region of Afghanistan. Everything was flattened, all living things, inhabitants and their livestock were killed, and ripped apart by American cluster bombs. Among the scattered remains of what used to be human beings, their blood splashed on the rubble, sat a young boy, about 12 years old, with a split-open belly, still alive. It was a depressing picture.

In a casual social conversation with a fellow American, in which I mentioned that scene, he with military background listened with apprehension. He felt insulted by my believing that America is waging a brutal war against civilians. And then, as if having found the fitting defensive response he said: *"We Americans don't wage wars against civilians. In that case somebody had given the wrong coordinates."* The issue of the "coordinates" came back repeatedly, giving a technical flavor to our otherwise emotional conversation. On a televised news conference to a reporter's question about the same incident the Pentagon's spokesman in an irate tone said: *"America is not like those terrorists who flew the planes into the WTC towers intentionally killing civilians. We Americans don't target civilians. In wars there are collateral casualties. It is possible that somebody fed the wrong coordinates into the bombers' computers, or it could be the malfunctioning of the guiding mechanism of the bombs."* The argument sounded militarily professional. For some it could even be convincing. Not for me. Only a few years ago I heard the same excuses when American bombs killed the fleeing Albanians in Kosovo. The spokesman at that time vehemently argued against any comments questioning America's conducting a war against civilians, but lately in Europe there are investigations of the case.

"We Americans don't target civilians." Well-sounding argument by the Pentagon spokesman, but not for those of us who lived through the bombing raids on the European cities in the Second World War. Did the spokesman forget the terror bombing of the many cities, among them Dresden, in which quite intentionally two hundred thousands fleeing civilians had been slaughtered? Had he not heard about the horrors of Hiroshima and Nagasaki, where hundreds of thousands of non-combatants, women and children have been intentionally killed? None of those horrors were caused by "wrong coordinates," or resulted from the "malfunctioning of the guiding mechanisms of the bombs". Those were well-planned, intentional mass-murders of civilians, and were among the most deplorable war crimes against humanity in history.

My words may sound utterly un-American, which I am not. My recalling the long past may appear serving America's enemies, which I don't intend to do and do not condone. In the days of the drummed-up patriotism my thoughts may sound repulsively unpatriotic, which I am not either. Patriotism, as I want to practice it, is serving and preserving the highest moral standards of a nation; respecting and protecting human lives, rejecting any and all forms of violence, especially wars.

In the tragic days of the autumn of 2001, when in the dramatic retaliatory actions of a group of terrorists—or for some the self-sacrificing devotees of a cause—the World Trade Center towers crumbled, burying thousands under the rubble, when American bombs and missiles killed civilians in Afghanistan the land of the poorest in the world, when the Israelis and the Palestinians fought endless battles, on the television screen I saw three images; the praying Muslim Taliban, the praying Israeli Jew and the praying American Christian. They all prayed to their Gods, but were mortal enemies. The cold reality is that once again in history millions of praying people are in wars against each other. There are plenty of denials from all three sides that their wars have anything to do with religion, although, all three claim that their religion, their faith is the only true, the only holy one. The Muslims call those of the other faiths the "Infidels", the Jews claim that they are the "Chosen", the Christians preach that they are the true followers of Christ. All three believing what they claim to be; namely the only righteous.

The next scene was the corpses of children, women and men, Muslims, Jews and Christians, civilians and in uniform, devotees and bystanders, all victims of violence between the faithful. Those images were not at all unusual. A few months earlier similar images could be seen from the Balkans and Iraq, earlier from Libya, Panama, Lebanon, just to mention a few. The American Christians and Jews, viewing on the television the crumbling of the World Trade Center, listening to the news about the thousands of victims were in shock, feared more attacks by those whom they hated, but who officially could not be called the enemy; Islam. The American government opened a war and they called it a "Crusade", but that title was quickly dropped because of its religious connotation. Politically it was wrong to sell a war against a religion. The American Christians and Jews went to their churches and synagogues to pray, while their government sent the bombers and missiles to kill the followers of Islam. The Jews in Israel prayed at the Wailing Wall, while their bullets killed the Muslim Palestinians. The Islamic Palestinians prayed in their mosques, while in the name of Allah their fighters killed Jews in the Israeli streets. Absurd!

Muslims, Jews and Christians! Don't fool yourselves and each other about your goodness. Just hate and kill and be good fighters of your faith. There will be plenty others who will praise you for what you did. Just conduct the murderous crusades in the names of your Gods. There will be plenty who will pray for you.

INDICTMENT.

Regrettably, the tragedies of the Second World War were repeated many times. The minds of the people are still being poisoned with fabricated accusations, just to serve the planners of wars. Weapon technology, supported by the governments almost without limits, building airplanes and remotely guided missiles to deliver death and destruction to the unseen victims just by pushing a button, eased the task of the military. For that purpose national economies have been—and also are being—burdened, the capacities of human ingenuity were and still are mindlessly wasted. The technology applied in making nuclear bombs capable of destroying entire cities, and the means to deliver those bombs, are still matters of national pride. These are the realities.

Have we learned anything from the tragedy in which we were the players? Have we done enough to teach the new generations not to repeat the same mistakes, not to fight more wars, not to kill and destroy, but try to understand and reason out the differences? The events of history seem to prove that we have not. That is—as I see it—our most important moral responsibility. Those of us who lived through the horrors, saw, or suffered the brutalities, have failed. Violence bears counter violence, false security behind weaponry produces more insecurity, both leading to the vicious circle of militarism, which I was the victim of. If we want a better, a peaceful world, militarism, the business of making wars must be eradicated. We must not allow the new generation to be brainwashed to become "Blood thirsty killing machines." We must raise a new generation that will cherish human decency, tolerance, understanding, will reject any form of violence, will follow self-discipline without submission to senseless, proud obedience, will live by mindful loyalty to noble principles. I trust, and I hope that by putting my life story in the hands of the reader, I can serve that goal.

Where do I find the roots of the human tragedy of the Second World War, and of all the wars since? If there was—and still is—a human institution that is not restricted by national boundaries, by language or ethnic differences, it is the church. The Catholics worship the same God in America and in Europe, and obey the same Pope, who claims to be the caretaker of God's will. The Protestants read the same Bible on all continents; they all preach peace on earth, at least at Christmas time. The Jews claim to be God's chosen children. But, what have they collectively done to prevent wars? Nothing. They were silent. What absurdity it was when the churches blessed the flags as national symbols used by the governments in carrying out the most immoral acts of war. If there were institutions that could, and should have stood on the front lines to stop the senseless brutality, killing and destruction, those were the spiritual institutions. Have the churches—other than a few individual priests or ministers—ever raised an official protest against wars? Never. Instead, they used the Bible to justify wars. The only time in my memory when a church as institution stood up against the government was, when after the Second World War under the Bolshevik era the wealth of the church was threatened. Then, they loudly protested, and even created martyrs among themselves.

Education is another of the failing human institutions. From my early childhood I was raised to unquestionably obey the authorities, and accept what was taught to me as the absolute truth. The history of my country was presented as the holy crusade on the path to justice, to preserving and spreading Christianity, culture and humanity. It is still the case in some countries. After having lived through a tumultuous period of our contemporary history, in which I myself was a pawn, when I read the accounts of those periods in the textbooks I ask myself; are they writing about the same thing that I lived through? If the commonly taught history of the past reflects as much—or as little—of the truth and realities as that of the periods that I lived through, than I do not consider teaching it worthwhile. To gain a more objective understanding one has to read the accounts as presented from all sides, which is hardly available for most of us.

When I see the trusting, innocent faces of small children, who will inherit a world from us, I am deeply saddened knowing that their trust and innocence will be misused in shaping them to continue the same ugly path that we ourselves followed. For that we parents are responsible individually. It is not enough for the mothers to cry and grieve over the death of their soldier sons. They have to stand up against those who claim the right to take their sons away. For us fathers who were victims of lies and indoctrination, who had to take part in senseless killings of unknown men wearing different uniforms, just because somebody told us that they were enemies, it is not enough, and also it is not right to keep silent. It is our duty to tell all what wars really are, and do everything in our power not to send our sons to fight wars.

In my long life I was under many shades and forms of indoctrination, interestingly enough remaining immune to all of them. As a young child my mind was poisoned with hateful slogans directed against the neighboring nations, which occupied parts of my homeland. As a young man during the war years I was exposed to the propaganda depicting the Jews as the worst enemies of our society and of the nation. Now, once again I am targeted by the mind-manipulating efforts of the government and of the fanatical institutions. One of the striking outbursts of the mind-controlling government propaganda was during the Iraq War, to which I reacted with alarm and dismay. An outward symptom was the ever-presence of the national flag, seen on the car antennas, on postal stamps and on coat lapels. The television news presented the events with glorification of the "heroic" fighting against the evil enemy. The magnificent precision of our bombs, hitting only the military targets with absolute accuracy was constantly fed to the ignorant and culpable audience. The realities were quite different.

The seeds of hatred are still being systematically planted by the governments, by the political institutions and even by individuals. In a casual conversation with a man whom I met while shopping in a store, he said that in his mind every German is Nazi, murderer and terrorist, and they should be eradicated. In a prestigious newspaper of the cosmopolitan city of Seattle I read an article by a nuclear physicist promoting the building of more nuclear bombs in preparation for the "Inevitable future war against Germany". On the anniversary of the tragic bombing of Dresden, killing nearly 200,000 fleeing refugees, the only remembrance on the public and government-supported and much praised National Public Radio was the reading of a letter from a listener. In it he wrote: "The loss of the life of even one child in the concentration camps justified the killing of 200,000 German refugees". I find it shocking that on the day of remembrance for a human tragedy someone could write such a hate-filled letter, and the management of the nation-wide radio station was willing to present it to its audience. Yes, the loss of the life of even one child is tragic enough to learn from it, not to allow hatred to prevail.

"A LESSON TO PEACEMAKING."

In 2003 on the days of the worldwide demonstrations against the Iraq war, in which I participated, I received the following e-mail.

"Subject: A lesson to peacemaking.

With all this talk of war, many of us will encounter "Peace Activists" who will try and convince us that we must refrain from retaliating the ones who terrorized us all on September 11, 2001, and all those who support terror. Those activists may be alone or in a gathering…most of us don't know how to react to them. When you come upon one of those people, or one of their allies, here are the proper rules of etiquette:

1. *Listen politely while the person explains their views. Strike up a conversation, if necessary and look very interested in their ideas. They'll tell you how revenge is immoral, and that by attacking the people who did this to us, we will only bring more violence. They will probably use many arguments, ranging from political to religious to humanitarian.*

2. *In the middle of their remarks, without any warning, punch them in the nose.*

3. *When the person gets up off the ground, they will be very angry and they may try to hit you, so be alert.*

4. *Very quickly and calmly remind the person that violence only brings about more violence and remind them of their stand on this matter. Tell them if they are really committed to a no-violent approach to undeserved attacks, they will turn the other cheek and negotiate a solution. Tell them they must lead by example, if they really believe what they are saying.*

5. *Most of them will think for a moment and then agree that you are correct.*

6. *As soon as they do that, hit them again. Only this time hit them much harder. Square in the nose.*

7. *Repeat steps 2–5 until the desired results are obtained and the idiot realizes how stupid of an argument he/she is making.*

8. *There is no difference in an individual attacking unsuspecting victim or a group of terrorists attacking a nation of people. It is unacceptable and must be dealt with. Perhaps at big cost.*

We owe our military a huge debt for what they are doing for us and our children. We all must support them and our leaders at times like these. We have no choice. We either strike back, VERY HARD, or we will continue getting hit in the nose.

I pledge allegiance to the flag of the United States of America and to the republic for which it stands, one nation under God, indivisible, with liberty and justice for all.

Lesson over. Class dismissed.

Take care and God Bless America.

Cheers."

A FEW REFLECTIVE THOUGHTS.

The greatness of a society as seen from historical perspectives is measured by its cultural and humanitarian contributions and by its spiritual strength, not by its military and political successes. The ruling power of the ancient Chinese and Egyptian empires long have disappeared, their cultural and spiritual contributions remained admired by the later civilizations. The Roman Empire and its mighty military power ceased to exist. Its temples are standing as lasting monuments, and its artistic masterpieces remained the admired treasures of our museums. The magnificent creations of the Greeks, both intellectual and artistic, are still the shining examples of what a great society could be.

While today's governments, the militarists and politicians keenly propagate their war victories as proof of their greatness, the nations and the societies will be judged on their peacetime accomplishments. Although I am living in an era in which the national pride—to a large degree—is encompassed in its military power and in its successes in defeating others, a realization is emerging, which shows that not the destructive power, but the moral and creative-cultural strength are the signs of national greatness. The proudly celebrated military victories will long be forgotten, but the contribution—or lack thereof—to the evolution of a higher order human society will be the lasting imprints of our times. The question we face is; how do we want be judged by our descendants. The time will come—so I hope—when the pride in the successes in wars will become the shame, and the shame in persistent struggle for peace will become the pride. The Twentieth Century, in which I lived much of my life, will be judged—so I believe—not as the age of great cultural and humanitarian accomplishments, but as the culmination of total breakdown of morality, of social disorder and of human brutality.

"Modern" art with its distortion of the "real," with its grotesque interpretation of what nature produces with beauty, cannot remain as lasting treasure.
Art, like most of the social-cultural issues of my lifetime, became the tool of
ideological confrontation. The propagation of abstract art, its imposition on
the societies, had clear political-ideological goals. This was evident especially
in the 1930s, when the major ideological forces in Europe were on a collision
course. In some of the societies efforts had been made to preserve and revital-
ize the traditional form of the classical art, which could be seen in the esthetics
of the newly erected public structures and in the tradition-based urban and
rural development, was manifested in the illustrative art by praising and glorifying the family, purity of the tranquil country life, beauty of the human body.
At the same time abstract art in some of its extreme forms was propagated by
the ideologically opposing elements of the societies as their political-ideological statement. I see in some of those trends the signs of the social-cultural
anarchy. Did the traditional classical art of the past centuries exhaust its subjects and themes, as some claim? Did the technique of the classical art reach a
dead end, as some argue? Was the surging of abstract art the manifestation of
the search of the human soul and mind for the "new"? Arguable points for
both sides. But, I believe that was not the case. The stroke of the brush of the
abstract artists with the grotesque images of the human face, the distorted
illustration of objects, the chaotic visions of events, the tasteless obscenities,
had clear ideological purpose, quite arguably with a message to shock.

I wish not to argue on behalf of the traditional classical art, because it
served the powerful, whether it was moral or immoral, often glorified human
brutality. The culmination of the ideological-political confrontation in art
came in the 1920s and 1930s, when abstract art in some countries flourished,
while in others was repressed. That was followed after the war, when art produced by the artists of a certain era, whether it had any propagandistic motives
or not, was confiscated and was locked up in government vaults. Similar fate
was imposed even on music. Some compositions were not on the programs
because the composers were Jewish. Literary art did not fare any better either,
when burning of books and the removing of the statues of literary artists were
rampant manifestations of ideological bigotry.

On the humanitarian accomplishments of the 20th century I can draw an
even more pitiful conclusion. Searching through the records I could not find
one single event, which would stand out as a great humanitarian act, and even
among those few which might be considered as such, most came after the horrors of wars and of social conflicts, for which the burden lies on the human

institutions. In my lifetime mankind has spent more efforts, wasted more resources, directed more knowledge to building destructive weapons, then ever before. I was not a witness to the horrors of the First World War; only saw its victims without arms and legs. As a living witness to the horror of the Second World War, and certainly only to a small fraction of it at the early years of my life, I had all the reasons to be totally disillusioned with the moral-humanitarian values of the societies. Instead of turning away from the use of brutality, they plunged the world into the totally mindless rush to obtain the ultimate destructive power, namely the nuclear bomb.

In seeking some noble accomplishments of our times I considered the achievements of science. Although I was an insignificantly small pawn on the chessboard of the human knowledge, instinctively I had a degree of satisfaction of being a part of it. The impressions of my early childhood when in the evenings petrol lamp provided the light in my room, when listening to the radio was a near miracle for me, gave me the basis for the amazement in what technology and science achieved in my lifetime. In my mental exercises I listed the to me most important accomplishments. Being a layman I based my selection on what those accomplishments meant for me directly. The first on my list is Penicillin. It saved millions of lives, quite likely also mine. DDT, which later turned out to be a highly toxic substance and became outlawed, relieved millions, including me as a prisoner of war, from the fear of the deadly epidemic spread by lice. Polio Vaccine, which saved my children, myself and millions of others from the horrors of that dreaded disease. Those are only a few of the many scientific accomplishments, which served mankind. But, at the turn of the century none of the men behind those was on the front pages of the magazines as the "Man of the Century." The science, and the scientist of the Century were chosen from what our society admires as the most grandiose; nuclear energy, and its masters.

The last, but certainly the most important element of the human existence which received the least attention in my lifetime was spirituality. Not that there were no religious upheavals, not that there were no doctrinal confrontations, not that there were no pious words of Popes and priests, but when social or political crises arose, when human brutality gained power, the institutions of spirituality ceased to fulfill their holy responsibility, and became the servant of the powerful, leaving the individual souls to their own survival. Where were the great minds that could give a new direction to human conduct when the bombs were falling on cities, when millions were persecuted because of their race, religion or nationality? Where were the institutions without political boundaries, which claimed to be the "shepherds" of the human soul across and between continents, when millions cried out for help? There cannot be true spirituality either for the individual, or for the institutions without absolute opposition to violence, especially to wars. That is one of the realms of the human mind and soul, where all the societies of the Twentieth Century have failed, and failed most miserably. There has never been any period of human history when the extinguishing of so many human lives in so short a time had been tolerated. And it happened in the Christian world. That will be the sorrowful legacy of the Twentieth Century.

I saw pictures of noisy, emotion-filled masses enthusiastically celebrating their nations' entering wars. I also saw joyful parades of masses over ending wars. After each horror there was a strange sense of happiness over survival. For many, survival was the greatest joy whether it was celebrated in loud parades or in quiet prayers.

When the sound of the whistles filled the air, when the champagne bottles popped, when in celebration of entering the new Century ticker tape covered the streets, all the ills of the past were forgotten. There were speeches by those who in self-glorification praised what had been accomplished, made promises for a wonderful future. I heard the prediction of peace, coming from those whose vision of the future was as distorted and as self-serving, as it was of the past. I left the Twentieth Century with resentment, and entered the new Century with fear.

A MESSAGE TO MY ENEMIES.

To those of you who were my enemies, and I was yours, without knowing each other, who flew over my head shooting at the train on which I was riding, bombed the cities where I lived and went to school, who fired at me in battles, who stood guard around the prisoner of war camp where I was a captive, together with whom today I have the same homeland here in America, my message is that although those events are much too deeply engraved in my memories to forget, I understand why you did what you did. We all were victims of lies, of hateful propaganda spread by governments, yours and mine, of mindless loyalty and proud obedience that was implanted in our young minds. I was not a worse human being than you were, and you were not worse than I was.

Do I accuse you as my captors of intentionally starving me as a prisoner of war? No, I do not. I understand that the task of caring for us was immense. The war came to a sudden end, and in a matter of weeks millions of us soldiers surrendered and were taken prisoner. The roads, railroads and bridges were destroyed in the war, bringing transportation to a virtual halt in Germany. You Americans had to provide first for your soldiers.

Do I accuse the military strategists and planners of crimes against humanity? Yes, I do. The inhumane, indiscriminate carpet bombing and burning of cities, attacking the fleeing civilians were crimes against humanity. Any air marshal who ordered the bombing of cities, which had no military or industrial significance, just to terrorize and kill defenseless civilians was guilty of horrible crimes. I felt true hatred when after bombing raids I saw children and women ripped apart. Firing missiles, or dropping bombs on unseen defenseless civilians is no lesser a crime than stabbing them in the back.

For the heads of countries on all sides, for the generals and politicians, who failed to prevent violence, who so willingly cheated their nations into wars, for those who in their blind, mindless loyalty and proud obedience sacrificed the young and the old, I wish they be hounded forever by the agonies and sufferings of their victims.

For the heads of countries, generals and politicians, who not having learned—or not wanting to learn—from the tragedies of past, who still bathe in the glory of defeating others, who still want to fulfill their appetite for more and more weapons, for more and more killing power, who still are willing to sacrifice the young, I have my deepest repugnance.

To you, who were my enemies, who reading my lines are awakening to our immense responsibility for the future of the new generations, I extend my invitation to join me in my crusade against senseless hatred and killing in wars.

EPILOGUE.

What could have led to the deplorable state of affairs that threaten our exist-ence? Not the horrible weapons, but the lies that unleash those weapons, not the explosive power of the bombs measured in megatons, but the evil minds which by deception justify the launching of such bombs. Hearing and reading about the feverish development of even more horrible nuclear bombs I am wondering where will all that end. I do fearfully watch the silencing of the moderates and the slow death of the institutions, which have been established to control violence in the world. Those institutions are now condemned to irrelevance. Yes, I am deeply depressed by seeing the path on which our soci-ety pursues its suicidal fate.

America could be—and should be—the land without enemies. It lies almost on an entire continent without facing territorial claims by anyone, oceans separate it from the other parts of the world, no hostile armies stand on its borders, it has a peacefully co-existing interethnic population, no national-istic strife is tearing it apart. Its society is tolerant to all racial, political, ideo-logical and religious lineage. It could be the ideal place, an example for the whole world. But, it is not. The worldwide opinion shown in the surveys from Asia to Europe depicts today's America as the greatest threat to world peace. We are viewed by the outside world—not only by our foes but also by our friends—as arrogant bullies, militaristic maniacs, conceited imperialists, our specially trained covertly operating commandos interfering in the affairs of nations. This view is quite in contrast to what our government and politicians attempt to plant in our minds, that America is the defender of freedom and liberty, that it can and will reshape the societies of the rest of the world into democracy.

The foreign media describes the events in Iraq and in the other Islamic countries quite differently than what we read and hear at home. The Middle-East crisis is extensively reported often with the details that we do not see in

our media. They often cite THE PATRIOT ACT as a return to the worst
times of deplored dictatorships. They report on the front pages America's
preparation for new wars, on the development of new weapons, on spending
enormous sums of money on armament. They view America's belligerency as a
religious-political war, a violent confrontation with the Islamic world. The
majority of the Europeans see it likewise. The events preceding the Iraq War,
the collisions at the United Nations between the views of the majority who
wanted to pursue a peaceful resolution of the crisis, versus the views of a small
but powerful minority that steadfastly argued for the war, their demeaning by
the establishment to "irrelevance", are still echoing not only in the media, but
also in the minds of the people. The calls by powerful American politicians for
boycotting the products of countries, which did not join in the war against
Iraq, are not forgotten. Anti-Americanism is not government-conducted propaganda, not the work of the media, but it comes directly from the people.
That is the reality

All these are happening around us while we are led to believe that we are
living in freedom, that we are the guardians of peace, that we are respected by
others. No, we are not. We live under the threat of laws in THE PATRIOT
ACT, which reminds me of the times when under the worst terror of the Bolshevik era "liberty and freedom for all" was the government's propaganda slogan, and nobody dared to question it. We are feared by others, but not
respected. The times of America's admiration are over, America bashing is in.
The days of unchallenged imperialism are over. This is shown by the growing
resistance on all levels, from the insurgents of the oppressed millions to the
institutions. America's monopoly on the most horrible weapons of mass-
destruction is an illusion. America the once untouchable is vulnerable. These
are painful thoughts, but these are the realities. America is at a crossroads;
either to remain the subservient to outside interests and pursue the suicidal
politics of worldwide confrontation, or become the true partner in the community of nations. The choice is ours; co-existence or co-extinction.

If some of my American readers may feel that I am overly critical on some
matters, especially concerning militarism and wars, I want to assure them that
it is not ill-intended. I ask them to understand that I view militarism and wars
from a perspective of my life, which was fundamentally affected by wars. I
want to present and justify my anti-war position on the basis of my personal
experience, not on spoon-fed "official information". It is true that academically I am not qualified to criticize the experts of politics, especially those in
high government positions. But, is it not the reality that after each failed polit-

ical or military attempt the powerful "hawks" were called to answer for their wrongdoing, in some cases paying dearly for it? If a post-event judgment is justified, why can't a pre-event criticism or warning be allowed, especially by someone, who as a victim of wars, of oppression, of the horrors of dictatorships, who by sharing his thoughts attempts to save others from the same? I wish they would understand that I saw the Second World War from the other side. For me it was happening not somewhere on another continent, but all around me. I was not one of the crew of the armada of the bombers, but was among the targets of their bombs. I was not the guard around the prisoner of war camps, but was the prisoner behind the barbed-wire fences. For me the horrors of the war were not written stories read in the comfort of an easy chair—or viewed on the television screen in the comfort of a living room—but were the daily realities. I lived through those horrors not as an aged man whose life was reaching its end, but as a young man dreaming about my future, the future that was being destroyed. In some respects I shared the agonies of those young Americans who were sent to fight wars away from home. We both believed that it was our moral and patriotic duty to defend our homelands against the feared enemy, but neither of us knew who our real enemies were.

For my Jewish readers who may feel that I am biased and prejudiced, or even racist, I wish to make clear that my intention is none of the above. I do not accuse or attack the Jews, but only the harmful radicals among them. For those who may feel that in my remarks about the war-years, especially regarding the racial-political persecution I gave a distorted picture, or even suggested justification for some of the events, my answer is that I wanted to show those times as they were, not as they could have been. In my recollection of the postwar times, particularly of those under the Bolshevik terror, I wanted to present the stark realities, as I was affected by them. My writings cover the tragic period of history when race and politics were intertwined, when extremism on both sides was the ruling power, when Jews and Gentiles could be turned against each other causing immeasurable suffering to each other. To deny that would be a distortion of the facts.

If my readers from the world of academia feel that my accounts on the events are historically inaccurate, I wish to remind them that my book is my subjective, personal story. I wrote about the events not on the basis of "Documentary evidence," but as I saw those as a child, as a young man whose dreams were being shattered, as a desperate family-man who feared for his children's' future. I did not see politics from the inner circles, but from the place of the "street-level people." Did I have all the facts, and did I understand all the issues for which the Second World War was fought, in which I voluntarily participated? Most certainly I did not. Did I have all the facts on the causes and reasons behind the 1956 Hungarian Revolution, on behalf of which I marched and built barricades in the streets of Budapest? Most certainly I did not. Did those who neither fought in the war, nor marched with the revolting crowd, but wrote about those events, have all the evidence? How could they? It might take lifetimes before all the evidence could be available, and before those can be analyzed. Can objective history be written without all the evidence from all sides? I believe it is impossible. Therefore, I am certain that nobody ever could write absolutely factual and objective history. Everything we read about the past is somebody's interpretation of the events, my book included. Whether those are objective or biased, one has to judge for himself. I rightfully ask the question; do the politicians, the policy makers and government propagandists who ardently argue on issues, who speaking to the public make every effort to present their stories believable really tell the facts? I don't claim credit to my account. Those are my interpretations.

Some of my critics may ask, why do I write about the Second World War, when it was over sixty years ago, and already much had been written about it. What can I as a layman add to it? My answer is that those were the events, which affected my life the most. Some might question why do I write about my wartime experiences, some of which contradict the official accounts. My answer is that, like everything else, wars also have two faces. It is true that the war was between nations, and it was a monumental historic event beyond the comprehension of the individual. But it is also true that it was the millions of individuals—among them myself—who carried the burdens, for whom the war was a personal matter.

Should I accept the propaganda that depicted the people, among whom I spent the last months of the war, as hateful fanatics, criminal murderers, when those I came in contact with—even in the most difficult times—had shown decency and morality? Should I join the chorus of those who in lack of personal experience like parrots repeat what the propaganda tells them? No, I am not willing to do that. Such an attitude would be the betrayal of the moral-intellectual principles by which I want to live. Quite certainly my accounts are only the macro-images of the monumental events, and are my very personal, subjective interpretations.

I do believe that unbiased, objective history writing and teaching—if that would ever be practiced—would greatly contribute to a peaceful world. The politically intentional, propagandistic distortions, which I still find in the strategies of the policy makers, on the television screen and in the news media, are among the most immoral and dangerous weapons, and are the fundamental causes of all wars. I had seen too much of it, and I refuse to surrender to it. No matter how powerful the propaganda might be, no matter how high-ranking the propagators are I am not willing to view the people of other nations as "Gooks," "Rogues" and "Outlaws," when they are human beings just as I am. I grew up with the war-propaganda, feeding me with hate-filled images of persons and of nations; I lived under the constant bombardment of the agitators trying to poison my mind with lies.

If my readers from the world of literature feel that I did injustice to their art, I wish to remind them that I am an immigrant and I am an engineer, that I did not author, but "engineered" my book. I wanted my writings to be a reflection of me, just as I am. It was not my intention to exercise my non-existing literary skill, it was not to entertain, but to share my experiences with my readers.

When I saw the vastness of the burning ruins of bombed-out cities, when I tumbled over torn-apart human bodies, I was frightened and also was angered. I thought that in the place of such devastation there were never going to be thriving communities again. But there are now. When in the horror of battles I despaired, I thought that there was no hope for my survival. But I survived. When in the hopelessness of captivity I lost the desire to live, I thought there was never going to be a recovery for me. But there was. When I had to live under the ruling of hateful ideologies I thought there was never going to be an escape from those. But there was. When I fled to the West, I thought I was going to be free of the ills of the human society. But I was not. There were wars fought with ferocity, killing millions. I still have to live under the threat of a nuclear war. The national resources are still being wasted on weapons. The politicians are still spreading hateful propaganda against their foes. There is still racial hatred and nationalistic bigotry. The young men and also women in uniform are still being brainwashed and trained to become "Blood thirsty killing machines." I still have a mission to fulfill.

My thoughts were presented in a modest attempt to unveil the memories, the pains of a human being, who together with you is dreaming about, and is hoping for a better world. I wanted to carve into your memory the horrors that I had seen as everlasting reminders of the wrongs of our world. If my book awakens you to what mankind had done in my lifetime, then I fulfilled an important life mission.

Before closing my book, please, pause for a moment and remember the millions of our fellow human beings, friends and foes, whose lives were extinguished in wars, who are among us maimed, orphaned, who still carry the painful burdens of wars, and ask yourself:

What are you willing to do to make the world a better place for us and for the new generations?

978-0-595-41154-2
0-595-41154-1

www.ingramcontent.com/pod-product-compliance
Lightning Source LLC
Chambersburg PA
CBHW030303290526
45785CB00001B/198